UBICOMM 2019

The Thirteenth International Conference on Mobile Ubiquitous Computing, Systems, Services and Technologies

September 22 - 26, 2019

Porto, Portugal

UBICOMM 2019 Editors

Konstantinos Kotis, University of the Aegean, Dept. of Cultural Technology and Communication, Intelligent Systems Lab, Lesvos, Greece

John Soldatos, Athens Information Technology, Greece

Printed from e-media with permission by:

Curran Associates, Inc.
57 Morehouse Lane
Red Hook, NY 12571

Some format issues inherent in the e-media version may also appear in this print version.

Printed with permission by Curran Associates, Inc. (2020)

International Academy, Research, and Industry Association (IARIA)
412 Derby Way
Wilmington, DE 19810

Phone: (408) 893-6407
Fax: (408) 527-6351

petre@iaria.org

Additional copies of this publication are available from:

Curran Associates, Inc.
57 Morehouse Lane
Red Hook, NY 12571 USA
Phone: 845-758-0400
Fax: 845-758-2633
Email: curran@proceedings.com
Web: www.proceedings.com

Table of Contents

UBICOMM 2019

Forward

The Thirteenth International Conference on Mobile Ubiquitous Computing, Systems, Services and Technologies (UBICOMM 2019), held between September 22-26, 2019 in Porto, Portugal, continued a series of evens meant to bring together researchers from the academia and practitioners from the industry in order to address fundamentals of ubiquitous systems and the new applications related to them.

The rapid advances in ubiquitous technologies make fruition of more than 35 years of research in distributed computing systems, and more than two decades of mobile computing. The ubiquity vision is becoming a reality. Hardware and software components evolved to deliver functionality under failure-prone environments with limited resources. The advent of web services and the progress on wearable devices, ambient components, user-generated content, mobile communications, and new business models generated new applications and services. The conference makes a bridge between issues with software and hardware challenges through mobile communications.

Advances in web services technologies along with their integration into mobility, online and new business models provide a technical infrastructure that enables the progress of mobile services and applications. These include dynamic and on-demand service, context-aware services, and mobile web services. While driving new business models and new online services, particular techniques must be developed for web service composition, web service-driven system design methodology, creation of web services, and on-demand web services.

As mobile and ubiquitous computing becomes a reality, more formal and informal learning will take pace out of the confines of the traditional classroom. Two trends converge to make this possible; increasingly powerful cell phones and PDAs, and improved access to wireless broadband. At the same time, due to the increasing complexity, modern learners will need tools that operate in an intuitive manner and are flexibly integrated in the surrounding learning environment.

Educational services will become more customized and personalized, and more frequently subjected to changes. Learning and teaching are now becoming less tied to physical locations, co-located members of a group, and co-presence in time. Learning and teaching increasingly take place in fluid combinations of virtual and "real" contexts, and fluid combinations of presence in time, space and participation in community. To the learner full access and abundance in communicative opportunities and information retrieval represents new challenges and affordances. Consequently, the educational challenges are numerous in the intersection of technology development, curriculum development, content development and educational infrastructure.

The conference had the following tracks:

- Ubiquitous software and security
- Ubiquitous networks
- Fundamentals

- Users, applications, and business models
- Ubiquity trends and challenges

We take here the opportunity to warmly thank all the members of the UBICOMM 2019 technical program committee, as well as all the reviewers. The creation of such a high quality conference program would not have been possible without their involvement. We also kindly thank all the authors that dedicated much of their time and effort to contribute to UBICOMM 2019. We truly believe that, thanks to all these efforts, the final conference program consisted of top quality contributions.

We also gratefully thank the members of the UBICOMM 2019 organizing committee for their help in handling the logistics and for their work that made this professional meeting a success.

We hope that UBICOMM 2019 was a successful international forum for the exchange of ideas and results between academia and industry and to promote further progress in the field of mobile ubiquitous computing, systems, services and technologies. We also hope that Porto provided a pleasant environment during the conference and everyone saved some time to enjoy the historic charm of the city.

UBICOMM 2019 Chairs

UBICOMM Steering Committee

Sathiamoorthy Manoharan, University of Auckland, New Zealand
Ann Gordon-Ross, University of Florida, USA
Jaime Lloret Mauri, Polytechnic University of Valencia, Spain
Radosveta Sokullu, Ege University, Izmir, Turkey
Michele Ruta, Technical University of Bari, Italy
Wladyslaw Homenda, Warsaw University of Technology, Poland
Hiroaki Higaki, Tokyo Denki University, Japan

UBICOMM Industry/Research Advisory Committee

Miroslav Velev, Aries Design Automation, USA
Cornel Klein, Siemens AG/Corporate Research and Technologies - Münich, Germany
Dmitry Korzun, Petrozavodsk State University, Russia
Carla-Fabiana Chiasserini, Politecnico di Torino, Italy
Volkan Gezer, German Research Center for Artificial Intelligence (DFKI), Germany
Shaohan Hu, IBM Research, USA
Elmano Ramalho Cavalcanti, Federal Institute of Education Science and Technology of Pernambuco, Brazil
Lars Braubach, Complex Software Systems | Bremen City University, Germany
Jon M. Hjelmervik, SINTEF Digital, Norway
Ming Jin, Lawrence Berkeley National Laboratory (LBNL) and UC Berkeley, USA

UBICOMM 2019

COMMITTEE

UBICOMM Steering Committee

Sathiamoorthy Manoharan, University of Auckland, New Zealand
Ann Gordon-Ross, University of Florida, USA
Jaime Lloret Mauri, Polytechnic University of Valencia, Spain
Radosveta Sokullu, Ege University, Izmir, Turkey
Michele Ruta, Technical University of Bari, Italy
Wladyslaw Homenda, Warsaw University of Technology, Poland
Hiroaki Higaki, Tokyo Denki University, Japan

UBICOMM Industry/Research Advisory Committee

Miroslav Velev, Aries Design Automation, USA
Cornel Klein, Siemens AG/Corporate Research and Technologies - Münich, Germany
Dmitry Korzun, Petrozavodsk State University, Russia
Carla-Fabiana Chiasserini, Politecnico di Torino, Italy
Volkan Gezer, German Research Center for Artificial Intelligence (DFKI), Germany
Shaohan Hu, IBM Research, USA
Elmano Ramalho Cavalcanti, Federal Institute of Education Science and Technology of Pernambuco, Brazil
Lars Braubach, Complex Software Systems | Bremen City University, Germany
Jon M. Hjelmervik, SINTEF Digital, Norway
Ming Jin, Lawrence Berkeley National Laboratory (LBNL) and UC Berkeley, USA

UBICOMM 2019 Technical Program Committee

Emad Abd-Elrahman, National Telecommunication Institute, Cairo, Egypt
Afrand Agah, West Chester University of Pennsylvania, USA
Dragan Ahmetovic, University of Turin, Italy
A. B. M. Alim Al Islam, Bangladesh University of Engineering and Technology, Bangladesh
Sadam Al-Azani, King Fahd University of Petroleum and Minerals (KFUPM), Saudi Arabia
Taleb Alashkar, Northeastern University, Boston, USA
Wael Alhajyaseen, Qatar University, Qatar
Mehran Asadi, Lincoln University, USA
Jocelyn Aubert, Luxembourg Institute of Science and Technology (LIST), Luxembourg
Fredrick Awuor, Kisii University, Kenya / Academia Sinica, Taiwan
Mohamed Bakhouya, University of Technologies of Belfort/Montbeliard, France
Ali Balador, RISE SICS Västerås, Sweden
Matthias Baldauf, FHS St.Gallen, Switzerland
Felipe Becker Nunes, Federal University of Rio Grande do Sul (UFRGS), Brazil
Oladayo Bello, Johns Hopkins University, USA
Fouad Ben-Abdelaziz, NEOMA Business School, Rouen Campus, France

Simon Bergweiler, DFKI GmbH, German Research Center for Artificial Intelligence, Germany
Aurelio Bermúdez, Universidad de Castilla-La Mancha, Spain
Nik Bessis, Edge Hill University, UK
Stefan Bosse, University of Koblenz-Landau, Germany
Lars Braubach, Complex Software Systems | Bremen City University, Germany
Juan Carlos Cano, University Politécnica de Valencia, Spain
José Cecílio, University of Coimbra, Portugal
Lamia Chaari, SFAX University, Tunisia
Bongsug (Kevin) Chae, Kansas State University, USA
Supriyo Chakraborty, IBM Thomas J. Watson Research Center, USA
Konstantinos Chatzikokolakis, MarineTraffic, UK
Chao Chen, Purdue University Fort Wayne, USA
Jingyuan Cheng, Technische Universitaet Braunschweig, Germany
Carla-Fabiana Chiasserini, Politecnico di Torino, Italy
Youngchol Choi, Korea Research Institute of Ships and Ocean Engineering (KRISO), Korea
Michael Collins, Technological University Dublin, Ireland
Carlos Henrique Corrêa Tolentino, IFTO - Palmas, Brazil
Giuseppe D'Aniello, University of Salerno, Italy
André Constantino da Silva, IFSP and NIED/UNICAMP, Brazil
Mauro Henrique Lima de Boni, Federal Institute of Education, Science, and Technology of Tocantins, Brazil
Claudio de Castro Monteiro, Federal Institute of Education, Science and Technology of Tocantins, Brazil

Teles de Sales Bezerra, Federal University of Campina Grande, Brazil
Alexiei Dingli, University of Malta, Malta
Choukri Djellali, University of Quebec at Rimouski, Canada
Roland Dodd, CQUniversity, Australia
Ali Dorri, UNSW / DATA61 CSIRO, Australia
Junzhao Du, Xidian University, China
Joyce El Haddad, University of Paris Dauphine, France
Ahmed El Oualkadi, Abdelmalek Essaadi University, Morocco
Ehab Helmy Elshazly, Egyptian Atomic Energy Authority, Egypt
Francisco Falcone, Universidad Publica de Navarra, Spain
Ramin Fallahzadeh, Stanford University, USA
Andras Farago, University of Texas at Dallas, USA
Muhamad Felemban, Purdue University, USA
Houda Ferradi, NTT Secure Platform Laboratories, Japan
Renato Ferrero, Politecnico di Torino, Italy
Aryan Firouzian, University of Oulu , Finland
Olivier Flauzac, University of Reims, France
Franco Frattolillo, University of Sannio, Benevento, Italy
Crescenzio Gallo, University of Foggia / University Hospital “Ospedali Riuniti", Italy
Vincent Gauthier, Telecom SudParis | CNRS SAMOVAR | University Paris-Saclay, France
Shahin Gelareh, IUT de Bethune | Universite d'Artois, France
Volkan Gezer, German Research Center for Artificial Intelligence (DFKI), Germany
Chris Gniady, University of Arizona, USA
Mikhail Gofman, Cal State Fullerton University, USA
Rossitza Goleva, Technical University of Sofia, Bulgaria /

Paulo Gondim, University of Brasilia, Brazil
Ann Gordon-Ross, University of Florida, USA
Weixi Gu, Tsinghua University, China / UC Berkeley, USA
Fikret Gurgen, Bogazici University, Turkey
Hedi Haddad, Dhofar University, Salalah, Oman
Zurina Mohd Hanapi
Md. Zoheb Hassan, University of British Columbia, Canada
Qiang (Nathan) He, Swinburne University of Technology, Australia
Hiroaki Higaki, Tokyo Denki University, Japan
Jon M. Hjelmervik, SINTEF Digital, Norway
Dong Ho Cho, KAIST, Republic of Korea
Wladyslaw Homenda, Warsaw University of Technology, Poland
Tzung-Pei Hong, National University of Kaohsiung, Taiwan
Sun-Yuan Hsieh, National Cheng Kung University, Taiwan
Shaohan Hu, IBM Research, USA
Yu-Chen Hu, Providence University, Taiwan
Edward Y. Hua, Janus Research Group, Inc., USA
Isabel Hübener, University of Kassel, Germany
Malinka Ivanova, Technical University of Sofia, Bulgaria
Nafaa Jabeur, German University of Technology in Oman (GUtech), Oman
Ming Jin, Lawrence Berkeley National Laboratory (LBNL), USA
Mehmet Karakoc, Alanya HEP University, Antalya, Turkey
Fazal Wahab Karam, COMSATS Institute of Information Technology, Pakistan
Sye Loong Keoh, University of Glasgow, UK
Djamel Khadraoui, Luxembourg Institute of Science and Technology (LIST), Luxembourg
BaekGyu Kim, Toyota InfoTechnology Center, USA
Cornel Klein, Siemens AG/Corporate Research and Technologies - Münich, Germany
Reinhard Klemm, Avaya, USA
Vitaly Klyuev, University of Aizu, Japan
Sönke Knoch, German Research Center for Artificial Intelligence - DFKI GmbH, Germany
Thomas Kopinski, University of South Westphalia, Germany
Dmitry Korzun, Petrozavodsk State University, Russia
Konstantinos Kotis, University of the Aegean, Greece
Abderrafiaa Koukam, Université de Technologie de Belfort-Montbéliard, France
Jarosław Koźlak, AGH University of Science and Technology, Poland
Brano Kusy, CSIRO, Australia
Michal Kvet, University of Zilina, Slovakia
Soo Kyun Kim, Paichai University, South Korea
Philippe Lalanda, Université Grenoble Alpes, France
Frédéric Le Mouël, INSA Lyon, France
Dongman Lee, KAIST, Korea
Gyu Myoung Lee, Liverpool John Moores University, UK
Pierre Leone, University of Geneva, Switzerland
Wenjuan Li, City University of Hong Kong, Hong Kong
Xiuhua Li, University of British Columbia, Canada
Mingming Liu, IBM, Ireland
Xiaodong Liu, Edinburgh Napier University, UK
Xiaoli Liu, University of Oulu, Finland

Politècnica de València, Spain
Ana Lucila Sandoval Orozco, Universidad Complutense de Madrid (UCM), Spain
José Santa Lozano, Technical University of Cartagena, Spain
Nurbek P. Saparkhojayev, Akhmet Yassawi University, Turkestan, Kazakhstan
Sarwar Sayeed, University of the West of Scotland, UK
Floriano Scioscia, Technical University of Bari, Italy
Zary Segall, UMBC, USA
Hugo Sereno Ferreira, University of Porto, Portugal
Hamed Shah-Mansouri, University of British Columbia, Vancouver, Canada
Alireza Shahrabi, Glasgow Caledonian University, UK
Vishakha Sharma, Georgetown University, Washington D.C., USA
Shih-Lung Shaw, University of Tennessee, Knoxville, USA
Haichen Shen, University of Washington, USA
Qi Shi, Liverpool John Moores University, UK
Kazuhiko Shibuya, Tokyo Metropolitan University, Japan
Tong Shu, Argonne National Laboratory, USA
Matteo Signorini, Nokia Bell Labs, France
Catarina Silva, Polytechnic Institute of Leiria, Portugal
Amita Singh, KTH Royal Institute of Technology, Sweden
Radosveta Sokullu, Ege University, Izmir, Turkey
Francesco Soldovieri, CNR IREA, Italy
Sebastian Soller, University of Passau, Germany
Angelo Spognardi, Sapienza University of Rome, Italy
Álvaro Suárez Sarmiento, University of Las Palmas de Gran Canaria, Spain
Chiranjib Sur, University of Florida, USA
Apostolos Syropoulos, Greek Molecular Computing Group, Greece
Ryszard Tadeusiewicz, AGH University of Science and Technology, Poland
Yoshiaki Taniguchi, Kindai University, Japan
Adrian Tarniceriu, PulseOn SA, Switzerland
Markus Taumberger, VTT Technical Research Centre of Finland, Finland
Aderonke F. Thompson, Federal University of Technology, Akure, Nigeria
Jean-Yves Tigli, Université Côte d'Azur, France
Angelo Trotta, University of Bologna, Italy
Chih-Cheng Tseng, National Ilan University, Taiwan
Ion Tutanescu, University of Pitesti, Romania
Hamed Vahdat-Nejad, University of Birjand, Iran
Miroslav Velev, Aries Design Automation, USA
Juan Vicente Capella Hernández, Universitat Politècnica de València, Spain
Dario Vieira, EFREI, France
Fabio Viola, ARCES - University of Bologna, Italy
Jie Wang, Dalian University of Technology, China
Xianzhi Wang, University of Technology, Sydney, Australia
Xuyu Wang, California State University, Sacramento, USA
Tomi Westerlund, University of Turku, Finland / Wuxi Institute of Fudan University, China
Jian Yu, Auckland University of Technology, New Zealand
Bo Zhou, German Research Center for Artificial Intelligence, Kaiserslautern, Germany
Eugenio Zimeo, University of Sannio, Italy
Claudia Liliana Zúñiga-Cañón, University of Santiago de Cali, Colombia

Copyright Information

TPM Feature Set: a Universal Algorithm for Spatial-Temporal Pressure Mapping Imagery Data

Bo Zhou, Paul Lukowicz

German Research Center for Artificial Intelligence and
Technical Universiy of Kaiserslautern
bo.zhou@dfki.de, paul.lukowicz@dfki.de

***Abstract*—There have been many studies in recent years using the Textile planar Pressure Mapping (TPM) technology for computer-human interactions and ubiquitous activity recognition. A TPM sensing system generates a time sequence of spatial pressure imagery. We propose a novel, comprehensive and unified feature set to evaluate TPM data from the space and time domain. The initial version of the TPM feature set presented in this paper includes 663 temporal features and 80 spatial features. We evaluated the feature set on 3 datasets from past studies in the scopes of ambient, smart object and wearable sensing. The TPM feature set has shown superior recognition accuracy compared with the ad-hoc algorithms from the corresponding studies. Furthermore, we have demonstrated the general approach to further reduce and optimise the feature calculation process for specific applications with neighbourhood component analysis.**

***Index Terms*—textile pressure mapping; data analysis; machine learning algorithm.**

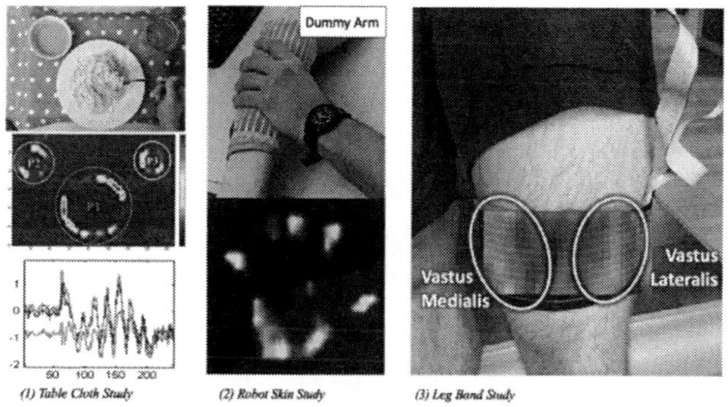

Figure 1. Illustration of the three datasets used in the evaluation: (1) *tablecloth study* [11], (2) *robot skin study* [12], and (3) *leg band study* [13].

I. Introduction

Textile Pressure Mapping (TPM) is an emerging technology for ubiquitous and wearable activity recognition. TPM technology measures the distribution of the planar pressure force on a surface, which is omnipresent during all sorts of physical interactions and activities. Dementyev et al. [1] used a wrist-worn Force Sensitive Resistor (FSR) array to detect hand gestures. Cheng et al. [2] proposed a system to detect tongue control gestures with a face-worn TPM patch. Pressure mat placed on the chair surfaces to detect seating postures have also been studied in [3] [4]. Sundholm et al. [5] have demonstrated that sports exercises can be recognized from a sports mat which sense the pressure distribution. Schneegass et al. [6] investigated using a pressure matrix as a sleeve for the forearm to recognize writing gestures.

Many of the researches mentioned above are ad hoc designed on the hardware, software, and algorithm levels. Since each of these studies encloses many aspects, including the hardware, software and activity recognition, none of them are focused on discussions in the algorithm.

Efforts have been devoted to bringing forward a unified solution to push the pressure mapping technology forward in the field of ubiquitous computing and the internet of things. A general hardware architecture to implement TPM sensing systems in [7] . In [8], a framework is proposed to as a unified solution to help developers who are new to the technology to build and evaluate TPM-enabled activity recognition studies. However, there lacks a comprehensive investigation into the algorithms of processing the TPM data, especially which features are contributing to the classification results.

TPM imagery has a spatial-temporal data format. Some computer vision techniques for video processing has been applied, such as the work in [9], where neural networks trained for video classification is used to recognize identity from footprint on a TPM carpet. However, TPM imagery is cleaner than camera images in terms of the background scene or objects, obstruction of view, etc. The neural networks also require substantial computational power and are not easily explainable, i.e. which feature or part of the network contributes more to differentiate different activities. Thus many computer vision techniques can be considered over-engineering for processing the TPM imagery. Maximilian et al. [10] proposed a generic feature extraction method on time series. To the best of our knowledge, there lacks a comprehensive and explainable feature analysis scheme that is suitable for the spatial-temporal TPM imagery.

In this paper, we propose the TPM feature set, which comprehensively analyses the TPM data through the time and space domains. The TPM feature set is evaluated with datasets from three empirical studies with different application scenarios. We also investigate which features are contributing more positively to the classification through neighbourhood component analysis. The streamlined methods proposed in this paper can be used to analyse and optimise new datasets from future TPM studies.

In Section II, the general format of the pressure mapping data and terminologies are introduced. Section III explains the detailed generic method, the TPM feature set, to extract information from space and time domains. In Section IV, the spatial and temporal domains are discussed in depth to investigate which features are more relevant with established empirical study datasets. Section V concludes the paper.

II. TPM Data in the Spatial-Temporal Domains

TPM sensors generate a multi-channel, spatial-temporal data format, which describes the localization of the pressure distribution along the time axis.

Every sensing point is defined as a *pixel*:

$$p(x, y, t) \tag{1}$$

where x and y are the coordinates in the spatial dimensions, and t is the specific time.

At any time t, the entire mapping M of the sensor is defined as a *Frame*:

$$F(t) = \{p(x, y, t) \mid (x, y) \in \{M\}\} \tag{2}$$

A temporal sequence from a time window T of *Frames* is defined as a data *Stream*:

$$S_T = \{F(t) \mid t \in \{T\}\} \tag{3}$$

Individual sensing points have limited information about the activity; therefore, some descriptive values of the frame at a given time t are calculated as *Frame Descriptors*:

$$des_i(t) = Func_i(F(t)) \tag{4}$$

Another approach to abstract the *stream* from a time window is to perform per-pixel operations along the time axis, resulting in individual frames that represent the stream. We call these frames as *Key Frames*:

$$KF_i(t) = Func_i(S_T)) \tag{5}$$

III. The TPM Feature Set

Figure 2 shows the general workflow of calculating the TPM feature set from the space and time domains. Temporal features are extracted from sequences of simple frame descriptors $des_i(t)$. Spatial features are calculated from 2-dimensional key frames $KF_i(t)$. The initial version of the TPM feature set includes 663 (17×39) temporal features and 80 (8×10) spatial features.

A. Frame Descriptors

Treat $F(t)$ as a set, the TPM feature set calculates the following $des_i(t)$:

- average value

$$des_1(t) = mean(F(t)) = \frac{1}{|M|} \sum_{(x,y)}^{\{M\}} p(x, y, t) \tag{6}$$

- variance

$$des_2(t) = \frac{1}{|M|} \sum_{(x,y)}^{\{M\}} (p(x, y, t) - mean(F(t)))^2 \tag{7}$$

- range

$$des_3(t) = p_{MAX}(t) - p_{MIN}(t) \tag{8}$$

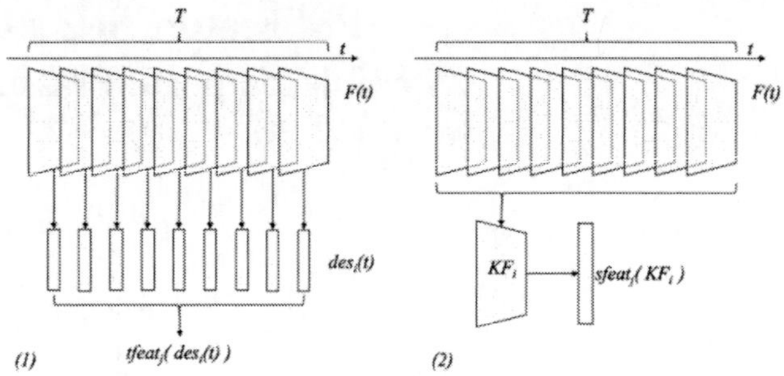

Figure 2. (1) Temporal and (2) spacial feature extraction process.

- entropy

$$des_4(t) = - \sum_{(x,y)}^{\{M\}} p(x, y, t) \cdot log_2\, p(x, y, t) \tag{9}$$

- mean absolute deviation

$$des_5(t) = \frac{1}{|M|} \sum_{(x,y)}^{\{M\}} (p(x, y, t) - mean(F(t))) \tag{10}$$

- the center of mass (CoM) coordinate x and y (weighted by pixel value) $des_6(t)$ and $des_7(t)$
- the centroid coordinate (unweighted, only considering the contour after filtering the frame with a threshold). $des_8(t)$ and $des_9(t)$. Here the threshold is defined as

$$mean(F(t)) - 0.25 \cdot (mean(F(t)) - p_{min}(t)) \tag{11}$$

- area (the count of pixels that are above the threshold) $des_{10}(t)$
- $des_{11}(t)$ to $des_{17}(t)$ Hu's seven image moments [14]

For a matrix of binary values, the CoM is identical to the centroid; but for a matrix with multi-values that describes a profile, the CoM shows how the pixel value density is focused while the centroid shows only the geometric center. $des_1(t)$, $des_6(t)$ and $des_7(t)$ are mathematically identical to the first three central moments in the literature on image moments.

B. Temporal Features

Any sequence of frame descriptors is denoted as $des_i(t) \in \{des_1(t), des_2(t), ...\}$. Then, from the temporal sequence within a window of length T (sliding window or spotted event), temporal features can be calculated:

- average

$$tfeat_1 = \frac{1}{|T|} \sum_{t}^{\{T\}} des_i(t) \tag{12}$$

- variance

$$tfeat_2 = \frac{1}{|T|} \sum_{t}^{\{T\}} (des_i(t) - tfeat_1)^2 \tag{13}$$

- range

$$tfeat_3 = des_{i_{MAX}} - des_{i_{MIN}} \tag{14}$$

- skewness, that describes the asymmetry of the data

$$tfeat_4 = \frac{\frac{1}{|T|} \sum_t^T (des_i(t) - tfeat_1)^3}{\left(\frac{1}{|T|} \sum_t^T (des_i(t) - tfeat_1)^2\right)^{3/2}} \tag{15}$$

- kurtosis, that measures how outlier-prone the temporal sequence's distribution is

$$tfeat_5 = \frac{\frac{1}{|T|}\sum_t^T (des_i(t) - tfeat_1)^4}{\left(\frac{1}{|T|}\sum_t^T (des_x(t) - tfeat_1)^2\right)^2} \quad (16)$$

- waveform length [15]

$$tfeat_6 = \sum_t^T -1(des_i(t+1) - des_i(t)) \quad (17)$$

- sum of values greater than mean

$$tfeat_7 = \sum_t^T (des_i(t) \mid des_i(t) > tfeat_1) \quad (18)$$

- the power spectrum density of des_i is calculated with fast Fourier transform as $PSD(n)$, $n \in N$ is the frequency in the spectrum. Following features are calculated from $PSD(n)$: average magnitude

$$tfeat_8 = \frac{1}{N}\sum_n^N PSD(n) \quad (19)$$

- mean frequency

$$tfeat_9 = \frac{\sum_n^N n \cdot PSD(n)}{\sum_n^N PSD(n)} \quad (20)$$

- N is divided to 5 equal frequency bands, the average values of each band is $tfeat_{10}$, $tfeat_{11}$, $tfeat_{12}$, $tfeat_{13}$, $tfeat_{14}$.
- A wavelet transform scalogram is calculated with the LTFAT toolbox [16], with $J = 4$ filterbank iterations. The coefficient vector of each filterbank is $C(j), j \in [0, 4]$.
- $tfeat_{15}$, $tfeat_{20}$, $tfeat_{25}$, $tfeat_{30}$, $tfeat_{35}$ are the mean value of each coefficient vector;
- $tfeat_{16}$, $tfeat_{21}$, $tfeat_{26}$, $tfeat_{31}$, $tfeat_{36}$ are the variance of each coefficient vector;
- $tfeat_{17}$, $tfeat_{22}$, $tfeat_{27}$, $tfeat_{32}$, $tfeat_{37}$ are the range of each coefficient vector;
- $tfeat_{18}$, $tfeat_{23}$, $tfeat_{28}$, $tfeat_{33}$, $tfeat_{38}$ are the skewness of each coefficient vector;
- $tfeat_{19}$, $tfeat_{24}$, $tfeat_{29}$, $tfeat_{34}$, $tfeat_{39}$ are the kurtosis of each coefficient vector;

C. Key Frames

From a time window, a *key frame* can be one particular frame that has special frame descriptor values, such as the maximum or minimum of $des_i(t)$. A *key frame* can also be calculated from the stream of the window through pixel-wise operations. 8 key frames are calculated in the TPM feature set:

- per pixel average of all frames

$$KF_1 = \frac{1}{|T|}\sum_t^{\{T\}} F(t) \quad (21)$$

- sum of per pixel differences

$$KF_2 = \sum_t^{\{T-1\}} (F(t+1) - F(t)) \quad (22)$$

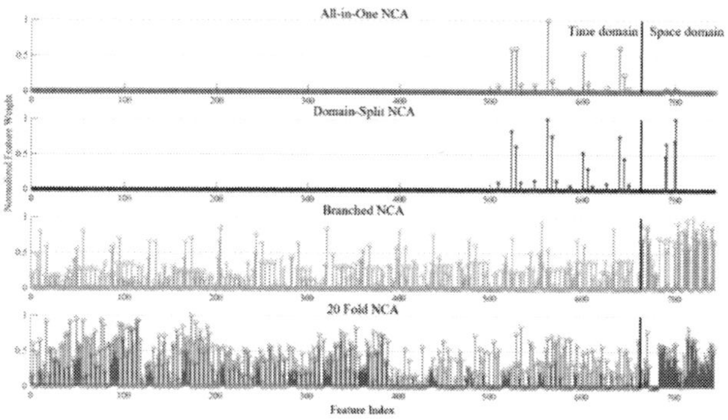

Figure 3. Feature weight distributions of different NCA division methods (tablecloth dataset)

- sum of only the positive or negative values of per pixel differences

$$KF_3 = \mid \sum_t^{\{T-1\}} ((F(t+1) - F(t)) > 0) \mid \quad (23)$$

$$KF_4 = \mid \sum_t^{\{T-1\}} ((F(t+1) - F(t)) < 0) \mid \quad (24)$$

- the frame which has the maximum mean pixel value as KF_5 and the frame with the minimum mean value as KF_6
- the frame with the maximum standard deviation from the stream as KF_7
- the per pixel average of the frames, whose pixel value is greater than the frame pixel average

$$KF_8 = \frac{1}{|T|}\sum_t^{\{T\}} (F_p(t)) \quad (25)$$

$$F_p(t) = \begin{cases} p(x,y,t) & \text{if } p(x,y,t) \geq mean(F(t)) \\ 0 & \text{if } p(x,y,t) < mean(F(t)) \end{cases}$$

D. Spatial Features

Various image processing techniques can then be used to extract information from those key frames. Image moments are proven to be helpful shape descriptors as spatial features $sfeat_j(KF_i)$ through previous studies. In the TPM feature set, we use the 3 central moments and Hu's 7 invariant moments [14], which are rotation, translation and scale invariant.

IV. Evaluation and Feature Selection

In this section, we evaluate how different combinations of frame descriptors - temporal feature pairs, and key frame - spatial feature pairs contribute to the classification accuracy. The datasets used are from various past studies in different setting scenarios.

A. General Approach

The evaluation process can be divided into four parts:

1) Convert the data stream into features: From the time domain, first, temporal sequences of the 17 frame descriptors $des_i(t)$ are calculated from every stream. Within every $des_i(t)$, a sliding window is performed. Every window is denoted as $n \in N$. The data in the window is multiplied with a Tukey window with $r = 0.2$, to bring the start and end of the window to zero. For every sliding window, 39 temporal features $tfeat_j(des_i), j \in 1, 2, ...39, i \in 1, 2, ...17$ are calculated. In the spatial domain, first the input data stream is cropped with the same window size and window step as the sliding window for $des_i(t)$, but the outputs are the smaller length of streams, and no Tuken window is applied. Within each window of streams, 8 key frames KF_i are calculated. Overall 10 spacial features is calculated from every key frame $sfeat_j(KF_i), j \in 1, 2, ...10, i \in 1, 2, ...8$.

2) Baseline cross-validation: To carry out balanced training, all classes are trimmed to the same amount of windows by random selecting. The amount of windows is the class that has the least windows. K-fold cross-validation is performed with multiple classifiers, and the accuracy is used to compare different classifier's results.

3) Feature selection: The feature weight evaluation is performed using neighbourhood component analysis (NCA) [17]. The method ranks the most relevant features that contribute to the classification. Since the features are calculated from two levels of information: temporal features are calculated first by reducing the space domain to frame descriptors, then to the time domain features; as spatial features are calculated first by reducing the time domain to key frames. Thus, the feature weight result can either be presented as a *feature weight vector* or as a *feature weight matrix* for either the temporal or spacial feature methods.

4) Feature reduction: The top-weighted features are selected to perform the same cross-validation. For comparison, the least weighted features are also evaluated separately.

Principle Component Analysis (PCA) [18] is another commonly used technique for reducing feature dimensions. The method removes redundancy and outputs a set of eigenvectors that best describes the variance of the dataset. Each component is orthogonal to the preceding one so that the eigenvectors are uncorrelated and thus without redundancy. However, PCA itself does not take the class label information, it only analyses the data distribution to remove redundancy but not irrelevant features. Typically, PCA is used as a step after calculating the features, and before feeding the information to classifiers. Therefore, we use NCA instead of PCA to find the features that are more contributive to distinguishing different classes.

B. Datasets

Three past studies are taken for comparison, they are codenamed as: *tablecloth* [11], *robot skin* [12], and *leg band* [13] as shown in Figure 2.

In the tablecloth study [11], a TPM fabric with a 30-by-42 matrix is placed on a dining tablet to detect dining related actions. A main dish plate, a salad bowl, and a glass are placed on it. Participants eat various food of different textures, that would require different actions for dining the food with a knife and a fork. The force of the actions can propagate through the cutlery and plates to the tablecloth surface. The 7 action classes are: stir, scoop, cut, poke, scoop, collect and replace. The sliding window is chosen with 2 second period and 1 second window step. 10 participants each took part in 8 recordings.

In the robot skin study [12], a TPM fabric with a 20-by-20 matrix is used to detect 7 emotionally related touch gestures onto a dummy arm or a surface, including grab, poke, press, push, scratch, pinch and stroke. The gestures are already segmented based on matrix activation, since when there is no gesture, the matrix is not being pressed. In total, 24 participants took part in 2 recordings. Each recording includes 16 repetitions of every gesture.

In the leg band study [13], a TPM fabric with an 8-by-16 matrix is embedded in an elastic compression band that is placed on the thigh as users take part in gym leg exercises. The sensor detects the surface pressure of the leg muscles as planar pressure mechanomyography. The 5 activity classes are: working out with a cross trainer, leg press, seated leg curl and leg extension, plus a class contains all non-workout activities. Based on the activity's characteristic, the sliding window is chosen as 4 seconds wide, the window step is 20% of the window size. Six participants have recorded 4 sessions each.

In this paper, all the participants' data are merged together as one dataset for every study (person independent - inclusive case). Every sliding window or gesture is one sample. The tablecloth dataset has 10815 samples, robot skin 5376 samples, and leg band 28425 samples.

C. Neighborhood Component Analysis (NCA)

This subsection briefly explains the NCA method published in [17] and implemented in Matlab as `fscnca`. The NCA method assumes a feature weight vector w as a variable to be multiplied with the features, and uses an approximate solver to find the optimal weight vector that maximizes the correct classification probability (the objective function). (The mathematical symbols for NCA explanation are not related to the rest of this paper for the TPM feature set.)

For a d-dimensional dataset of N training points, all the points from the dataset are taken as a query point once x_i. For each query point, the other points can be taken as its reference point as a probability p_{ij} derived from their weighted distance enclosed in a kernel function. The probability that this query point x_i is correctly classified is defined as the probability summation of the reference points that has the same class, similar to a K-nearest neighbour classifier.

The objective function is the average of all the points' correct classification probability. After unfolding the relationship, the objective function can be written as a differentiable function of the feature weight vector, with a tunable parameter λ which is multiplied with the weight vector's term in the objective function:

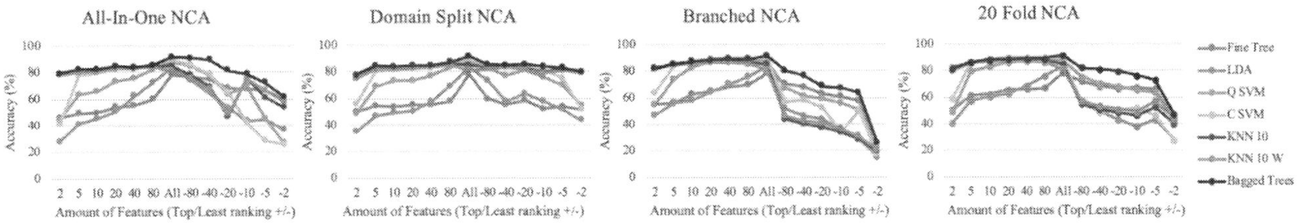

Figure 4. Accuracy with varying amount of selected features comparison of four NCA division methods (tablecloth dataset)

$$F(w) = \sum_{i=1}^{N} \left(\sum_{j=1, j \neq i}^{N} P_{ij} y_{ij} - \lambda \sum_{l=1}^{d} w_l^2 \right) \quad (26)$$

where $y_{ij} = 1$ if the query point and the reference point has the same class. Since $F(w)$ is differentiable, its maxima can be approximated with algorithms, such as stochastic gradient descent (SGD) [19], to find out the feature weight vector w that maximizes the objective function $F(w)$. In other words, NCA finds the best feature weight combination that yields the highest correct classification probability.

D. NCA division approaches on high dimensional features

A problem of NCA is that when most of the features contribute to the classification, the approximation may return to only very few highly weighted features while the others remain close to zero weight. This leaves the classification result relatively low with selected high weighted features. Our solution is to segment these features and perform NCA on smaller batches, then combine the feature weights. In this work, four NCA division approaches are investigated:

- All-in-One: all the features are taken under NCA as once.
- Space-time domain split: features are split into two groups: spatial domain features and temporal domain features.
- Branched: features are more detailed separated into branches. In the time domain, a branch is all the temporal features from one frame descriptor; in the space domain, a branch is all the spatial features from one key frame.
- K-fold: all features are randomized and split into K equal partitions. One NCA is performed for each partition.

In the segmented feature groups, the resulting feature weight vectors are normalized within each group before being concatenated into one vector. The results of the four different feature division approaches on the smart tablecloth data are shown in Figure 3. From the result, All-in-One and domain-split NCA return similar weight for the time domain features, with zero weight for most of the features. The domain split NCA gives higher weight on the spatial features as a result of normalization before merging, but the feature indexes that are higher than approximate zero are the same between the two approaches. In the branched and 20-fold NCA, however, many more features are given higher weight.

To compare which approach is better, cross-validation with the highest ranking features, in comparison with the lowest ranking features can be used. A better approach should meet the following criteria:

- Higher accuracy with the same number of top ranking features compared to other approaches.
- Greater difference between highest accuracy and the accuracy with the least ranking features, than the difference between highest accuracy and the accuracy with the top ranking features.
- With the same amount of features, top ranking features should in general result in higher accuracy than least ranking features.

E. NCA Evaluation

To evaluate which approach yields better feature selection, cross-validation from the top or least ranking features are performed. For performance reasons, top or least 2, 5, 10, 20, 40 and 80 features are chosen. The NCA algorithm should have greater influence on the KNN classifiers since the basic principle is similar (Euclidean distance to the training data samples). In this evaluation, a variety of classifiers are chosen:

1) classification tree with 100 maximum splits and Gini's diversity index split criterion (Fine Tree)
2) linear discriminant analysis (LDA)
3) support vector machine with a quadratic kernel (Q SVM)
4) support vector machine with a cubic kernel (C SVM)
5) K-nearest neighbor with equally weighted Euclidean distance and K=10 (KNN 10)
6) K-nearest neighbor with squared inversely weighted Euclidean distance and K=10 (KNN 10 W)
7) Ensemble of 30 decision tree learners (Bagged Trees)

The results are shown in Figure 4.

For many classifiers, all-in-one and domain split NCA has a near symmetric accuracy distribution centered at all features; sometimes with the least ranking features, there are higher accuracy points than the corresponding top ranking features. From this, we concluded that the feature weights derived by these two methods are no better than random selection. Branched and 20 Fold NCA, on the other hand, in general, meet the criteria listed above, and have a similar trend of the accuracy values. The highest ranking features result in higher accuracy values than the lowest ranking features.

The top 2 ranking features already result in over 80% accuracy for Bagged Trees and the two KNN classifiers. While for the other classifiers, Fine Tree, LDA and SVM, the accuracy values are significantly lower. This may because these classifiers work by separating the feature space with modelled boundaries, while KNN and bagged trees do not use such boundaries to distinguish different classes. The data's nature may not fit very well with the classifiers' algorithms, e.g., the data may not have clean-shaped boundaries, or the same class may have several clusters. However, this cannot be further investigated at this point due to the high dimensionality.

The least 2 ranking features result in close to chance level (14.3% for 7 classes) accuracy values, thus means the NCA successfully identify the less relevant features. As the number of features taken grows, the accuracy of both top and least ranking features increase, but the top ranking features give higher accuracy than the least ranking ones.

As branched NCA is not a generic approach, and K-Fold NCA can be performed on any feature sets, this work will continue with K-Fold NCA. Figure 5 shows the top ranking features but with more amount of taken features until all of them are chosen. From it, the accuracy has come to a stable level close to 90% between 10 to 160 features for most classifiers except for LDA and Fine Tree; while from 240 features on, the accuracy has another increase that is on the similar level with all the features. This shows that only the top 10 features are sufficient for this dataset for moderately high accuracy, and 240 features are adequate to explain all the class discriminant as good as with all features.

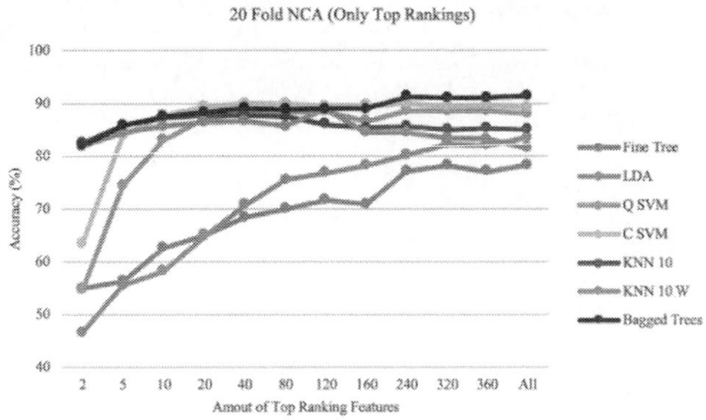

Figure 5. Top ranking features of the 20 fold NCA on the tablecloth dataset to locate the optimal amount of features.

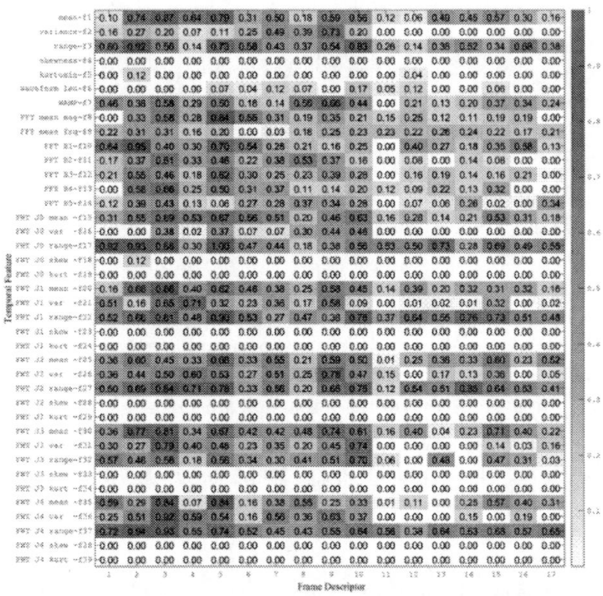

Figure 6. Temporal feature weight - Smart tablecloth dataset.

F. Application Variance and Discussions

To be displayed only as a linear vector of values as in Figure 3 is not sufficient to tell which feature calculation method is more relevant. Therefore, the feature weight vector is reshaped into two 2-dimensional matrices according to the frame descriptor - temporal feature combination or key frame - spacial feature combination as a feature weight matrix (FWM). For the tablecloth dataset, the temporal feature weight matrix FWM_t is shown in Figure 6, and the spacial feature weight matrix FWM_s is in Figure 9(1). From FWM_t, it can be seen that some temporal features have no contribution, such as skewness, kurtosis, including the skewness and kurtosis for the wavelet transform. Some frame descriptors are more important, such as des_2 variance, des_3 range, des_5 mean absolute deviation. All the 7 Hu's moments des_{11} to des_{17} are less important. It is possibly a result that in this dataset, the objects are all plates or glasses, and their footprints are all circular. Hence, the shape descriptors are not contributing to the activity. From FWM_s, the key frames describe the static values, such as KF_1 and KF_2 are less contributive, while the key frames that describe the dynamic changes all have greater feature weights.

Two other datasets are evaluated with the same process, and the resulting plots of 'number of features' - accuracy plots are in Figure 10. (SVM classifiers are not used for evaluation here due to performance constraints.) Referring to the NCA evaluation criteria, NCA has effectively located relevant features in all datasets. Feature weight matrix are shown in Figure 7, Figure 8, and Figure 9(2)(3). Table I compares the accuracy of the original studies with the TPM feature set. The top 20 features from each dataset are further listed in Table II.

Comparing the FWM_t and FWM_s of all datasets, highest ranking features are different for specific applications. There are only three features that are present in all datasets' top 40 features. For example, skewness and kurtosis have relatively high weight for the robot skin dataset, and also have higher weights in some of the frame descriptors for the leg band dataset. The FFT features have almost no weight in the robot skin dataset, while these features are significantly relevant in the tablecloth and leg band dataset. And when FFT features have more weight, wavelet transform features also have more

TABLE I. ACCURACY COMPARISON OF THE ORIGINAL STUDIES AND THE TPM FEATURE SET

Dataset	Original Study	TPM Feature Set
Tablecloth	91.2%	91.4 %
Robot Skin	92.7%	94.7 %
Leg Band	81.7 %	98.2 %

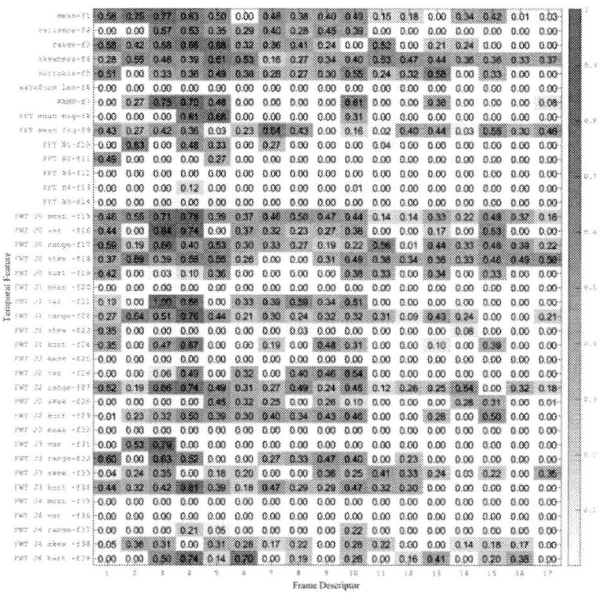

Figure 7. Temporal feature weight (robot skin dataset)

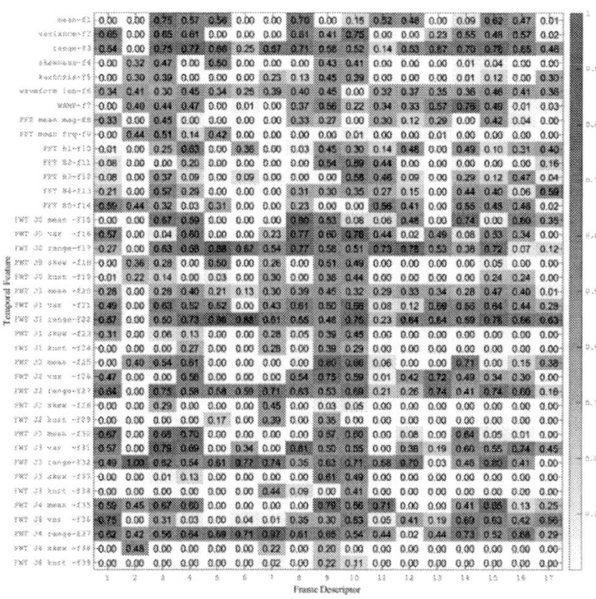

Figure 8. Spatial feature weight (leg band dataset)

weight. This is expected since both FFT and wavelet transform describes frequency information. In the leg band dataset, Hu's 7 moments as frame descriptors have significantly higher weight than the other two dataset. Spatial features on average have less weight in the tablecloth and robot skin datasets than in the leg band datasets.

The key conclusion is that, for different applications, the TPM sensor data exhibit different natures.

G. Performance Benchmark

We evaluated the computational performance with a dataset recording file (.mat format) of 286MB (Leg Band dataset person 1 recording 1). The benchmark was carried out on a 2018 MacBook Pro with a six-core 2.6GHz Intel Core i7 processor, and Matlab 2019a. The total frame descriptors calculation took 43.87s and total key frames 2.47s. All the temporal features from all frame descriptors took 350.05s and the spatial features 0.765s. During the temporal feature calculation, the most time consuming process is the fast wavelet transform, which takes 281.35s out of the 350.05s. The 20 fold NCA with all the recordings from the leg band dataset took 926.83s.

However, since the feature set is meant to help explore the useful features for specific data set offline, the computational requirement is less important. With the NCA optimization method, developers can further reduce and select the features to be computed based on their specific requirements.

TABLE II. TOP RANKING FEATURES

Tablecloth dataset

Ranking	1	2	3	4	5	6	7	8	9	10
Des/KF	5	2	2	3	2	1	3	2	5	3
Feature	17	10	37	37	17	17	36	3	22	17
Domain	T	T	T	T	T	T	T	T	T	T
Ranking	11	12	13	14	15	16	17	18	19	20
Des/KF	3	3	14	5	5	3	3	6	10	3
Feature	1	20	27	35	8	35	27	3	3	22
Domain	T	T	T	T	T	T	T	**S**	T	T

Robot Skin dataset

Ranking	1	2	3	4	5	6	7	8	9	10
Des/KF	3	3	4	4	4	3	4	6	3	4
Feature	21	16	34	8	1	31	15	7	1	22
Domain	T	T	T	**S**	**S**	T	T	**S**	T	T
Ranking	11	12	13	14	15	16	17	18	19	20
Des/KF	3	2	4	4	4	3	4	3	3	4
Feature	7	1	27	39	16	1	7	6	15	2
Domain	T	T	T	T	T	**S**	**S**	**S**	T	**S**

Leg Band dataset

Ranking	1	2	3	4	5	6	7	8	9	10
Des/KF	2	7	6	5	5	15	8	15	9	8
Feature	32	37	22	17	22	35	31	32	25	1
Domain	T	T	T	T	T	T	T	T	T	**S**
Ranking	11	12	13	14	15	16	17	18	19	20
Des/KF	8	9	3	15	12	15	8	4	8	6
Feature	15	35	31	3	17	22	16	3	17	32
Domain	T	T	T	T	T	T	T	T	T	T

V. CONCLUSION

A generic feature calculation method, the TPM feature set, is proposed in this paper. Built upon various relevant studies, it can be used to extract information from both the space and time domains for the TPM imagery. Through our evaluation, our approach shows superior accuracy compared to the original studies in which the datasets were published with ad hoc algorithms. Not all features contribute equally, and the

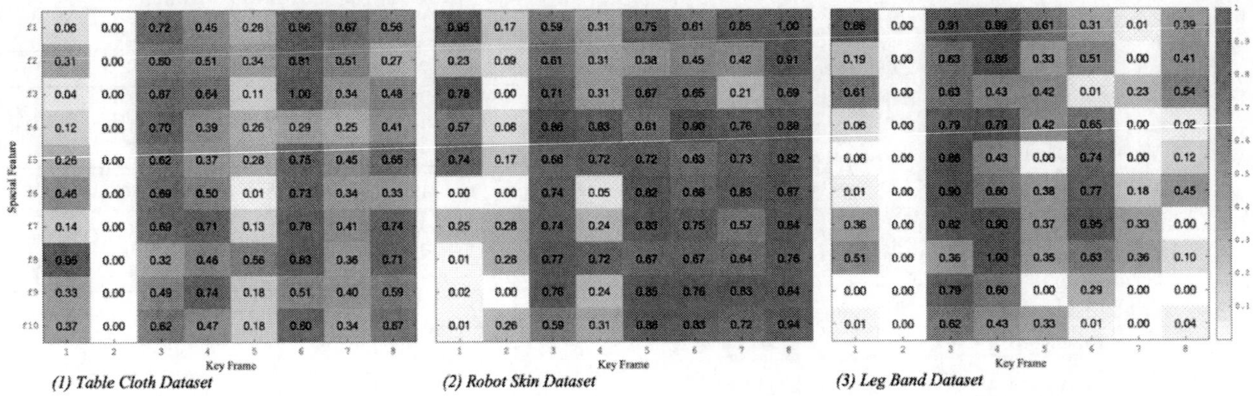

Figure 9. Spatial feature weight matrices of the three datasets.

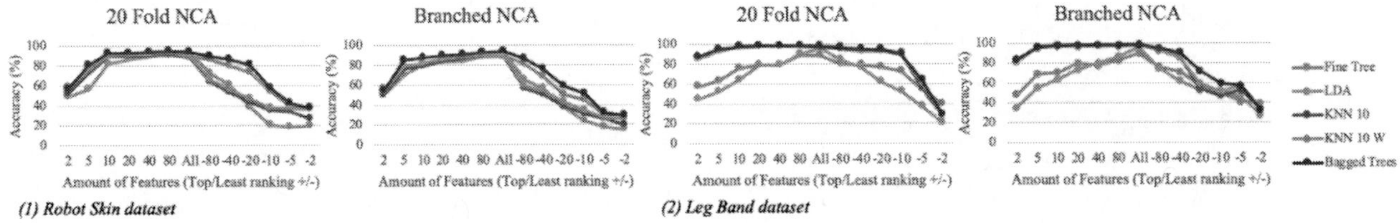

Figure 10. Feature number against accuracy for the Robot Skin and Leg Band dataset with 20 fold and branched NCA.

feature weights vary with different applications. Neighborhood component analysis can be used to locate and explain the more contributing features and further optimise a system by reducing feature calculation efforts.

REFERENCES

[1] A. Dementyev and J. A. Paradiso, "Wristflex: low-power gesture input with wrist-worn pressure sensors," in Proceedings of the 27th annual ACM symposium on User interface software and technology. ACM, 2014, pp. 161–166.

[2] J. Cheng et al., "On the tip of my tongue: a non-invasive pressure-based tongue interface," in Proceedings of the 5th Augmented Human International Conference. ACM, 2014, p. 12.

[3] S. Mota and R. W. Picard, "Automated posture analysis for detecting learner's interest level," in 2003 Conference on Computer Vision and Pattern Recognition Workshop, vol. 5. IEEE, 2003, pp. 49–49.

[4] B. Zhou et al., "Smart blanket: A real-time user posture sensing approach for ergonomic designs," in International Conference on Applied Human Factors and Ergonomics. Springer, 2017, pp. 193–204.

[5] M. Sundholm, J. Cheng, B. Zhou, A. Sethi, and P. Lukowicz, "Smart-mat: Recognizing and counting gym exercises with low-cost resistive pressure sensing matrix," in Proceedings of the 2014 ACM international joint conference on pervasive and ubiquitous computing. ACM, 2014, pp. 373–382.

[6] S. Schneegass and A. Voit, "Gesturesleeve: using touch sensitive fabrics for gestural input on the forearm for controlling smartwatches," in Proceedings of the 2016 ACM International Symposium on Wearable Computers. ACM, 2016, pp. 108–115.

[7] B. Zhou, J. Cheng, M. Sundholm, and P. Lukowicz, "From smart clothing to smart table cloth: Design and implementation of a large scale, textile pressure matrix sensor," in International Conference on Architecture of Computing Systems. Springer, 2014, pp. 159–170.

[8] B. Zhou et al., "Tpm framework: a comprehensive kit for exploring applications with textile pressure mapping matrix," in UBICOMM 2017 : The Eleventh International Conference on Mobile Ubiquitous Computing, Systems, Services and Technologies. IARIA, 2017.

[9] M. S. Singh et al., "Transforming sensor data to the image domain for deep learning—an application to footstep detection," in 2017 International Joint Conference on Neural Networks (IJCNN). IEEE, 2017, pp. 2665–2672.

[10] M. Christ et al., "Time series feature extraction on basis of scalable hypothesis tests (tsfresh–a python package)," Neurocomputing, vol. 307, 2018, pp. 72–77.

[11] B. Zhou, J. Cheng, P. Lukowicz, A. Reiss, and O. Amft, "Monitoring dietary behavior with a smart dining tray," IEEE Pervasive Computing, vol. 14, no. 4, 2015, pp. 46–56.

[12] B. Zhou et al., "Textile pressure mapping sensor for emotional touch detection in human-robot interaction," Sensors, vol. 17, no. 11, 2017, p. 2585.

[13] B. Zhou, M. Sundholm, J. Cheng, H. Cruz, and P. Lukowicz, "Measuring muscle activities during gym exercises with textile pressure mapping sensors," Pervasive and Mobile Computing, vol. 38, 2017, pp. 331–345.

[14] M.-K. Hu, "Visual pattern recognition by moment invariants," IRE transactions on information theory, vol. 8, no. 2, 1962, pp. 179–187.

[15] Z. O. Khokhar, Z. G. Xiao, and C. Menon, "Surface emg pattern recognition for real-time control of a wrist exoskeleton," Biomedical engineering online, vol. 9, no. 1, 2010, p. 41.

[16] Z. Průša, P. L. Søndergaard, N. Holighaus, C. Wiesmeyr, and P. Balazs, "The Large Time-Frequency Analysis Toolbox 2.0," in Sound, Music, and Motion, ser. Lecture Notes in Computer Science, M. Aramaki, O. Derrien, R. Kronland-Martinet, and S. Ystad, Eds., 2014, pp. 419–442.

[17] W. Yang, K. Wang, and W. Zuo, "Neighborhood component feature selection for high-dimensional data." JCP, vol. 7, no. 1, 2012, pp. 161–168.

[18] H. Hotelling, "Analysis of a complex of statistical variables into principal components." Journal of educational psychology, vol. 24, no. 6, 1933, p. 417.

[19] E. Moulines and F. R. Bach, "Non-asymptotic analysis of stochastic approximation algorithms for machine learning," in Advances in Neural Information Processing Systems, 2011, pp. 451–459.

Multi-device Notifications: A Comparison Between MQTT and CoAP

Luís Augusto Silva*, Gabriel de Mello*, Bruno A. da Silva*, Gabriel Villarrubia González‡, Juan De Paz Santana‡, Paula Prata†, Valderi R. Q. Leithardt*†
*Laboratory of Embedded and Distributed Systems, University of Vale do Itajai (UNIVALI), Brazil, 88302-901
†Instituto de Telecomunicações, Delegação da Covilhã Departamento de Informática
Universidade da Beira Interior-PT, Portugal 6201-001
‡ Expert Systems and Applications Lab, Faculty of Science, University of Salamanca
Plaza de los Caídos s/n, 37008 Salamanca, Spain
Email: {luis.silva, gabrieldemello, silvabruno}@edu.univali.br,
{fcofds, gvg}@usal.es, {valderi.leithardt, pprata}@ubi.pt

***Abstract*—New devices generate, send, and display messages about their status, data retrieval, and device information. An increase in the number of notifications received, tends to reduce their tolerance. This article sets out a notification management system focused on user profiles and environments. The solution involves transferring notifications in a multi-device scenario using MQTT and CoAP technologies, while also adopting privacy criteria. It consists of three modules, the first of which was a prototype and evaluated using real devices, the second is a decision module and the third which was a dispatcher module for processing the messages.**

Keywords–Notifications management; data privacy; internet of things.

I. INTRODUCTION

Ubiquitous computing is currently an everyday phenomenon in which we are surrounded by mobile devices, such as smartphones, tablets, clocks, televisions, and other smart devices. According to [1], the computer has been imperceptibly shipped into the environment for the user. These devices also meet the demands of the users and, in turn, collect data from them [2]. In light of this, there has been a comparable growth in mobile device networks, and as [3] and [4] state, devices can be used to process an extensive collection of data from the most wide-ranging events and points of interest.

The devices have become ubiquitous, and as a result, there has been a rise in the number of notifications delivered. This delivery requires a management system that can deal with multiple devices since the number of interruptions caused by so many notifications can distract the user's attention. According to [5], there is a need to bring together communication, the user, and the devices being employed, to ensure data privacy is protected. This task entails providing accurate information to the right recipient, establishing rules for timely decision-making, as well as choosing the location.

This work requires using the control and management notifications with a suitable network for transferring messages through devices using CoAP and MQTT protocols. The CoAP was defined by the IETF [6] in 2014 and is the most recent protocol of the two. The method of using CoAP is similar to HTTP, since it follows the client/server model, and makes use of REST. Its mode of operation includes HTTP methods such as POST, PUT, UPDATE and DELETE. However, the UDP-based communication of this protocol is different from that of HTTP. The MQTT is an application layer protocol that is already designed for devices with low computational power and it uses the publish/subscribe architecture. This means that when a client posts a **M** message on a particular topic, each client enrolled in the **T** topic will receive the M message. In the same way as the HTTP, the MQTT depends on the TCP protocol and IP that are involved. However, compared with HTTP, MQTT is designed to have a lower cost in the protocol stack.

The main difference between CoAP and MQTT is that the former runs on UDP, while the latter runs on top of TCP. Since UDP is not reliable in its acknowledgment of a receipt, CoAP provides a reliability mechanism. This is carried out by using both confirmable and non-confirmable messages. Confirmable messages are entirely dependent on a commit message, while non-confirmable messages do not need acknowledgment. Another difference between CoAP and MQTT is the availability of different levels of QoS. The MQTT defines three levels of QoS while the CoAP does not offer different levels.

This paper is structured into six sections: Section II presents the related works; Section III is dedicated to the description of the proposed solution and comparison between MQTT and CoAP are presented in Section IV; Section V presents the prototype and the experimental results and, finally; in Section VI, we present the conclusions and contributions obtained.

II. RELATED WORK

The papers selected in this chapter emerged from a systematic review of the literature. In the search for the best time for the delivery of notifications and breakpoint discovery methods [7], the authors sought to execute the task directly on the mobile device. The application can detect breakpoints and then deliver notifications.

In [8], a study was conducted to predict the most opportune time for delivering the notification to the user employing a dataset obtained from the Android system which displays a pop-up notification format. The process ends after a pairing device and browser. In the study by [9], it is stated that before notifications can be delivered effectively to a user with IoT devices, it is first necessary to understand the user's real need. The main challenge is determining the user´s interest, which may vary according to his/her status.

The work of [10] is a provisional study and only attempts to predict which device should be selected to deliver the notification. Although the dataset of notification is used to train the algorithms, the solution is based on different machine learning algorithms and allows the system to be evaluated. The result is to some extent synthetic and assumes that the data available for the notification are precise. As early as [9], the author examines an approach to access user notifications, (usually for registration purposes), by establishing an open-source framework for searching notifications on mobile devices.

III. PRISER

The solution that was found makes use of UbiPri's privacy and control management middleware [11], which differs from other existing solutions by providing a generic privacy management and control model. One of the components refers to services; this is called PRISER [12] and is responsible for managing notifications. The application involves assigning a lifetime value to the notification. In the case of a device without Internet access, in a given environment, it should be possible to send medium and high priority notifications in another way, such as by sending an SMS.

In PRISER, a mobile device application was developed to gather, and record notifications executed in the second plan. All the requirements and running jobs in the second plan are reliable and can be run in almost all android versions. After granting users rights to manage services, this service is executed in the second plan on a permanent basis and receives a callback when a notification is added to or removed from the system. The Notifications are stored in the device memory and can be navigated by the device administrator. A JSON object comprises all the notification information. The infrastructure is based on open standards and used on the Internet and IoT devices, such as the CoAP protocol and the MQTT message queuing protocol for low-capacity devices. The proposed architecture is composed of three modules: the collector mentioned above, the decision and dispatcher. These modules are highlighted in blue in Figure 1.

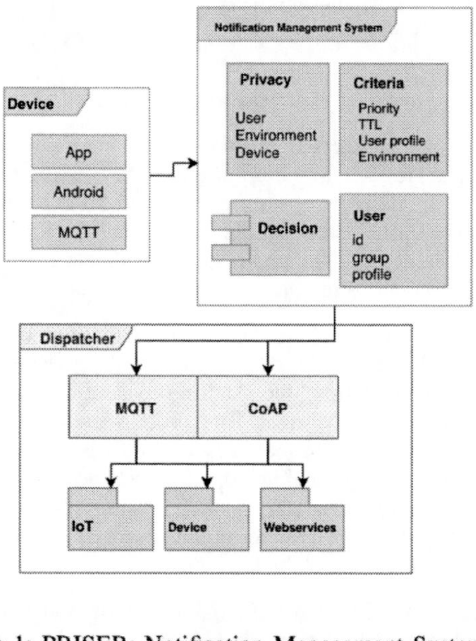

Figure 1: PRISER: Notification Management System [13]

A. Notification Collector

The notifications of the device are stored in the device memory and can be navigated by the device administrator. An Android app was used for this test, and its installation was based in [5]. A JSON object comprising all the notification information is obtained, in accordance with the items mentioned above.

B. Decision Maker

The main purpose of the decision module in the notification management system is decision-making, and receiving information concerning the privacy of the environment, the device or even the user. The module seeks to answer the following questions: *(i)* what is the best location to receive the message?; *(ii)* when is the best time to show the notification to the chosen user? *(iii)* in which device will the chosen users receive the notification? and *(vi)* what is the best way to send the notification?. The most important feature of this module is the way it is used to make decisions.

According to [10], a decision tree algorithm creates a flowchart pattern, in which each internal node represents a test attribute, each branch represents the test result, and each node in the sheet represents a label. The root- to-leaf paths represent the classification rules for issuing the notification This module also aggregates criteria information about the user context (e.g., location, status, current activity), as well as information related to the notification for a lifetime. The criteria serve important purposes in the NMS, such as the way information is used to choose the device and to alert the user (e.g., vibration, sound or light) or to display notifications received that are based on the user's location.

C. Dispatcher

Finally, the dispatcher adapts the notifications to the chosen target devices and then sends them. When handling notifications that are only intended for one device, this causes certain problems. The first point is that the user must always be charging the device, or remain close to it. The second point refers to connectivity, during which the device that the user uses may become disconnected, or even be without a battery. The dispatcher module is based on an architecture that uses multiple devices as shown above in Figure reffig:diagrama1. Both MQTT and CoAP can be used in the dispatcher. Routing messages for IoT include smart-things and devices and provide a web service for third-party applications. The MQTT and CoAP applications are described below.

IV. MQTT AND CoAP

This section is dedicated to experiments performed on multiple devices, including proposals for message transmission and notifications between devices using the MQTT and CoAP message protocols. Packet transmission times and tests from notification quantities were used.

A. Collect and Share using MQTT

The notifications collected in an Android device are shared with the decision module through the publish/subscribe that implements an MQTT protocol. The WebSocket unit provides the communication layer between a combination of the client-side and the server-side for MQTT. The reaper unit receives heartbeat events from operational devices and the component for connecting the devices is called triproxy because it deals with three endpoints instead of the usual two. They can have more than one instance of running simultaneously, and then give a comma-separated list to the provider.

The unit below uses a provider in the dispatcher module unit for making a connection to the Android Debug Bridge (ADB) and starting worker processes for each device. It then sends and receives commands from the processor. Its purpose is to send and receive requests from the app units and distribute them across the processor among the units.

B. Collect and Share using CoAP

In the case of CoAP, the notification system employs a request/response system for transferring messages to other devices. A gateway called COSGP-IoT was implemented that relied on the methods and other resources provided by the libcoap2 library, which is the default system for limited capacity devices. This method makes the server responsible for assigning the appropriate working logic of the GET, PUT and DELETE methods defined by the CoAP protocol specifications. It follows the Constrained Restful Environment (CORE) architecture, that includes the Write / Read and Full / Partial of the OSGP model. Also, it supports Pending Events Descriptors (PEDs), which act as the Pending Activator Tables, that are essential for maintenance and general scalability. It should be noted here that there is an absence of a POST function, which can be explained by the lack of an analog method from the OSGP model; thus, it is not necessary to implement the type of request in question.

The following are invoked for its use: a) the gateway function, b) an individual call for each request and response, and c) a corresponding translation method and d) , mapping the data when extracting certain attributes, such as a message identifier, request/response, packet size and token. The data repository of the CoAP server is one of the resources that can be added in the context of the application, and it is through this that the methods must be called. When used for the CoAP requests, this work carried out the implementation of a client in Python, owing to the practicality of the language and ease of use of the libraries available for the platform.

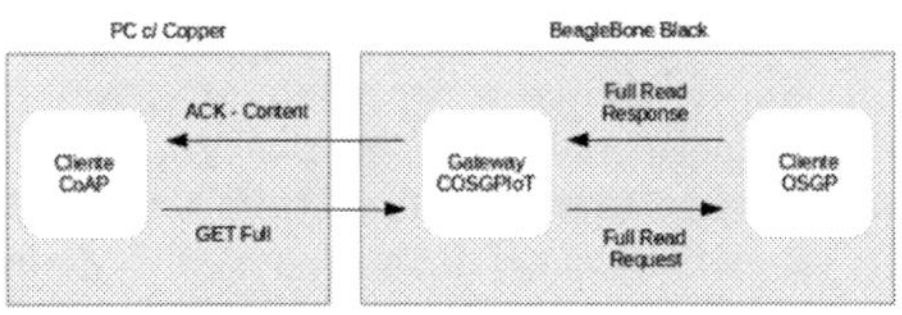

Figure 2: GET Full method for received message.

The testing environment consisted of the hardware implementation of the code developed. The chosen development platform, that was focused on integrating implementations planned in the work, were divided between the client and server. In the case of the CoAP client, it was decided to use the BeagleBone Black microcontroller, which has 512MB of RAM and an ARM Cortex A8 AM3358 CPU with a core operating at 1GHz, while running the Debian 9.4OS and Raspberry Pi model 3 which has 1GB of RAM and an ARM Cortex-A53, 1.2GHz.

V. Prototype and Experimental Results

The initial tests of the collector module proved that, depending on the number of notifications a user receives, the collection process can alternate between every 10 and 60 seconds. A large accumulation of notifications of just the operating system was noticed when using notification by application. The application used for the tests were initially developed by Weber et al. [5] and described in PRISER [13]. This application is shown in Figure 3. Only the message transmission control part and the protocols were used for this work. This resulted in a comparison System for Notifications x Notifications of an application shown in Figure 4.

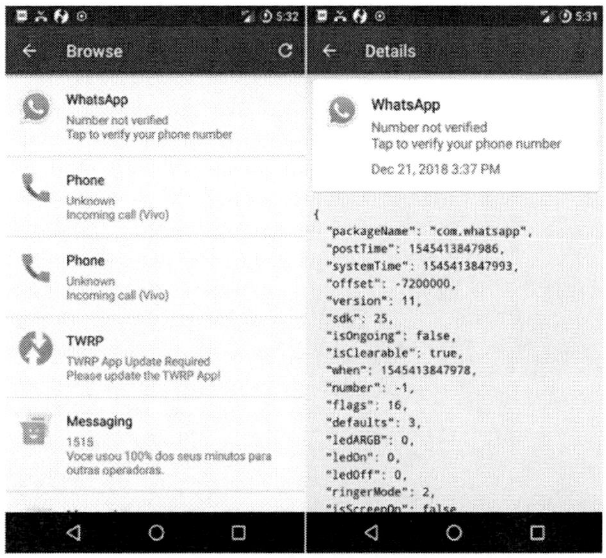

Figure 3: NMS Notification collector. [13]

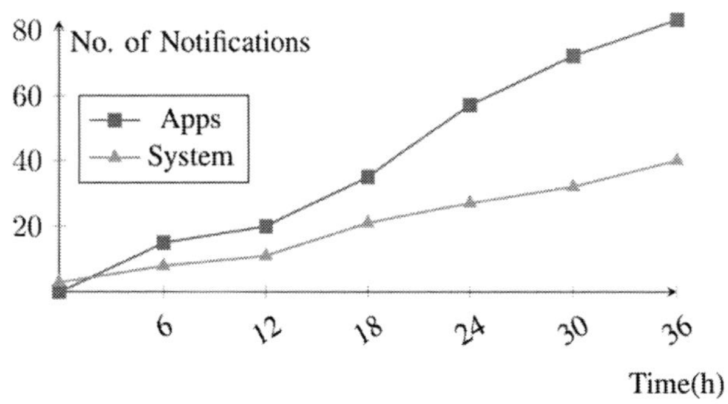

Figure 4: Notification by System x Notification by App per hour.

A. MQTT Results

The purpose of the second experiment is to compare the MQTT transfer and latency to forward a notification. First, a transmission was carried out by dividing the packets into the MQTT. 64, 128, 256 and 512 bytes were used for a total load of 1024, 2048, 4096 and 8192. In every case, a JSON file was simulated. The results are shown in Figure 5.

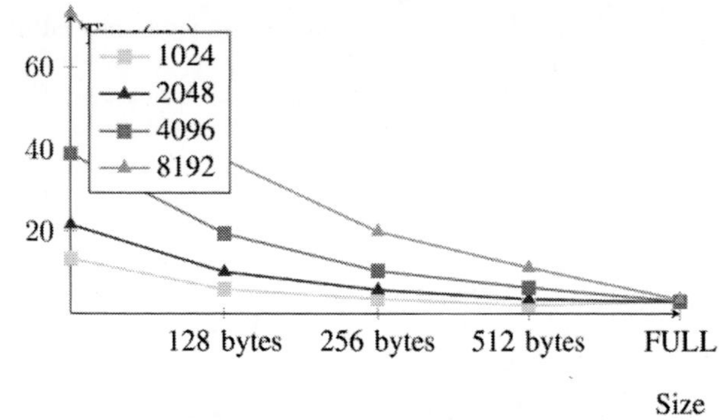

Figure 5: MQTT Publish transmission splited in packets on Beaglebone Black microcontroller.

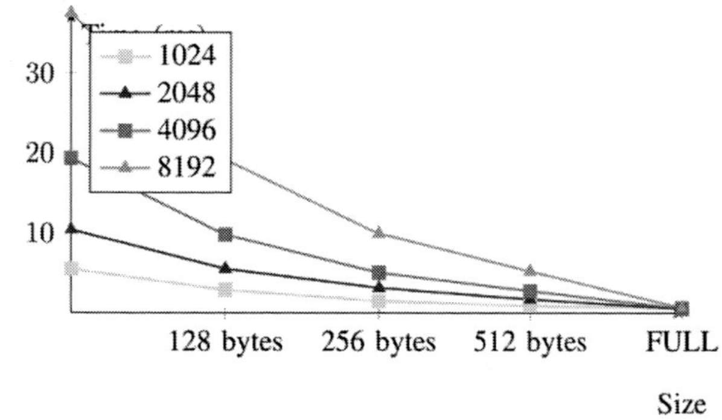

Figure 6: MQTT publishing with split packages on Raspberry Pi device.

The results obtained through the comparison showed that the CoAP is efficient for a low volume of messages but when the volume increases the MQTT is more efficient; further tests must be carried out to measure the degree of efficiency during the work. This result is shown in Figure 7.

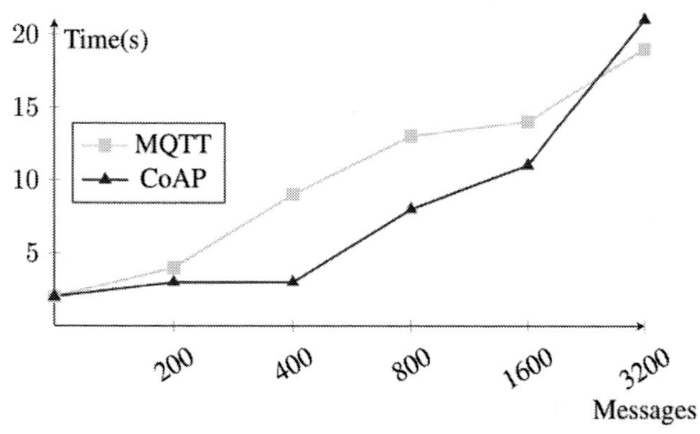

Figure 7: MQTT vs CoAP.

The requirements imposed on NMS were based on the taxonomy and continued as rules and regulations in accordance with research in the literature. The evidence obtained from this article is as follows.

B. CoAP Results

The performance results of CoAP and the translation functions, together with the resources coming from the standard C language libraries, were obtained directly from the source code of the gateway. The results are arranged in milliseconds in the graphs below. The communication latency between the devices was discounted . Only the PUT and GET Fulls methods were tested, in view of the complexity involved in describing the results and the nature of the article. The payloads of the CoAP packages had JSON files of sizes varying between 1024, 2048, 4096 and 8192 bytes. These were divided into packets smaller than 64 bytes, which allowed a larger sample and greater control. Each method was tested 4 times, making a total of 960 packets for each of the two methods tested. The first test can be seen in Figure 8.

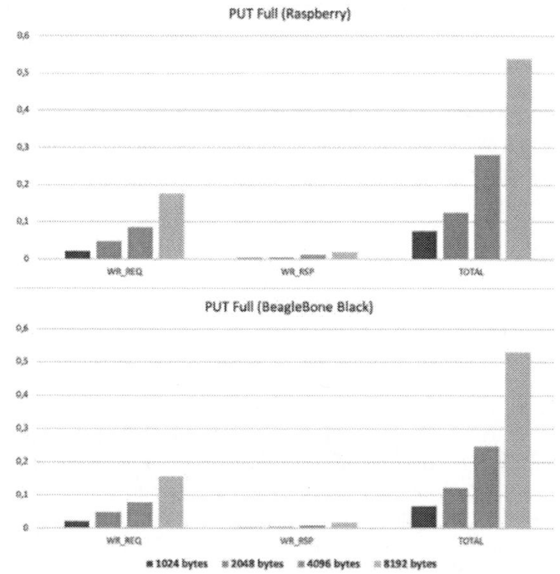

Figure 8: Comparative graphs between the Raspberry and BeagleBone microcontroller for the PUT Full method.

There is a difference between the processing time of the PUT Full requests made by the two microcontrollers. The requests for translation from the CoAP script to OSGP took up more time (between 0.021 ms and 0.175 ms) than the response translations (0.002ms to 0.018 ms), owing to the number of fields and amount of information used by the OSGP packages. The total time for the method ranged from 0.076 ms to 0.538 ms. However, in Figure 9, the processing time between both types of hardware is technically the same (except for the fluctuation rates that may occur) for the GET Full method.

The read response translations from OSGP to CoAP were predictably the most detachable, with times varying between 0.41ms and 0.318ms. The requests were given in the order of 0.003ms to 0.027ms and the total amount of time ranged from 0.083ms to 0.608ms.

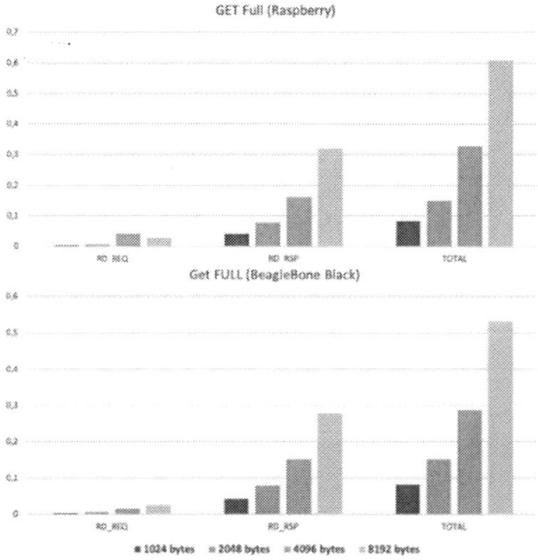

Figure 9: Comparative graphs between the Raspberry and BeagleBone microcontroller for the GET Full method.

VI. Conclusion and Future Work

Throughout this work, stress was laid on the importance of using the privacy criteria with regard to the environment and the hierarchy assigned to the user, and the taxonomy discussed earlier was highlighted. In this way, we were able to contribute to applications of different types of environments and deal with different types of notifications. In addition, it was possible to ensure that relevant notifications were sent and received in compliance with the defined rules. Our architecture is divided into three key modules to manage the notifications received.

A simplified version of the architecture was prototyped, and a preliminary validation was made of the collection module. Besides, the transfer of messages between devices was tested through CoAP and MQTT. New tests must be conducted to determine the variables and make comparisons. Also, a careful evaluation of the decision algorithms had to be implemented, so that different algorithms could be employed and compared. Finally, the prototype must be improved by including an assessment of a large numbers of users.

Acknowledgment

This study was financed in part by the Coordenação de Aperfeiçoamento de Pessoal de Nível Superior—Brasil (CAPES)—Finance Code 001. Supported by project PLATAFORMA DE VEHÍCULOS DE TRANSPORTE DE MATERIALES Y SEGUIMIENTO AUTÓNOMO — TARGET. 463AC03.

Project co-financed with Junta Castilla y León, Consejería de Educación and FEDER funds. This work was partially funded by FCT- Fundação para a Ciência e a Tecnologia through national funds and when applicable co-funded by FEDER – PT2020 partnership agreement under the project UID/EEA/50008/2019. Operação Centro-01-0145-FEDER-000019 – C4 – Centro de Competências em Cloud Computing, co-financed by the Programa Operacional Regional do Centro (CENTRO 2020), through the Sistema de Apoio à Investigação Científica e Tecnológica – Programas Integrados de IC&DT. Including a cooperation with the project international cooperation project Control and History Management Based on the Privacy of Ubiquitous Environments—Brazil/Portugal.

References

[1] M. Satyanarayanan, "Pervasive computing: Vision and challenges," IEEE Personal Communications, vol. 8, no. 4, 2001, pp. 10–17, DOI:10.1109/98.943998.

[2] F. Viel, L. A. Silva, R. Q. Valderi Leithardt, and C. A. Zeferino, "Internet of things: Concepts, architectures and technologies," in 2018 13th IEEE International Conference on Industry Applications (INDUSCON), Nov 2018, pp. 909–916, dOI:10.1109/INDUSCON.2018.8627298.

[3] M. Stolpe, "The internet of things: Opportunities and challenges for distributed data analysis," ACM SIGKDD Explorations Newsletter, vol. 18, no. 1, 2016, pp. 15–34, DOI:10.1145/2980765.2980768.

[4] S. K. Goudos, P. I. Dallas, S. Chatziefthymiou, and S. Kyriazakos, "A survey of iot key enabling and future technologies: 5g, mobile iot, sematic web and applications," Wirel. Pers. Commun., vol. 97, no. 2, Nov. 2017, pp. 1645–1675, DOI:10.1007/s11277-017-4647-8.

[5] D. Weber, A. Voit, and N. Henze, "Notification log: An open-source framework for notification research on mobile devices," in Proceedings..., ser. UbiComp '18, International Joint Conference and 2018 International Symposium on Pervasive and Ubiquitous Computing and Wearable Computers. New York, NY, USA: ACM, 2018, pp. 1271–1278, dOI:10.1145/3267305.3274118.

[6] Z. Shelby, K. Hartke, and C. Bormann, "Constrained application protocol (coap) - draft-ietf-core-coap-18," ago 2019, https://datatracker.ietf.org/doc/draft-ietf-core-coap/.

[7] T. Okoshi, J. Nakazawa, and H. Tokuda, "Attelia: Sensing user's attention status on smart phones," in Proceedings of the 2014 ACM International Joint Conference on Pervasive and Ubiquitous Computing: Adjunct Publication, ser. UbiComp '14 Adjunct. New York, NY, USA: ACM, 2014, pp. 139–142, DOI:10.1145/2638728.2638802.

[8] A. Sahami Shirazi, N. Henze, T. Dingler, M. Pielot, D. Weber, and A. Schmidt, "Large-scale assessment of mobile notifications," in Proceedings of the 32Nd Annual ACM Conference on Human Factors in Computing Systems, ser. CHI '14. New York, NY, USA: ACM, 2014, pp. 3055–3064, DOI:10.1145/2556288.2557189.

[9] Z. Pan, X. Liang, Y. C. Zhou, Y. Ge, and G. T. Zhao, "Intelligent push notification for converged mobile computing and internet of things," in 2015 IEEE International Conference on Web Services, June 2015, pp. 655–662, DOI:10.1109/ICWS.2015.92.

[10] F. Corno, L. D. Russis, and T. Montanaro, "A context and user aware smart notification system," in 2015 IEEE 2nd World Forum on Internet of Things (WF-IoT), Dec 2015, pp. 645–651, DOI:10.1109/WF-IoT.2015.7389130.

[11] V. R. Leithardt, L. H. A. Correia, G. A. Borges, A. G. Rossetto, C. O. Rolim, C. F. Geyer, and J. M. S. Silva, "Mechanism for privacy management based on data history (ubipri-his)," Journal of Ubiquitous Systems and Pervasive Networks, vol. 10, no. 1, 2018, pp. 11–19.

[12] L. A. Silva, D. dos Santos, R. Dazzi, J. S. Silva, and V. Leithardt, "PRISER - Utilização de BLE para localização e notificação com base na privacidade de dados," Revista Eletrônica Argentina-Brasil de Tecnologias da Informação e da Comunicação, vol. 2, no. 1, 2018, DOI:10.5281/zenodo.1336806.

[13] L. A. Silva, V. R. Q. Leithardt, C. O. Rolim, G. V. González, C. F. R. Geyer, and J. S. Silva, "Priser: Managing notification in multiples devices with data privacy support," vol. 19, no. 14, 2019. [Online]. Available: https://www.mdpi.com/1424-8220/19/14/3098

EARTH COURSE Pilot: NEWTON Project Support for STEM Education

Cristina Hava Muntean
National College of Ireland, School of Computing
Dublin, Ireland
cristina.muntean@ncirl.ie

Diana Bogusevschi
Dublin City University, School of Electronic Engineering
Dublin, Ireland
diana.bogusevschi@dcu.ie

Abstract— **This paper presents NEWTON Earth Course large scale pilot developed and deployed as part of the NEWTON Project. The pilot consists of a number of innovative applications that teach STEM topics part of the primary school curriculum. A demo of the Earth Course Pilot will be provided during the presentation session.**

Keywords: STEM Education; technology enhanced learning; augmented reality; game based learning.

I. Introduction

Technology-Enhanced Learning (TEL) methods are currently one of the proposed teaching solutions for the increasing lack of interest in science, technology, engineering and mathematic (STEM) subjects. These subjects are perceived as boring and difficult to be studied. Therefore, many students seem to become disengaged in such topics, especially if they are struggling to understand certain complex concepts leading to diminishing grades. TEL solutions offer various teaching approaches that help students to understand better STEM topics, thus increasing their interest and engagement. It has been observed in primary schools the majority of students are interested in STEM topics and it is important to continue fostering students' interest in these throughout their education, from primary to secondary and third-level institutions.

The NEWTON project [1] is an EU Horizon 2020-funded project involving 14 partners from seven countries. The main objectives of the project include building a networked platform to facilitate integration and dissemination of many technology-enhanced learning (TEL) materials and innovative learning approaches. NEWTON also investigates the impact of using various forms TEL materials, such as serious games, virtual labs, fabrication labs, augmented reality, virtual reality, and innovative learning approaches, such as problem-based learning, on students' learning outcome and affective states. Various courses covering STEM subjects were developed and deployed in European educational institutions [2]-[4].

II. Earth Course Pilot

Earth Course is one of the NEWTON Project's large-scale pilots that focuses on primary school education and it was carried out across Europe in Ireland, Slovakia and Romania, 172 students have participated in the study. The Earth Course pilot includes a set of educational applications developed in an effort to attract children to STEM subject. The educational applications cover a set of topics part of four main areas: Atmosphere, Geosphere, Biosphere and Astronomy. The applications use various technologies and innovative pedagogical methods (e.g., Augmented and Virtual Reality, gamification, game-based learning and problem-based learning) to achieve the learning objectives specific to the primary school curriculum specific to the 5th grade and 6th grade and to improve learning satisfaction. The applications are also suitable for children with special educational needs, specifically hearing impairments.

The main applications (see Fig.1) employed in this pilot are:

- *Water Cycle in Nature*, focusing on precipitation formation and related topics, such as vaporisation, evaporation and condensation;
- *Wildlife*, focusing on a set of terrestrial animals, such as deer, brown bear, lynx, wolf, wild boar, fox, hare and moose;
- *Sea-Life*, focusing on the aquatic world and presenting educational material on sea creatures such as sharks, stingrays, dolphins, puffer fish, jellyfish, octopus, orc, turtle, clownfish, seahorse;
- *Final Frontier* game, presenting the rocky planets, the giant gas planets and an astronomical bodies such as the Moon part of the Solar System;
- *Geography* application, focusing on educational content about Ireland and United Kingdom, including its monuments and archaeological sites.

The deployment of the Earth Course pilot was done using the online NEWTON project platform called NEWTELP (NEWTON Technology Enhanced Learning Platform) and it involved all applications, knowledge tests and questionnaires for assessing learner experience, usability of the platform and applications as well as knowledge gain evaluation. The pilot was deployed in three European schools and results presented in various papers [4]-[7]. Eight separate learning sessions were carried out employing digital educational content developed as part of the NEWTON project.

Focus groups and interviews were carried out with learners and teachers, in order to assess the effect and benefits of the pilot. Noteworthy is that the children participating in this course enjoyed each session, and got excited every time when the NEWTON team was setting up the classroom for another Earth Course session. Some children already came up with ideas on other applications and what other interesting subjects they might like to learn.

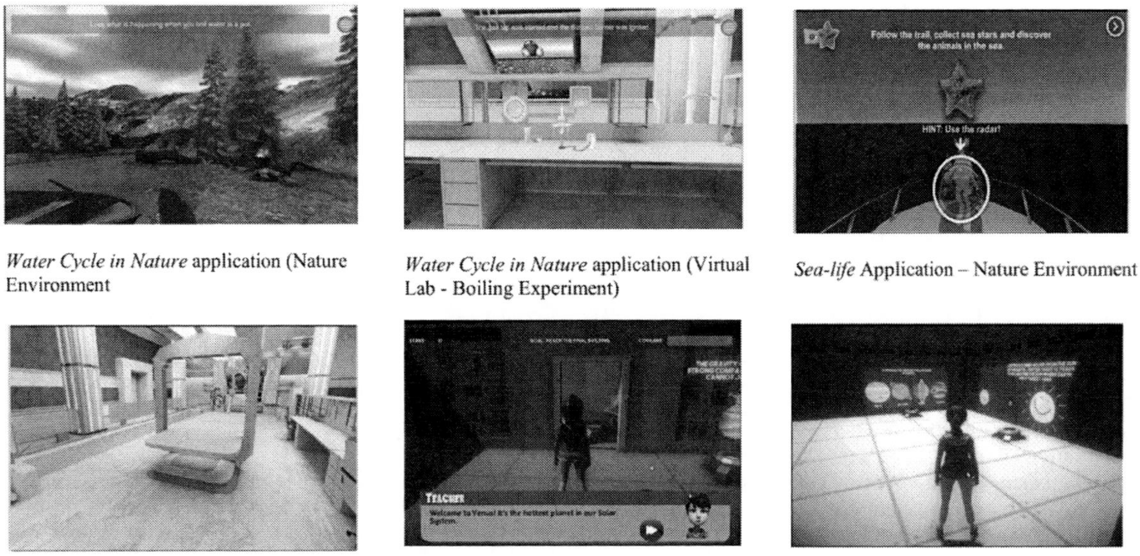

Water Cycle in Nature application (Nature Environment

Water Cycle in Nature application (Virtual Lab - Boiling Experiment)

Sea-life Application – Nature Environment

Sea-life application – Virtual Lab

Final Frontier Game - Venus

Final Frontier game – Virtual Library

Figure 1. Water Cycle, Final Frontier and Sea-life applications part of the NEWTON Earth Course Pilot

The overall feedback from teachers that applied the Earth Course pilot in their class was positive. They all noted the enjoyment students exhibited during these sessions as well as their engagement in each topic. Teachers are very open to using novel technologies seeing the benefits of the NEWTON-based lessons. However, schools' infrastructure were sometimes lacking the necessary equipment. Teachers also noted that it is imperative to have a more established communication between TEL designers and teachers, emphasizing the need to improve teachers' familiarity and involvement with TEL approaches.

In terms of learner satisfaction, the majority of the students who exhibited positive learning satisfaction following NEWTON-based lessons were students who already have positive attitudes to school and they were used to employing technology as well as those students who do not have issues with STEM subjects. It is notable the fact that students who do not like school reported significant improvements in knowledge assessment tests, specifically preferring to use NEWTON apps when learning STEM topics and an increased enjoyment level during NEWTON-based lessons compared to their usual STEM classes.

III. Conclusions

Summarizing, learner's experience and knowledge results analysis show that the NEWTON approach lessons applied in primary schools increased children's interest in Technology Enhanced Learning, which also improved their engagement in STEM subjects. NEWTON approach also provided a beneficial support in terms of knowledge acquisition and can be employed by teachers as an aiding tool to better illustrate to children various STEM concepts.

Acknowledgment

This research is supported by the NEWTON project [1] funded under the European Union's Horizon 2020 Research and Innovation programme, Grant Agreement no. 688503.

References

[1] NEWTON Project, http://newtonproject.eu Retreived: September 12, 2019

[2] A. Chis, A.N. Moldovan, L. Murphy, P. Pathak, and C.H. Muntean, "Investigating Flipped Classroom and Problem-based Learning in a Programming Module for Computing Conversion Course" Journal of Educational Technology & Society, 21(4), pp. 232-247, 2018

[3] D. Bogusevschi, C.H. Muntean and G.M. Muntean, "Teaching and Learning Physics using 3D Virtual Learning Environment: A Case Study of Combined Virtual Reality and Virtual Laboratory in Secondary School", in Society for Information Technology & Teacher Education International Conference. Las Vegas, NV, USA, pp. 721-728, 2019

[4] D. Bogusevschi, C.H. Muntean and. G.M. Muntean, "Earth Course: Knowledge Acquisition in Technology Enhanced Learning STEM Education in Primary School", in EdMedia + Innovate Learning Conference, Amsterdam, Netherlands, pp. 1261-1270, 2019

[5] D. Bogusevschi, C.H. Muntean, N.E. Gorji and G.M. Muntean, "Earth Course: A Primary School Large-Scale Pilot on STEM Education", in 10th EDULEARN Conference, Palma de Mallorca, Spain, pp. 3769-3777, 2018

[6] C.H. Muntean, J. Andrews and G.M. Muntean, "Final Frontier: An Educational Game on Solar System Concepts Acquisition for Primary Schools", in 17th IEEE ICALT Conference, Timisoara, Romania, pp. 335-337, 2017

[7] N. El Mawas, I. Tal, A. N. Moldovan, D. Bogusevschi, J. Andrews, G.-M. Muntean and C.H. Muntean, "Final Frontier Game: A Case Study on Learner Experience", in 10th International Conference on Computer Supported Education (CSEDU), Madeira, Portugal, pp. 122-129, 2018

AHRS Calibration for a Drill String Sensor Network Application

E. Odei-Lartey, K. A. Hartmann
Zentrum für Sensorsysteme (ZESS),
Universität Siegen, D-57076
Siegen, Germany
email: (elartey,hartmann)@zess.uni-siegen.de

H. Roth
Regelungs- und Steuerungstechnik, Fakultät IV,
Universität Siegen, D-57076
Siegen, Germany
email: hubert.roth@uni-siegen.de

Abstract— **In this paper, we illustrate a practical way to determine the systematic error of a micro-electro-mechanical systems inertia measurement unit sensor-based altitude and height reference system mounted on a drill-head for underground navigation. This enables for calibration purposes and for alignment of the system in a designated global reference frame. Furthermore, an extension of this is to enable for onboard real-time calibration in the field with direct access to required parameters over a designed underground wireless ad hoc sensor network telemetry system. This contribution is in line with the embedded systems component of the ubiquitous devices and operative systems track of the conference.**

Keywords-calibration; deterministic; stochastic; AHRS; MEMS; sensor guided drill process;

I. INTRODUCTION

Recent developments in the field of wellbore drilling has seen the gradual migration towards the concept of digitalization of key aspects of the entire drilling operation [1]. This has therefore seen the move towards the optimization of drilling operations utilizing the so-called modern technology tools so as to gain economic advantage by way of improving the efficiency of the drilling process [1]. There is therefore a push towards sensor-controlled deep drilling process so as to provide suitable sensor data continuously in real-time. This requires a deeper understanding of multimodal sensors/sensor networks and their conditions of use. Therefore, for field test verification, we have realized an appropriate ad-hoc sensor network along the entire drill string. We also describe the necessity for using a suitable calibration process and give an outlook on how we can generate training data in the next steps to provide a deep neural network solution to process the sensor data.

In our Micro-Electro-Mechanical Systems (MEMS)-based Altitude and Height Reference System (AHRS) for bottom hole trajectory tracking, the main concept is to minimize the errors associated with the IMU sensors before the application of a suitable mathematical model in order to obtain an optimal estimation of the orientation and therefore improve the trajectory of the well path. To facilitate this process is our in-house designed and developed underground wireless ad hoc sensor network borehole telemetry system which allows for real-time data exchange during a drilling operation irrespective of the drill depth. An extension of this will be to enable the calibration process to be done directly on the field while only communicating the required parameters for the process.

In general, the contribution of this paper is to provide a methodology for MEMS sensor positioning and calibration which can be applied (on-field) by making use of a robotic arm-mounted miniature drill-head where different orientations can be simulated thus representing a multi-position platform for effective sensor calibration. Our robotic-arm-mounted IMU-based AHRS drill-head is programmed at preset orientations whose positions are accurately known from the settings on the robotic arm and used in the estimation of the deterministic errors. The known orientation angles are used with the known local gravity vector to establish the resolved known MEMS accelerometer output data from each of the 3 orthogonal axes which is then used in the determination of the calibration parameters.

Sensor system testing and calibration for Inertial Measurement Unit (IMU)-based navigation systems is of critical importance and has significant consequences in terms of cost and performance of the host vehicle. Basically, the testing and calibration techniques employed needs to reflect the type of application and importantly, the environment in which the sensor and systems are to operate [2]-[6]. Testing is done to enable the output signals to be calibrated and to understand the behavior of the device unit in various situations and environment. In other terms, sensors are calibrated by comparing the analogue or digital signals produced by the sensor with the known input motion. So, for instance, from the rate transfer tests, the output signals from a gyroscope can be compared with the accurately known rotation rate and the scale factor deduced. Also, using gravity vector as an accurate standard, the scale-factor of an accelerometer can be defined. Application of error compensation is then utilized to correct the effects of a predictable systematic error. A basic requirement is that an error process can be represented by an equation and modelled mathematically, and that a signal corresponding to the disturbing effect such as temperature or acceleration, is available and can be measured to the required accuracy [4]. The accuracy that may be achieved from the application of compensation techniques is dependent on precisely how the coefficients in the "error" equations represents the actual sensor errors. The representation can often vary as a function of time, the environment in which the sensor is used and how often it is used. For more demanding applications, it may be necessary to re-calibrate the sensor regularly, to ensure that the compensation routines are as effective as required by the particular application. Usually, the sensor system is mounted on a multi-axis table or on a rig. The unit may be rotated through a series of accurately known angles and positioned in different orientations with respect to the local gravity vector. The dominant sensor errors may then be determined from static measurements of acceleration and turn rate taken in each orientation of the unit.

In Section II of our paper, we provide an overview of the related works on the approach utilized for IMU sensor calibration. Section III then outlines the general equation model representation for the combined form of the deterministic and stochastic model of the IMU sensor output data. In Section IV, we discuss the calibration process and the methodology for determination of the calibration parameters for finding the deterministic errors associated with two mounted inexpensive MEMS IMU sensors used for the wellbore trajectory tracking process. We then discuss an experimental setup for verification of our calibration process. In Section V, we give the conclusion and an overview of ongoing research in view of the adaptation of deep-learning techniques to improve the calibration process.

II. RELATED WORKS

Introduction to topics surrounding AHRS fail to sufficiently describe the error characteristics of the inertial systems. Inertial system design and performance prediction depends on accurate knowledge of sensor level behavior and therefore it is important to be able to understand and analyze the intrinsic noise characteristics of the IMU sensors to develop the necessary stochastic model to be used in the AHRS model. Generally, the IMU sensor errors are composed of the deterministic and stochastic parts. The main deterministic errors are the bias and misalignment errors. The misalignment errors are composed of the scale factor and the non-orthogonal errors of the sensor [3]-[5]. Laboratory calibration procedures are normally employed in the elimination of these deterministic errors. El-Diasty et al. [3] discussed two calibration methodologies used to find the calibration parameters in order to remove the deterministic errors (systematic errors); inertial biases (bias offset), scale factor and non-orthogonality errors. This involves the six-position static test (up and down position for the inertial sensor axes) [3]-[5]. Basically, the non-orthogonality error is as a result of the imperfect mounting of the IMU sensors along the orthogonal axis at the time of manufacturing. However, in most cases, upon the final integration of the IMU sensor in the final application hardware, there is also the need for a re-calibration of the IMU sensor output as a result of imperfection in the alignment of the IMU sensor with respect to the final application hardware, which in this case is the drill-head. In the field, there is the difficulty or lack of adequate means to properly re-calibrate the inertial sensors after physically mounting of the hardware on the respective device. This approach therefore provides a means to utilize the drill tube holder which has the ability to be oriented at different angular positions like that of a robotic arm to be utilized for the purposes of calibration.

El-Diasty et al. [3] work is based on the premise that the IMU sensor is in alignment with local gravity vector and therefore gives a general description of how the calibration parameters are determined using the two-position static tests in the zenith direction for the case of the MEMS accelerometer. In their approach, the calibration was done by inducing an excitation signal as input to MEMS accelerometer which is done with local gravity as the excitation/reference signal [3]. In the case of the MEMS gyroscope, the test is done by the use of a two-position dynamic test in any direction [4]. This involves a gyro excitation signal input in the form of a known rotation rate using a calibration turn-table. They discuss further the so-called six position direct method and the six-position weighted least square method approach to determine the inertial bias, scale factor and non-orthogonal deterministic errors. However, for certain applications, this zenith position is determined by the geometry (physical structure) of the application hardware of interest which for our case would be the bottom hole assembly or the drill-head. The sensor reference frame is defined by the body to which the IMU MEMS sensor is strapped unto. This therefore necessitates the need to determine the alignment of the IMU MEMS sensor relative to the body frame of bottom hole assembly or drill-head on which it is mounted. So basically, the final deployment would require for a re-alignment of the IMU MEMS sensors with respect to the drill-head orientation.

III. GENERAL MODEL OF THE IMU SENSOR

The output from the IMU MEMS accelerometer and gyroscope illustrating both the deterministic and stochastic errors is given as shown in (1) and (2). For the MEMS gyroscope triad with instantaneous output $\underline{\omega}_m$, we have

$$\underline{\omega}_m = \left(\mathrm{M}_g + \delta\mathrm{M}_g\right) \cdot \underline{\omega} + \underline{b}_g + \underline{\delta b}_g + \underline{w}_g \qquad (1)$$

and for the MEMS accelerometer triad with instantaneous linear acceleration output $\underline{f}_m$, we have

$$\underline{f}_m = \left(\mathrm{M}_a + \delta\mathrm{M}_a\right) \cdot \underline{\omega} + \underline{b}_a + \underline{\delta b}_a + \underline{w}_a \qquad (2)$$

where $\underline{\omega}$ is the true instantaneous output of the gyroscope triad and M_a and M_g represent the 3x3 matrices of the misalignment (scale factor and non-orthogonal) errors of the accelerometer and gyroscope respectively. $\underline{b}_a$ and $\underline{b}_g$ are

the biases in m/s^2 and deg/s respectively for the accelerometer and gyroscope respectively. δM_a and δM_g are 3x3 matrices comprising of the residual scale and non-orthogonal errors (non-diagonal elements), $\delta \underline{b}_a$ and $\delta \underline{b}_g$ are residual biases, $\underline{w}_a$ and $\underline{w}_g$ are the zero mean white noise (deg/s for gyros and m/s^2 for acceleration).
So basically the deterministic part of the scale factor and non-orthogonality and the bias can be determined in the laboratory calibration approach that allows for the direct estimation of the bias and misalignment which can be removed from the raw measurements say ω_m and f_m [3]; the raw gyroscope and accelerometer output, before being used in the implementation of the inertial machination equations. The corrected measurements in body reference frame is given as

$$\underline{\omega}_{ib}^{b} = \delta M_g \cdot \underline{\omega} + \underline{\delta b}_g + \underline{w}_g \tag{3}$$

$$\underline{f}^{b} = \delta M_a \cdot \underline{f} + \underline{\delta b}_a + \underline{w}_a \tag{4}$$

Basically $\underline{\omega}_{ib}^{b}$ and $\underline{f}^{b}$ still contain random errors: δM_g and δM_a matrices comprising residual scale errors (diagonal elements) and residual non-orthogonal errors (non-diagonal elements) for gyro and accelerometer respectively. El-Diasty et al. [3] also elaborates on the different stochastic models as random constant, random walk, Gauss-Markov process that is used with the Kalman filter for optimal estimation of the gyroscope and accelerometer outputs to provide accurate and continuous navigation solution.

IV. CALIBRATION IN THE GLOBAL REFERENCE FRAME FOR DETERMINISTIC ERRORS

The calibration of our IMU-based AHRS miniature drill-head involved finding the parameters/coefficients that map the measured MEMS accelerometer and gyroscope triad outputs from each sensor's reference frame unto our designated navigation reference frame shown as the global reference frame in Figure 1.

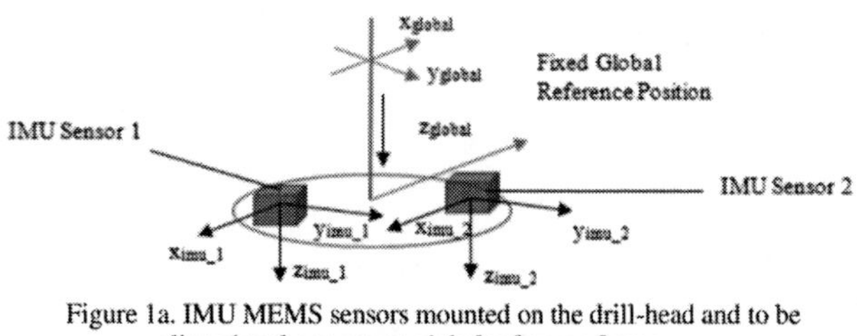

Figure 1a. IMU MEMS sensors mounted on the drill-head and to be aligned to the common global reference frame

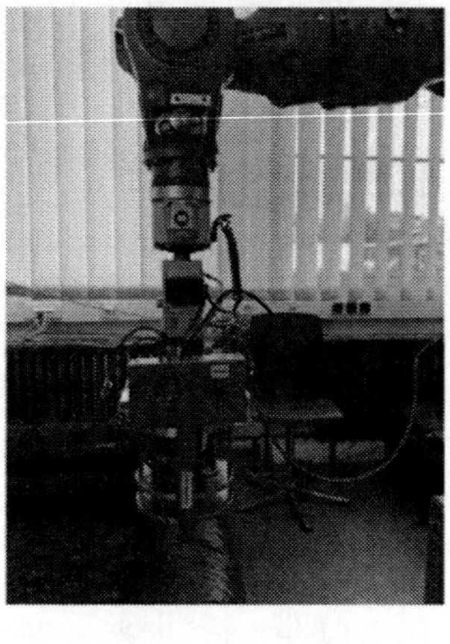

Figure 1b. Sensors mounted on the miniature drill-head and further mounted on the KUKA robotic arm

In our setup, for the IMU sensors, we used the Vectornav-100T and the MPU-9255 MEMS sensors which are of industrial and consumer grade respectively. The IMU MEMS accelerometer output data model is represented by the linear equation given as

$$\underline{f}_m = M_a \cdot \underline{f}_g + \underline{b}_a + \underline{w}_a \tag{5}$$

where $\underline{f}_m$ is the observed measurement acceleration vector consisting of the outputs of the x, y and z axes of the MEMS accelerometer triad IMU sensor , $\underline{f}_g$ is the resolved accelerometer vector at a preset orientation, M is the misalignment matrix with the unknown parameters, $\underline{b}$ represents the static bias and $\underline{w}$ denotes the zero-mean white Gaussian noise. The equation represents that for which a linear regression analysis by which an attempt to find the best, in the least-square sense, straight line to fit a given set of data can be made.

A. Experimental setup and description

Our experimental setup consisted of the two IMU sensors mentioned earlier; Vectornav-100T and the MPU-9255, each composed of a MEMS gyroscope accelerometer triad with axis orthogonal and mounted on a miniature drill-head to form our AHRS integrated system. Eight preset orientations at predefined and accurately measured angles on the Kuka Robot was programmed. At each defined orientation, 1000 measurements were recorded from both sensors at a data rate of 20Hz. This was then used in the formulation given in (6) to generate the unknown regression parameters for the misalignment and bias which minimizes the errors using the maximum likelihood estimation method. Given a set of parameter values with the matrix representation and observations, the estimated regression parameters were determined. The general equation is written in the form.

$$\underline{Y} = \Pi \cdot \underline{\Theta} + \underline{\delta r} \tag{6}$$

This is represented as

$$\underline{Y}_i = \begin{bmatrix} f_{mx_i} \\ f_{my_i} \\ f_{mz_i} \end{bmatrix} \tag{7}$$

$$\Pi_i = \begin{bmatrix} 1 & 0 & 0 & f_{a\_x_i} & f_{a\_y_i} & f_{a\_z_i} & 0 & 0 & 0 & 0 & 0 & 0 \\ 0 & 1 & 0 & 0 & 0 & 0 & f_{a\_x_i} & f_{a\_y_i} & f_{a\_z_i} & 0 & 0 & 0 \\ 0 & 0 & 1 & 0 & 0 & 0 & 0 & 0 & 0 & f_{a\_x_i} & f_{a\_y_i} & f_{a\_z_i} \end{bmatrix} \tag{8}$$

$$\underline{\Theta} = \begin{bmatrix} b_x & b_y & b_z & M_{xx} & M_{xy} & M_{xz} & M_{yx} & M_{yy} & M_{yz} & M_{zx} & M_{zy} & M_{zz} \end{bmatrix}^T \tag{9}$$

$$\underline{\delta r}_i = \begin{bmatrix} w_x & w_y & w_z \end{bmatrix}^T \tag{10}$$

$$\hat{\underline{\Theta}} = \left(\Pi^{\mathrm{T}} \cdot R^{-1} \cdot \Pi\right)^{-1} \Pi^{\mathrm{T}} \cdot R^{-1} \cdot \underline{Y} \tag{11}$$

where $\underline{\delta r}$ is the zero-mean white Gaussian noise vector and R is the noise covariance matrix, f_{mx_i} is the x component of the ith measured acceleration. The converted output in the global reference frame is given as

$$\underline{f}_g = \mathrm{M}^{-1} \cdot \left(\underline{f}_m - \underline{b}\right) \tag{12}$$

Considering the calibration of our drill-head mounted MEMS IMU sensors after mounting both on the robotic arm, as mentioned earlier, the robotic arm was preset to assume a number of orientations to enable the sensor data in the respective orientations to be recorded and used for the calibration process. The calibration entailed the determination of the mapping misalignment matrix and bias vector for the transformation of the sensor output from the sensor reference frame to our designated global/navigation reference frame. In our case, the recordings were done twice in each preset orientation position as observed in Table 1.

TABLE I. CALCULATED X,Y,Z VALUES FOR THE TRUE ACCELERATION VALUES IN A GIVEN ORIENTATION

		h_p	p_1	p_2	p_3	p_4	p_5	p_6	p_7	p_8
Axis	Pitch:	0°	-10°	10°	0°	0°	-10°	10°	0°	0°
	Roll:	0°	0°	0°	-10°	10°	0°	0°	-10°	10°
x	Cal.	0	-0.18	0.18	0.00	0.00	-0.18	0.18	0.00	0.000
y		0	0.00	0.00	-0.18	0.18	0.00	0.00	-0.18	0.176
z		1	0.99	0.99	0.99	0.99	0.99	0.99	0.99	0.985

Table I shows the true accelerometer output approximated to three decimals places for the different orientation positions (p) preset on the robotic arm with respect to our designated global/navigation reference frame. The recorded measurement in the respective orientation from both MEMS IMU accelerometer sensors is given in Table II. At each orientation position, up to 1000 readings were taken and then afterwards averaged to obtain the respective output on each axis. The output from the Vectornav-100T accelerometer is labelled as the vn_ax, vn_ay and vn_az for the respective x, y, and z axes while for that of the MPU-9255 accelerometer is labelled mpu_ax, mpu_ay and mpu_az respectively.

TABLE II. ACTUAL ACCELEROMETER OUTPUT IN THE CORRESPONDING ORIENTATION

	vn_ax	vn_ay	vn_az	mpu_ax	mpu_ay	mpu_az
hm_pos	-0.245	0.109	10.276	-0.004	-0.003	1.010
pos_1	0.400	1.681	10.131	0.129	-0.115	0.996
pos_2	-0.883	-1.466	10.123	-0.137	0.110	0.997
pos_3	-1.811	0.749	10.081	0.108	0.129	0.995
pos_4	1.333	-0.533	10.175	-0.116	-0.136	1.000
pos_5	0.368	1.709	10.126	0.132	-0.113	0.996
pos_6	-0.916	-1.436	10.124	-0.133	0.112	0.996
pos_7	-1.848	0.778	10.070	0.111	0.132	0.993
pos_8	1.296	-0.505	10.179	-0.113	-0.133	1.000

The recorded MEMS accelerometer triads output data shown in Table 2 were then used as the observation representation in equation (6) and the maximum likelihood method was used to determine the systematic mapping bias vector and scale factor and non-orthogonal mapping matrix that is used for the transformation from each sensor's reference frame to our designated global/navigation reference frame.

The results for the generated Vectornav-100T misalignment and bias were found to be:

$$M_{VN\_a} = \begin{pmatrix} -3.820 & 8.100 & -1.465 \\ -9.005 & -3.826 & 0.966 \\ -0.012 & 0.293 & 9.625 \end{pmatrix}$$

$$\underline{b}_{VN\_a} = \begin{pmatrix} 1.188 \\ -0.822 \\ 0.644 \end{pmatrix} \tag{13}$$

The generated MPU-9255 accelerometer misalignment and bias was determined to be:

$$M_{MPU9255\_a} = \begin{pmatrix} -0.754 & -0.658 & 0.082 \\ 0.658 & -0.753 & 0.010 \\ 0.001 & 0.016 & 1.061 \end{pmatrix}$$

$$\underline{b}_{MPU9255\_a} = \begin{pmatrix} -0.076 \\ -0.093 \\ -0.052 \end{pmatrix} \quad (14)$$

Conceptually, an unlimited or arbitrary number of different preset locations can be utilized for generating the true outputs to be used in the bias vector and misalignment vector determination process. However, the number of observations/measurements should be equal or greater than the number of unknown parameters to ensure a non-underdetermined system.

For the determination of the calibration parameters of the MEMS IMU gyroscope triad, the high resolution, high accurate calibration turn-table was utilized. With rotation in the clockwise direction considered positive, two preset rotation speeds of equal magnitudes at 200 degrees per second (°/s) but in opposite directions were applied to each axis while the axis of interest was aligned with gravity in the upwards direction on the turn table as shown in Figure 4.

TABLE III. THE PRESET RATE OF 200°/S APPLIED BOTH CLOCKWISE (C.W.) AND ANTI-CLOCKWISE (A-C.W.) TO THE TURN TABLE WITH EACH AXIS IN TURN ALIGNED WITH GRAVITY IN THE UPWARDS DIRECTION

axis	rate	x c.w. (°/s)	x a-c.w (°/s)	y c.w. (°/s)	y a-c.w (°/s)	z c.w (°/s)	z a-c.w (°/s)
x	200 °/s	200.00	-200.00	0.00	0.00	0.00	0.00
y	200 °/s	0.00	0.00	200.00	-200.00	0.00	0.00
z	200 °/s	0.00	0.00	0.00	0.00	200.00	-200.00

Again 1000 readings were taken and then afterwards averaged to obtain the respective output on each axis as shown in Table 4. The results of the readings from Table IV were then used as the observations representation in equation (6) and the maximum likelihood method again used for the determination of the misalignment and bias mapping matrix and vector respectively. Temperature dependency was considered such that the misalignment and the bias were recalculated according to the corresponding sensitivities per degree increase in temperature of both MEMS IMU accelerometer and gyroscope triads.

TABLE IV. RECORDED VECTOR-100T GYROSCOPE OUTPUT IN THE RESPECTIVE POSITIONS

axis	x c.w. (°/s)	x a-c.w (°/s)	y c.w. (°/s)	y a-c.w (°/s)	z c.w. (°/s)	z a-c.w (°/s)
x	-185.875	185.741	74.060	-74.429	0.068	-0.353
y	-72.021	71.948	-186.627	186.225	0.156	0.418
z	-2.667	2.601	0.633	-1.004	199.412	-199.75

The generated Vectornav-100T gyroscope misalignment and bias was determined to be:

$$M_{VN\_g} = \begin{pmatrix} -0.929 & -0.360 & -0.013 \\ 0.371 & -0.932 & 0.004 \\ 0.001 & -0.001 & 0.998 \end{pmatrix}$$

$$\underline{b}_{VN\_g} = \begin{pmatrix} -0.046 \\ -0.190 \\ -0.008 \end{pmatrix} \quad (15)$$

TABLE V. RECORDED MPU-9255 GYROSCOPE OUTPUT IN THE RESPECTIVE POSITIONS

axis	x c.w. (°/s)	x a-c.w (°/s)	y c.w. (°/s)	y a-c.w (°/s)	z c.w. (°/s)	z a-c.w (°/s)
x	127.8232	-127.678	154.0631	-154.038	2.809	-2.849
y	-154.261	154.480	126.568	-126.565	0.930	-1.047
z	-0.976	1.120	-0.001	-0.013	200.138	-200.338

The generated MPU-9255 gyroscope misalignment and bias was determined to be:

$$M_{MPU9255\_g} = \begin{pmatrix} 0.639 & -0.772 & -0.005 \\ 0.770 & 0.633 & 0.000 \\ -0.014 & 0.005 & 1.001 \end{pmatrix}$$

$$\underline{b}_{MPU9255\_g} = \begin{pmatrix} 0.085 \\ 0.002 \\ -0.059 \end{pmatrix} \quad (16)$$

B. Verification of Calibration

For the verification of our calibration process, the Kuka robotic arm was then programmed for motion along a specified trajectory. The trajectory involved the movement of the drill head from a station position A, through station position B and finally settling at position point C. In this setup the vertical displacement from A to B was made with a distance of 0.5m. The position C was then set at an inclination angle of about 30° from station position B and also with a displacement of 0.5m from B. We then established the ground truth of our drill-head trajectory based on the Kuka robots coordinate system with the points A, B and C as shown in Figure 2. The points of the station positions A, B and C were referenced to a central reference point on the robot. To determine the true geometric measurements, the numerical values of the positions given as vector coordinates indicated by the robotic PLC read out was used. Note that the measurements were given in millimeters. For actual verification of the trajectory of the miniature drill-head, a recording of the changing position vector coordinates was made and graphed to give a good representation of the ground truth from the perspective of

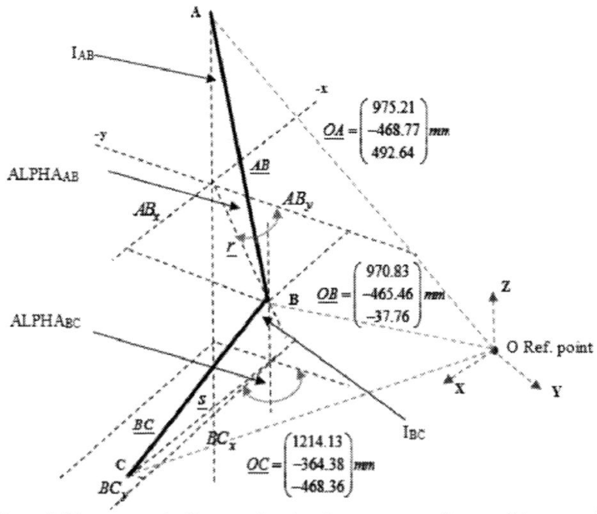

Figure 2. The geometric diagram showing the vector coordinates of the station positions A, B, and C on the Kuka Robot and from which the true trajectory of the drill-head is determined

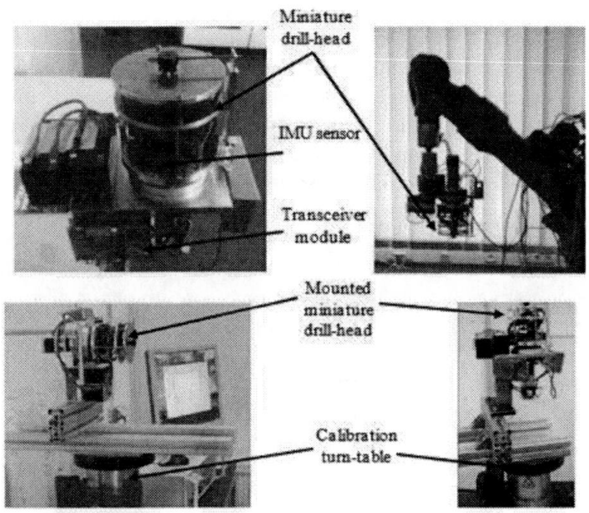

Figure 3. Top left is the miniature drill-head (AHRS) with the mounted IMU sensors and a wireless transceiver module for data acquisition. Top right is it mounted on the robotic arm. Bottom is the calibration turn-table with it mounted for calibration of the MEMs gyroscope triad.

the robotic arm. Only the trajectory and drill-head orientation were of interest. In Figure 3, the mounting positions of the miniature drill-drill head on the robotic arm as well as the turn-table for the static measurements are shown. From the station position vector coordinates, A, B, C, the distance traversed from station A through station B to station C is determined from the readout of the robot coordinate system. From the Figure 2 information, we can easily compute the respective displacement vectors and consequently the distance from position A to position B.

Figures 4-7 show the output of the two MEMS accelerometer and gyroscope triads; MPU-9255 and vectornav-100T, during translational motion in both the body frame of reference and the designated global/navigation reference frame. The two IMU sensors were mounted on different positions on the drill-head setup. Figure 4 shows the respective 3-axis accelerometer output which reflects difference in mounting positions. After application of the determined bias vector and misalignment matrices, the resulting converted outputs of the respective MEMS accelerometer and gyroscope triads in the global reference frame were plotted as shown in Figure 6. The outputs of both sensors show the expected similarity in values after the removal of the deterministic bias offset, scale factor and non-orthogonal systematic errors.

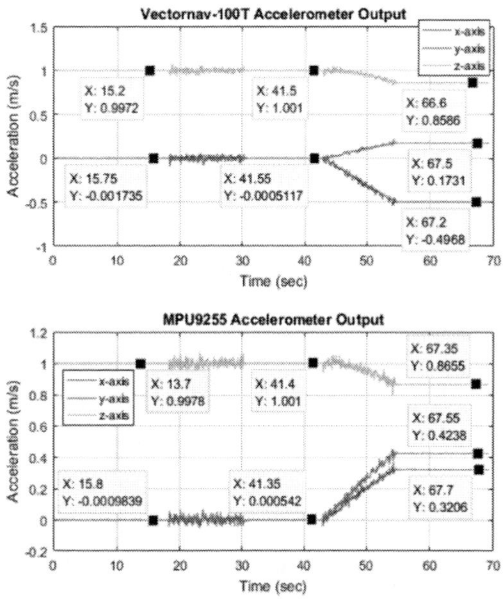

Figure 4. Measured IMU accelerometer output BEFORE conversion to global reference

This converted output data, after denoising, is then used as the input source in the AHRS model for the respective orientation estimation and consequently the overall the wellbore trajectory determination. Slight differences in output can be explained as the effects of temperature variations within the laboratory environment. The random errors left afterwards are the residual bias and residual misalignment errors which could then be stochastically modelled and utilized in the optimal estimator for the trajectory tracking process.

Improvement of the overall accuracy of the measurement can also be attributed to both the number and performance specification of the individual sensors used within a cluster or single node which is calibrated.

V. CONCLUSION, ONGOING RESEARCH AND OUTLOOK

The aim is to enable an adoptable concept of the algorithm to be directly implementable on the onboard microprocessor with the required parameters transferred to all sensor node modules over the underground wireless ad hoc network to facilitate the calibration process in real-time. Taking into consideration recent trends in machine learning and neural networks [11], a possible extension of this calibration process is with the use of multiple point measurements with the respective output data as training data within a neural network. Investigation into the possibility of improving the estimation of well-bore trajectory tracking utilizing the concept of artificial neural networks for predicting the orientation of the drill-head or bottom hole assembly would be of great interest.

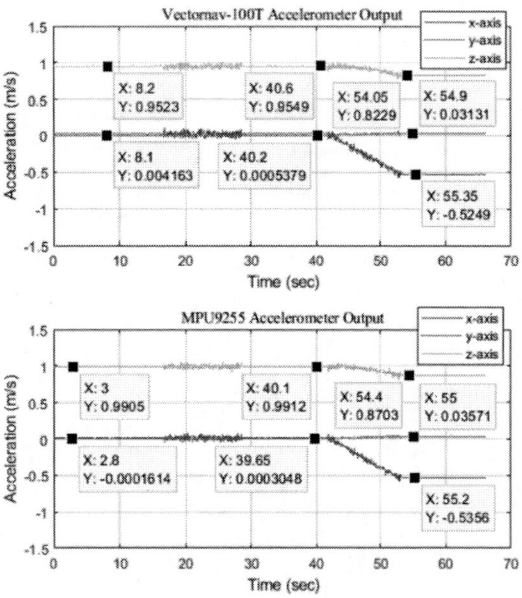

Figure 5. Measured IMU accelerometer output AFTER conversion to global reference

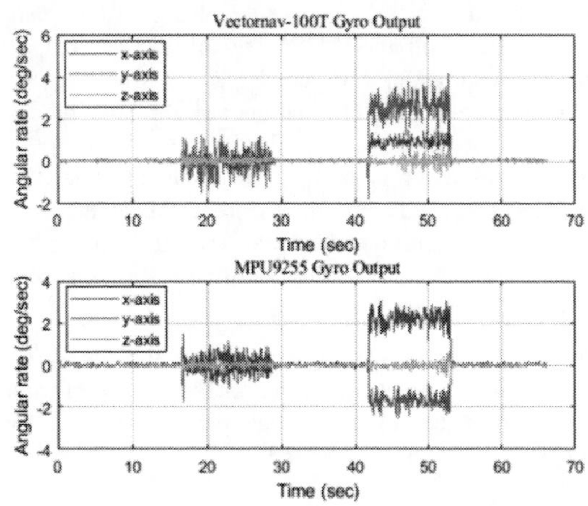

Figure 6. Measured IMU gyroscope output BEFORE conversion to global reference

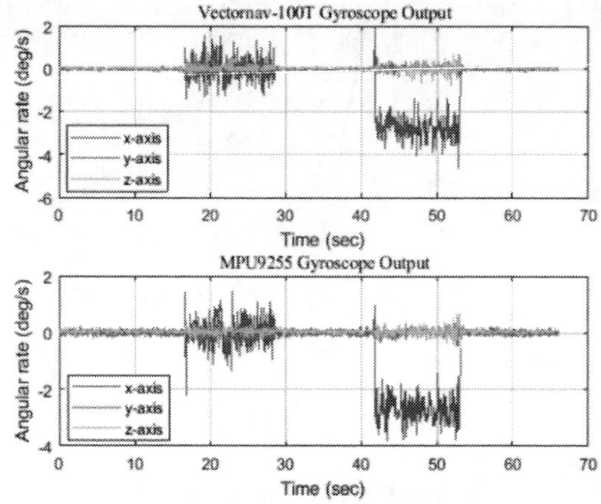

Figure 7. Measured IMU gyroscope output AFTER conversion to global reference

This notwithstanding, will not completely discard the current concept of using appropriate navigation models, such as the AHRS mathematical model in conjunction with an optimal estimator for continuously tracking the drill-head/bottom hole assembly, but would rather serve to complement the other. The concept for a laboratory setup is to use the miniature drill-head-mounted on the robotic arm to generate training data to be used in determining the different orientations of the drill-head during underground borehole navigation. The aim is to generate a proper set of coordinates characterizing a set of landmarks as inputs from the relevant sensors and the outputs characterizing the correlating orientation positions or the transformed orientation position. Theoretically, there will be an infinity of positions in the input landmark set or data points which will capture all possible orientations of the drill head relative to a designated frame of reference. In practicality, a couple of important beacon positions with their corresponding output landmarks set could be carefully selected and used as training data. This can then be extrapolated to capture all possible representations of the orientation. Controlled temperature (and pressure condition) could be included in the training data set to capture the effect of temperature rise on the IMU sensor data output.

The machination equation will be used in the optimal estimator filter in the classical sense for estimation of the bottom hole assembly/drill head orientation and the output fused or used as extra information in addition to the output generated by the artificial neural network. This technique would serve as an extension to find a more accurate estimate of the overall well-bore trajectory estimation. A comparison of the results of the optimal filter to that of the artificial neural network could be evaluated and further used as training data set to improve the neural network.

ACKNOWLEDGMENT

Thanks goes to Peter Sahm of the RST robotic laboratory, Faculty IV, Universität Siegen for his assistance in the KUKA robotic arm setup and programming to enable for the measurements to be taken. Also, thanks to Bodo Ohrndorf and Peter Hof for their technical assistance in the miniature drill-head and turn-table setup.

REFERENCES

[1] "The digital oilfield" Drilling Contractor, International Association of Drilling Contractors (IADC), Vol. 75, No. 4, July/August 2019

[2] P. Maybeck, "Stochastic Models, Estimation and Control: Volume 1", Department of Electrical Engineering, Air Force Institute of Technology, Wright-Patterson Air Force Base, Ohio, Academic Press, New York, Inc.

[3] M. El-Diasty and S. Pagiatakis, "Calibration and Stochastic Modelling of Inertial Navigation Sensor Errors", Dept. of Earth & Space Science & Engineering, York University, Journal of Global Positioning Systems, Vol.7. No. 2: 170-182, pp. 170-182, 12/2008.

[4] H. Titterton and J.L. Weston, "Strapdown Inertial Navigation Technology – 2nd Edition," The Institute of Electrical Engineering and Technology, London, United Kingdom and The American Institute of Aeronautics, Reston, Virginia, USA, 2004.

[5] A. Quinchia and G. Falco, E. Falletti, F. Dovis, C. Ferrer, "A Comparison between Different Error Modeling of MEMS Applied to GPS/INS Integrated Systems", Open Access, Sensors, ISSN 1424-8220, July 2013.

[6] IEEE Standard Specification Format Guide and Test Procedure for Single-Axis Interferometric Fiber Optic Gyros; IEEE Std 952-1997; IEEE: New York, NY, USA, 1998.

[7] A. G. Quinchia, G. Falco, E. Falletti, F. Dovis, and C. Ferrer, "A Comparism between Different Error Modeling of MEMs Applied to GPS/INS Integrated Systems," Open Access, Sensors ISSN 1424-8220,p. 9549, 08/2013.

[8] N. El-Sheimy, H. Hou, and X. Niu, "Analysis and Modeling of Inertial Sensors Using Allan Variance," IEEE Transactions on Instrumentation and Measurement, Vol. 57. No. 1, pp. 140-149, January 2008.

[9] A. Radi, S. Nassar, and N. El-Sheimy, „Stochastic Error Modeling of Smartphone Inertial Sensors for Navigation in Varying Dynamic Conditions", ISSN 2075-1087, Gyroscopy and Navigation, Vol. 9, No. 1, pp. 76-95, 2018.

[10] O. Woodman, "An introduction to inertial navigation" Technical Report, University of Cambridge Computer Laboratory Number 696, United Kingdom, ISSN 1476-2986, 2007.

[11] B. Zhang, I. Horvath, and J. Molenbroek, C. Snijders, "Using artificial neural networks for human body posture prediction", International Journal of Industrial Ergonomics, ScienceDirect, Elsevier, 2010.

Predicting User Interests Based on Their Latest Web Activities

TSUCHIYA Takeshi, HIROSE Hiroo, YAMADA Tetsuyasu
Dept. of Applied Information Engineering
Suwa University of Science
Chino city, Nagano, Japan
{ tsuchiya, hirose, yamada }@rs.sus.ac.jp

YOSHINAGA Hirokazu
Logly Inc.
Tokyo, Japan
yoshinaga@logly.co.jp

KOYANAGI Keiichi
Waseda University
Kitakyushu City, Fukuoka, Japan
keiichi.koyanagi@waseda.jp

***Abstract*—This paper discusses and proposes a method for predicting information interesting to users based on their recent online behavior. Analysis of user activities on the web aims to investigate and acquire some information about user interests through websites. Therefore, we assume that recent interests of users can be predicted by analyzing the characteristics of acquired web contents. Our proposed method identifies these user interests based on the clicked log of web advertisement by using neural networks, and makes it possible to predict information by regression to the learned user model. It means that flexible information service can be constructed using predictions based on user presence. The evaluation indicates that the method is effective and practical in comparison to the conventional model which statistically analyzes web activities.**

Keywords - user interests; content prediction; web advertisement.

I. INTRODUCTION

Online advertising, which is the essential business model, is interactive in comparison to conventional billboard advertisement and TV commercials. A representative example is listing advertisements adapted to displayed contents, and another example is targeting advertisements based on user behavior displayed based on web history.

These are core approaches to web advertisement, which comprise strategy and analysis to effectively pass product information to target users. As a benchmark indicating the importance of web marketing, the amount of advertising expense in Japan has grown 657 times from 1995 to 2014 [1]. However, the growth rate has remained unchanged recently. This is because the component technology is not making any significant changes in the amount of investment in advertising as well as business type of advertising.

Several kinds of web services/Social Network Service (SNS) utilize registered individual information and service usage history to display personalized advertisements [2] . However, these services require active registration of personal information, and it is difficult to personalize advertising without entering personal information. Behavioral targeting advertising utilizes cookies generated on each website for personalization purposes; however, the stored information may be outdated and might therefore not reflect user's current interests.

User interests can be roughly classified into the following two types: continuous long-term interests regardless of the time or period such as hobbies and intentions, and short-term interests which last for a certain period of time and are focused on current tasks or investigations. Therefore, we focus on the information that the user has acquired most recently in order to predict the user interest and the transition of the user interest. By using our proposed method, we expect applications such as conventional web marketing, advancement of web advertisement, and dynamic design of information system to be based on prediction of user behavior.

It is assumed that the short-term interest of the user is limited to the latest 30 minutes [3], and the acquired web content by each user will include current interest information within this period. For feature analysis of each user interest, supervised learning is used for predicting user interest by regression of user acquired information. In this paper, the data used for learning is online behavioral history collected through the clicked log of web advertisements on several real web services. The effectiveness of the proposed method is evaluated in comparison with the general method that uses the statistical method of words embedded in web content.

Section 2 describes and discusses how to acquire information indicating user interest to the analysis based on web activities. Section 3 clarifies the proposed way of analyzing this information. Section 4 evaluates the proposal, and section 5 gives consideration. Section 6 concludes this paper.

II. USER INTERESTS

This section discusses how information related to current user interests can be determined from their web behavior.

A. Related Research

Regarding related research, Siriaraya et al. [4] proposes a method for analyzing the potential interest of the long-term/short-term user based on the analysis of user activities on the web in the same way as it is done in this paper. Feature analysis compares the Fully Qualified Domain Name (FQDN) of the site visited by the user and the category of the website. It is clear that the method using website category has better performance, and the long and short analysis period has no relation to prediction performance. Compared with the proposed method, which uses web content for analysis, the analysis load of learning features based on FQDN and website category involves less processing load caused by no text processing than the proposed method. However, using this information for feature analysis only makes it possible to classify website features. In other words, it only predicts the classification of user interest information. On the other hand, the method proposed in this paper analyzes the information contained in the content as a feature although the processing load increases. It is possible to make judgment based on similarity considering the content in more detail than the classification of interest information. It is also clarified that the prediction performance can be expected to improve by introducing Recurrent Neural Network (RNN) to consider the order of browsing history. The use of order reveals the context of browsing history. And the effect of emphasizing the interest information of short–term users can be expected compared to the conventional method.

Van den Poel et al. [5] proposes a method that predicts consumer behavior from the behavior before and after making a purchase through an EC site. In particular, a model based on the logit model is proposed. However, since the method is based on statistical prediction, it cannot predict user interest. It is impossible to predict behavioral patterns that have not occurred before. Since this paper analyzes the information of the acquired content itself, it is possible to predict user interest information from the viewpoint of similarity and correlation among contents.

B. Information Indicating User Interests

This research assumed that user interests at each point in time are included in information retrieved around that time. By analyzing the acquired information and its characteristics, current user interests could be elucidated.

As such interests change over time, it was assumed that the same interest lasted up to 30 minutes at most. Therefore, user web behavior history characteristics ware used to derive user interests. Fig. 1 shows the web behavioral history of users at each point in time ($t = 0$).

C. Web Behavioral History

The web behavioral history URLs used in this study were collected by executing a script when acquiring web content, after which information was stored with the user ID generated from the first access and time on the database. The data were then analyzed for user interests by automatically scraping the content from the collected URLs for each user using PhantomJS [9] and Selenium [10] headless browser, which sequentially accessed each URL to acquire content.

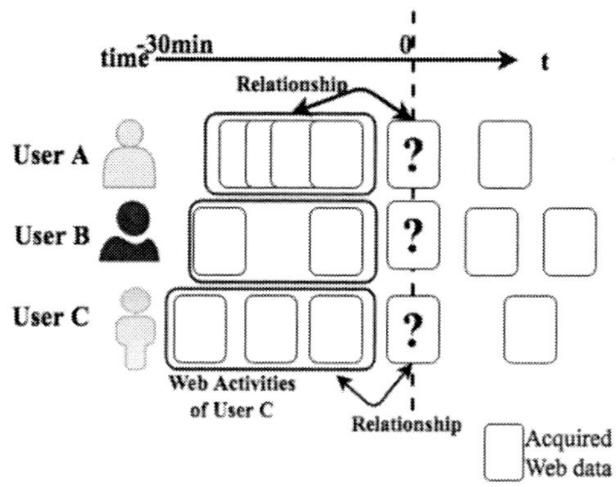

Figure 1: User Interests

D. Extracting the Main Content

There are numerous methods for extracting main content, e.g., presumption based on learning the web content context using the natural language method [6] or learning content placement within a webpage using machine learning [7].

Yamamoto et al. [8] assumed that the main content had the most sentences (number of characters). The main content occupied an average of 78.8% of all texts in the web content, which was the largest ratio obtained from the analysis of real web pages. Therefore, in this paper, it was assumed that the main content locations were based on the ratio of block size to the entire text volume from <body> tag to </body> tag. Therefore, it was only necessary to count the characters on the web page, which lessened the extraction load compared to learning the web context.

E. Deriving Information from the Content

Almost all targeted web contents were written in Japanese. Therefore, it was necessary to analyze each word in order to extract the characteristics; note that some words were combined with their postpositional particles or auxiliary verbs. Therefore, unlike the extraction of English words, it was necessary to analyze the words in texts using morphological analysis, after which the words unrelated to the information context such as particles, conjunctions, or numerals were removed to avoid performance degradation and reduce processing load. This study used the open source segmentation library MeCab [11] for morphological analysis.

III. Model Construction

This section presents a learning model, which is constructed on the basis of the information extracted from each user. Fig. 2 provides an overview of the proposed method.

A. Data for Learning

The web information acquired by the user, who clicks the web advertisement as shown in Fig. 2, is used as the data for learning. As shown in Section 1, the current web advertisement is selected as the advertisement which has an attribute related to or similar to that of the web content

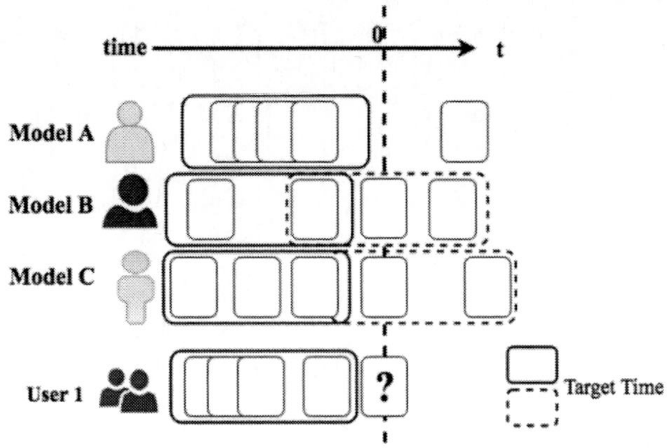

Figure 2: Overview of Constructing Models

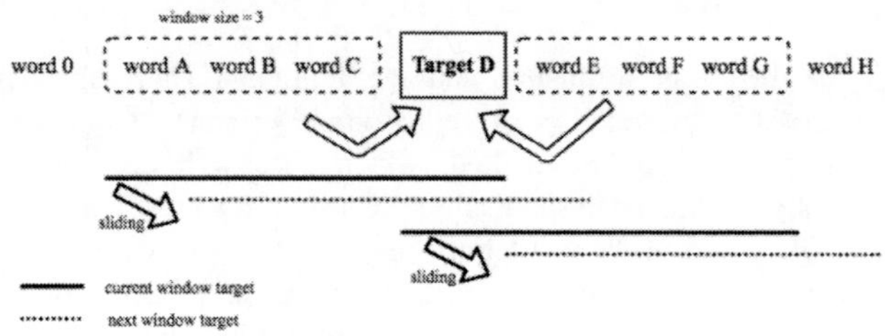

Figure 3: Context Learning

for the ad space in web pages. Delivered advertisements are dynamically determined by bidding for advertisements that are adapted to the attributes of acquiring user (static information such as age and living area, dynamic information such as past web history). Therefore, the user who clicks on the advertisement displayed on the web content could be considered as currently interested in the web advertisement. By increasing the number of target data, it can be considered that the number of users who are more interested in web advertisements and clicked on them increases than the users who accidentally clicked on the web advertisements. Therefore, the acquired information from the users who clicked this web advertisement can be considered as the indication of their current interests, and is used as the data for learning.

B. Context Learning

A paragraph vector–distributed memory (PV–DM) model [12] was used to learn the order of the words included in the information. At the time, the PV–DM model determines the learning contexts in the information as the words in the window are treated as input, and the next word is adjacent to the neural network window, as shown on the left side of Fig. 3.

In Fig. 3, the parameter, "window size," is set to three words. In an environment where the parameter "window size = 3 words" is set, the information context learning proceeds by designating "wordA" ∼" word C" in the window as the information contexts in order to output "target word D." The output is then learned by moving the window for all words included in the information. By sliding the target to the right, the learning proceeds by designating "word B" ∼ "word D" as the contexts in order to predict "word E." The proposed method also learns in the opposite direction; that is, by designating the input window on the right side in Fig. 3 ("wordE" ∼ "word G"), the output is the previous word ("target word D"). In short, the proposed method learns on a neural network so that it can predict words on both sides of the defined window parameter "window size," which enables effective learning even if only a few words are included the window. Based on these processes, the learning model is structured by using the derived information, from which it forms the learned word vectors and information vectors.

C. Prediction

In order to predict the user interest, vectorization of the latest acquired information is executed by using the constructed model as in the case of the data for learning. The vectorized acquisition information of each user includes the feature of their interest. (corresponding to the "?" of User 1 in Fig. 1).

Therefore, the predicted information is regressed to a vector indicating a similar feature. However, such vector information is not useful as it is for the predicted information. Therefore, the candidates of predicted information (e.g., the web advertisement and web content) are vectorized in advance. The similarity between the vectorized candidates of predicted information and the vectorized users interest is derived, and the one closest candidate information to the user interest is taken as the predicted information. In other words, the most similar information is determined by the cosine similarity, which measures the angle formed by two vectors.

IV. EVALUATION

This section evaluates the proposed method for determining the user interests from user behaviors acquired from the real web services.

A. User Behaviors on the Web

The user behavior extracted for the evaluation is clicked as the log of web advertisement mentioned in Section 3.1 as for learning and evaluating, which is collected from various unspecified web services on various domains. The data used in this paper use the log of web advertisement notified to the advertisement network. It is information shared among the advertisement frames (media) for displaying the recommendations and advertisements within the web content, called the advertisement network.

It is not located at a specific domain, but at unspecified websites on various domains. The data included user IDs and the URL entries for the executed sites. The user ID was generated randomly when each user first accessed any of the corresponding websites. Then, the same user ID was used when the same script was executed in any of their websites; that is, the user web behaviors were traced using this ID. This evaluation used about $5,000$ user behaviors (the number of user was $1,300$) for the learning, and another 150 user behaviors for the evaluation test.

B. Evaluation Scenario

In this evaluation, the model was constructed based on the user behaviors, as shown in TABLE I, after which the evaluation data were vectorized to predict the user interests and derive the most similar behaviors. Then, the proposed method and a method using the statistical properties of words and web content were compared. The expression of statistical properties for appearing words is done by the LDA method [14], in which the use for probabilistic reduction of vector dimensions in the tf–idf [13] method weights the appearing words based on frequency.

To demonstrate the effectiveness of main content extraction, the performance comparison was also evaluated. TABLE II shows the development environment.

TABLE I. USER BEHAVIORS ON THE WEB

Environment	Specification
Number of User Behaviors	4500
Number of Users	1300
Number of Users for test	150User

TABLE II. DEVELOPMENT ENVIRONMENT

Environment	Specification
Pre-Processing	gensim [15]
Modeling	Tensor Flow 1.8 [16], Python 3.6.2
OS	Ubuntu 16.10
System	Docker 17.09

C. Results

Fig. 4 shows the evaluation results, in which the $x-$axis is the precision rate, and the $y-$axis is the recall rate. In the graph, "Proposal (only main)" refers to the method when only the main content was used for the modeling, "Received all data" refer to the method when all acquired web content was used for the modeling, and "Conventional" was the statistical method based on the word frequency including the main content. In general, the graph on the upper right side of the graph shows a superior performance for the recall–precision rate, indicating that the proposed method was able to effectively express the information characteristics.

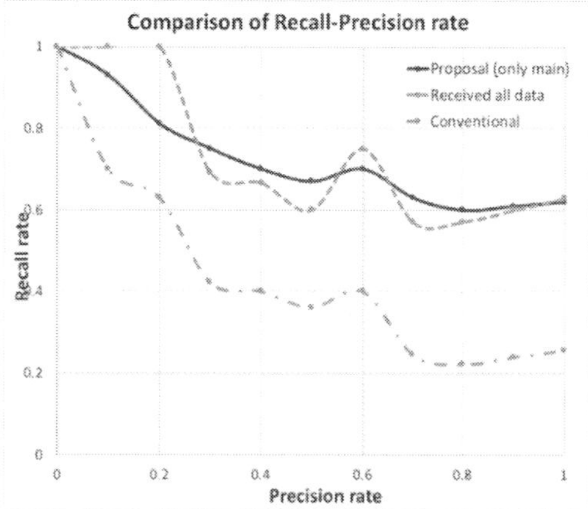

Figure 4: Comparison of R–P rate

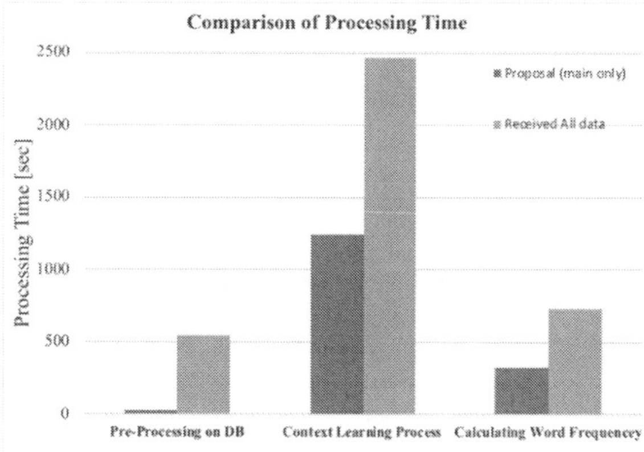

Figure 5: Processing Time

The "Received all data" case performed better than the "Proposal (only main)" case in some intervals, which was possibly due to the partial information loss. The main content characteristics were emphasized in the embedded web advertisements, which were similar to the main content in the sides and the header. The "Received all data" case dynamically generated the web advertisements and "search engine optimization" tags as well as the main content, which was based on the main content similarities and web history. Therefore, it was concluded that the "Received all data" performance was unstable, but the "Proposal (only main)" was stable at some intervals.

Fig. 5 shows the processing time comparisons for extracting and not extracting the main content from the web content. Specifically, it shows the time taken for each process from scraping to the extraction of the words from the contents on the DB; that is, as this difference was the difference in the information volume to be processed, accordingly, the impact increases in proportion to the target information volume.

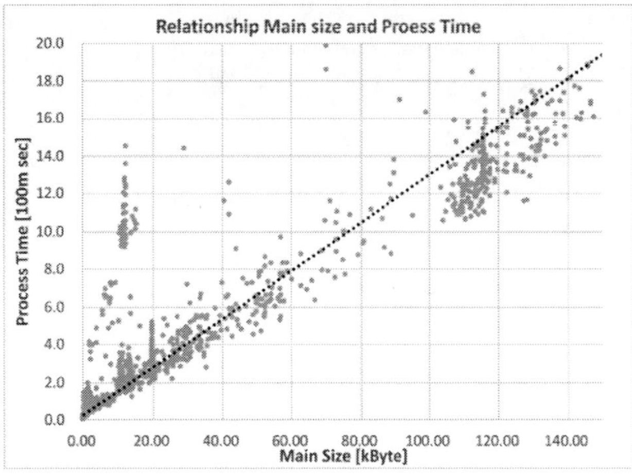

Figure 6: Processing time and Data Volume

V. CONSIDERATION

Based on the results, this section examines the effectiveness of the proposed method.

A. Based on the evaluation

Based on the evaluation results, the proposed method was found to be able to identify similar information related to the users web interests. In particular, extracting the main content by using the learned model rather than the statistical information showed a better and more stable performance. Due to the assumption that the acquired information was biased toward a specific field or topic (lack of comprehensive information), it was concluded that the conventional method had a poorer performance because of insufficient data as the $4,500$ items in TABLE I were inadequate for the method characteristics.

The proposed method only targeted the web content acquired by the users; therefore, the performance was more stable and the processing load was smaller as the main contents were previously extracted (this process corresponded to data cleansing). However, to predict the user interests, the following processes were necessary: acquiring the most recent information, extracting the main contents, and analyzing these contents; whereas, the conventional method use cookies. If the proposed method were to be applied to a real system, the key problems would be at the respective nodes, where these processes were to be executed.

The load processing for extracting the main content from each web page was then clarified for the $3,000$ randomly extracted websites by calculating the time for the pre–processing and word extraction from the main contents. Fig. 5 shows the relationship between processing times and targeted data volume.

In Fig. 6, the $x-$axis shows the size of the main contents [kByte], and the $y-$axis shows the extraction time for the main content and words, for which the average size of the main content to page size was 46.53%; that is the main content occupied 46% of the user' s acquired web contents. In addition, the main content was less than 150[kByte] for $2,800$ of the websites, which was a majority of the $3,000$ websites. Fig. 5 only plots this range on the graph, from which it can be seen that the processing time linearly increased with a slope of 0.13 in proportion to the main content size. However, to implement this method, the load balancing would need to be primarily dealt with as the load increases depending on the processing and extracting processes.

If it is assumed that each node simultaneously executed these processing steps with content acquisition, then it will take about 1 [sec] to process the average data size for each content; therefore, the processing load could be distributed to the nodes, leaving a possibility that the web usability of each user could be lost.

Therefore, for effective implementation, it would be necessary to design a system model which is focused on how this processing could be executed.

B. Future Work

This section discusses the possible improvements to the proposed method. The model based on the consideration of the user web behavioral history was able to effectively extract the information related to the user interests; therefore, the users who clicked or watched a displayed web advertisement corresponding to their interests could be targeted. As these users showed an interest in the display advertisement, these could be seen to have relevance to the user latest web activities and could be used as a part of the users' information history.

The user interest duration was assumed to be up to 30 minutes in this paper. However, this could change depending on the situation and the people. Accordingly, it could be possible to determine the user interest displacement and thought transitions from a correlation of the obtained web data. Therefore, a method could be designed to detect the user interest transition from the acquired data correlations, which could remove the non–target data from the training data and improve the quality and effectiveness of the proposed method.

The data used in this evaluation were focused on the user web behavioral history acquired from a web service on one day; however, it is necessary to evaluate this by extending the duration. If the proposed method were to be implemented on a real system, it would be necessary to solve the load problem for the acquisitions and analysis of the user web behavioral history data; therefore, a method to distribute this through networks could also be considered.

VI. CONCLUSION

In this paper, we assume that a web user latest interests would be included in their web behavioral history within the latest 30 minutes of web browsing. Therefore, a prediction method was proposed based on the analysis and extraction of the users' characteristics. The proposed method was found to more easily identify the latest user interests than the conventional method based on cookies. The evaluation also indicated that the proposed method was better able to predict the user interests than the current method based on the statistical information. Future works will improve the model performance to better categorize the user interests and develop a method to dynamically detect the interest duration.

ACKNOWLEDGMENT

This work was partly supported by MEXT KAKENHI Grant Number 17K01149

REFERENCES

[1] Dentsu, "Advertising Expending Reports in Japan", http://www.dentsu.com/knowledgeanddata/ad_expenditures/ , Retrieved September 8, 2019

[2] S. Hirose, "Textbook for Advertisement technology", Shoei-sya, 2016 (written in Japanese)

[3] Y. Watanabe and Y. Ikegaya, "Effect of intermittent learning on task performance: a pilot study", Journal of Neuronet, Vol.38 pp.1–5, 2017

[4] P. Siriaraya, Y. Yamaguchi, M. Morishita, Y. Inagaki, R. Nakamoto, J. Zhang, J. Aoi, and S. Nakajima, "Using categorized web browsing history to estimate the user' s latent interests for web advertisement recommendation", 4429-4434. 10.1109/BigData.2017.8258480

[5] V. den Poel and B. Wouter, "Predicting Online-purchasing Behaviour", European Journal of Operational Research 166, pp.557–575, 10.1016/j.ejor.2004.04.022

[6] B. Orkut, G. Hector, and P. Andreas, "Seeing the Whole in Parts: Text Summarization for Web Browsing on Handheld Devices" , Proc. 10th International Conference on World Wide Web, pp.652–662, 2001

[7] K. Nakamura, S. Tanaka, Y. Yamamoto, and S. Abiko, "Method of Filtering Harmful Information Considering Extraction Range of Word Co-occurrence", IPSJ Journal, Vol.54, No.2, pp.571–584, IPSJ, 2013

[8] Y. Yamamoto, K. Nakamura, S. Tanaka, and S. Abiko, "Proposal Research of Web Page Segmentation Method for Extracting and Describing Each Article in Detail", IPSJ Journal, Vol.55 No.2, pp.874–891, 2014

[9] PhantomJS,"http://phantomjs.org/", Retrieved September 8, 2019

[10] Selenium,"https://www.seleniumhq.org/", Retrieved September 8, 2019

[11] MeCab, "http://taku910.github.io/mecab/", Retrieved September 8, 2019

[12] Q. Le and T. Mikolov, "Distributed Representations of Sentences and Documents" , Proc. of Int. Conf. on Machine Learning, pp.1188–1196, 2014

[13] C.D. Manning, P. Raghavan, and H. Schutze, "Scoring, term weighting, and the vector space model", Introduction to Information Retrieval. pp100–123, 2008

[14] D. Blei, A. Ng, and M. Jordan, "Latent Dirichlet Allocation", Journal of Machine Learning Research, pp. 1107–1135, 2003

[15] topic modelling for humans, "https://radimrehurek.com/gensim/", Retrieved September 8, 2019

[16] TensorFlow, "https://www.tensorflow.org/", Retrieved September 8, 2019

UHD Panoramic Video Coding for Multi-Camera and Multi-Processor Acquisition Systems

Joao Duarte

Instituto de Telecomunicações
Leiria, Portugal
Email: joaoerduarte@gmail.com

Joao Carreira and Pedro Assuncao

Instituto de Telecomunicações
Politécnico de Leiria / ESTG
Leiria, Portugal
Email: {jcarreira, amado}@co.it.pt

Abstract—**This paper addresses the problem of encoding Ultra-High Definition (UHD) panoramic video in multi-camera and multi-processor systems, where a wide Field of View (FoV) is captured by multiple cameras, each one corresponding to a small FoV. The UHD panoramic images are then formed by stitching high-definition images captured by the individual cameras, covering a wide FoV around the acquisition viewpoint. A simulation study is carried out to evaluate the rate-distortion-complexity performance of multi-encoder systems using independent processors for encoding sub-images with small FoV, as part of a wider panoramic UHD resolution. This study uses an image partitioning scheme to distribute the UHD images with wide FoV over various processors and evaluates the rate-distortion-complexity performance of HEVC encoding in comparison with classic encoding of a single frame per processor. The results show that the rate-distortion performance of multi-processor systems is quite similar to single processor ones, which allows to distribute the huge computational requirements of HEVC encoding across several low-cost processors.**

Keywords–Panoramic video Coding; Multi-processor encoding systems; Rate-distortion-complexity.

I. Introduction

The increasing use of Ultra-High Definition (UHD) video, such as 4k and 8k resolutions, drives significant research efforts to develop efficient coding systems, not only to improve the rate-distortion performance, but also to cope with the demand of huge computational resources [1]. The latest encoding standard, High-Efficiency Video Codec (HEVC), also known as H.265, is currently the most adequate to encode UHD video [2]. However, the better compression efficiency in comparison with its predecessor H.264/AVC is achieved at the cost of much higher encoding time due to the heavy computational requirements. This poses limitations on the acquisition and coding of UHD video using low-cost equipment with reduced computational resources. In the case of UHD panoramic video, the technical challenges arise from the huge amount of data required to represent visual information with wide Field of View (FoV). Thus, acquisition, processing and coding of UHD panoramic video has been driving research efforts [3][4]. However, despite the existence of fast hardware to deal with the high resolutions of UHD panoramic video, the lack of low-complexity acquisition and encoding systems still limit the development of new applications for non-professional consumers. One of such low-complexity systems is described in [5], where nine low-power processing units are used to capture a panoramic image.

Current acquisition and encoding systems for UHD panoramic video can be found in both consumer and professional markets with quite different characteristics. On the one hand, cheap systems available for consumers using either one or two cameras with ultra wide-angle fisheye lenses, suffer from limited resolutions and optical distortions. On the other hand, professional equipment include several high quality cameras, each one capturing high resolution images with limited FoV. To use the best characteristics of both type of systems requires multiple cheap cameras and processors for capturing and encoding the whole FoV in a distributed manner by using low-cost processors.

This paper presents a contribution for the development of such systems by investigating the rate-distortion-complexity performance of a multi-processing system to encode UHD video using multiple independent processors to encode part of the panoramic visual data, i.e., a narrow FoV. A simulation study is carried out to evaluate whether the encoding performance achieved by distributing narrow FoVs across several encoders/processors is comparable with a single high-end encoder with only one processor for the full-FoV UHD panoramic images.

This paper is organized as follows. Next section presents an overview of related work. Section III describes the simulation study procedure and Section IV presents the results along with their discussion. Finally, Section V concludes the paper.

II. Related work

Recent improvements in the coding efficiency of predictive algorithms, when compared to the previous standards, are mostly achieved at the expense of a great increase in computational complexity [1]. For instance, the HEVC is very efficient at compressing video data, but it requires significantly more processing power when compared to the previous standards [6], making it difficult to deal with very high resolution video, such as UHD panoramic video. A possible approach to deal with such high computational power requirements is to use parallel processing, where the input video data is partitioned and independently encoded by multiple processors. There are different methods that are able to accomplish this goal, as explained below.

At high-levels of the video data hierarchy, one can use parallel processing on the basis of Groups of Pictures (GOP). In this approach, the input video is divided in temporal segments, each one assigned to a different GOP independently encoded by a different processor [7]. Although this is simple to implement, the overall latency of such coding process is non-negligible and does not allow to achieve real time communications [8]. Memory limitation may also pose problems because typical caches have insufficient storage space for multiple frames. To achieve a more fine control, parallelism can be defined at the frame-level, where several frames, in the same GOP, are encoded at the same time. However, such an approach imposes constraints to the temporal dependency between frames, which significantly reduces the motion estimation efficiency. Moreover, synchronisation between processing threads is required to guarantee that all prerequisites for motion estimation are encoded.

Alternatively, each frame can be divided into several slices to be processed in parallel. As each slice is independent from each other, it is straightforward to process multiple slices in parallel, without inter-process communication, except for motion compensation prediction. Although this is a simple approach, it incurs in substantial coding overhead due to the higher number of slice headers, and reduction of causal neighbours for prediction, due to lack of predictions across slice boundaries. In order to reduce the slice overhead, one can use tile partitioning. Then, each tile can be processed independently as defined in the HEVC standard [9]. Although the use of tiles is similar to slices, tiles are able to achieve efficiency frame partitioning for parallel processing with lower overhead [10].

Finally, each row of Coding-Tree Units (CTU) can be processed independently using the Wavefront Parallel Processing (WPP) mechanism proposed in the HEVC standard [11]. Contrary to slice and tile boundaries, no dependence is broken at each row boundary so the rate-distortion penalty is small when compared to other methods, as the context of the arithmetic coder is propagated between rows. However, to maintain the context, a delay of one CTU has to be introduced in each row. In this approach, the number of threads does not affect the coding efficiency, but the requirements of inter-process communication substantially increases.

Even though HEVC already has some parallel processing mechanisms to deal with the problem of high computational complexity, as mentioned before, they are often not enough, specially when using hardware with quite limited resources. Moreover, the techniques introduced in HEVC for parallel processing dependent on inter-processor communication and are not suitable for independent processing by different cores or processing units.

The idea of using multi-processor units was also investigated for system-on-chip [12] and in the case of multi-view video coding [13]. However, the relative performance of image data splitting into sub-images corresponding to a narrow FoV of a panoramic video remains mostly unknown. Thus, this study addresses the impact on rate-distortion-complexity performance of using multiple independent encoding processors, each one covering a limited FoV captured by independent cameras. This study fo Specifically, this work studies multiple schemes with FoVs of different sizes under different coding parameters and compares the impact on the coding efficiency. By evaluating how the coding performance varies with the video signal characteristics (e.g., spatial and temporal complexity), the amount of processing units and the size of each FoV, one can easily design efficient video acquisition and encoding systems based on multi-camera and multi-processor architectures.

TABLE I. TEST SEQUENCES USED IN THE EXPERIMENTS.

Sequence	SI	TI	Description
Beauty	10.6	8.35	Very high spatial details in some regions (hair) and flat background
Bosphorus	13.4	3.75	Boat shipping at low motion with moderate complex background
HoneyBee	8.24	2.54	High spatial detail, with one low motion object
Jockey	11.5	16.2	High motion with one horse rider
ReadySteadyGo	18.0	19.0	Very high motion with several horse riders

III. SIMULATION STUDY PROCEDURE

In the simulation study, the open source implementation of the HEVC encoder x265 was used [14].

The goal was to evaluate the rate-distortion-complexity of a multi-processor system, where each processor runs an independent encoder for sub-images of the full-FoV UHD resolution, i.e., partial FoV corresponding to a vertical stripe of the original image. The performance is evaluated in comparison with a conventional system using a single processor running only one encoder for the full-FoV UHD resolution. To make a fair comparison, the same video sequence is encoded in both systems. The small FoV sub-images captured by independent cameras are simulated by splitting the original images into multiple vertical stripes of equal size.

The five UHD video sequences presented in Table I were used in the experiments. These test sequences have 4k spatial resolution, i.e., 3840×2160 pixels, and were selected as they are commonly used for UHD HEVC evaluation tests and are public available [15]. As shown in Table I, the test sequences have different types of motion and texture complexity, demonstrated by the measures of spatial information (SI) and temporal information (TI), which follow the definitions given in [16]. These high resolution video sequences are used to simulate a wide FoV. Table II defines the six different sub-image splitting modes used in this study along with the corresponding spatial resolution of the resulting FoV. Figure 1 shows an example for the partition into six narrow FoVs.

After splitting the UHD images, each video sequence corresponding to either a full or limited FoV were encoded using five different native presets of the x265 encoder: 0-ultrafast, 3-fast, 5-medium, 7-very slow and 9-placebo, which have direct impact on rate-distortion and encoding time. These presets define various control variables within the encoding process such as maximum and minimum coding unit (CU) size, maximum consecutive B-frames, number of frames for lookahead

TABLE II. FOV PARTITIONS AND THEIR SPATIAL RESOLUTION.

Number of partitions	Spatial resolution of the FoV
One	3840×2160
Six	640×2160
Eight	480×2160
Ten	384×2160
Twelve	320×2160
Fifteen	256×2160

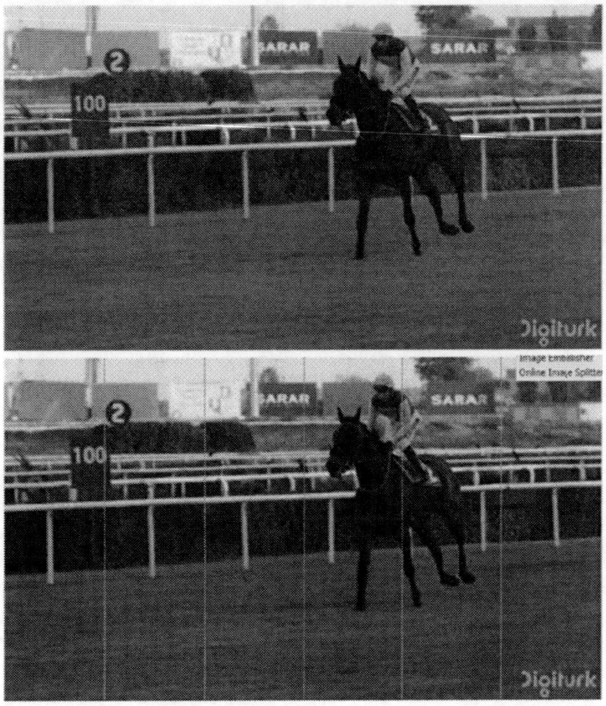

Figure 1. Example of a full-FoV UHD video frame (top) and its corresponding partitioning into 6 FoVs (bottom).

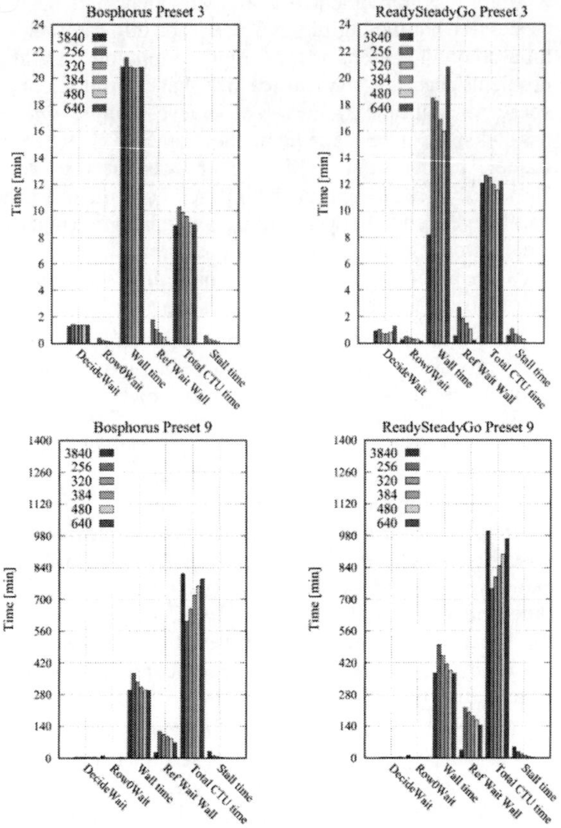

Figure 2. Encoding times for the for CRF 21 and different preset and FoV splitting.

slice-type decision, motion search algorithm, motion range and merge mode configuration [17]. For each preset, the Constant Rate Factor (CRF), which is used to control the Quantisation Parameter (QP) was also configured to the following values: 11, 16, 21 and 26 (lower CRF results in higher quality). Finally, each reduced FoV sequence is encoded 20 times to obtain valid average results for encoding times. Considering all possible encoding configurations and sequences, a total of 1200 encoding runs were performed in this simulation study.

From the output produced by the x265 software, the following time-related variables were extracted for each condition:

- *DecideWait*: time that the encoder waits since the previous frame was retrieved by the API thread, before a new frame is given for encoding. This is the latency introduced by slice-type decisions (lookahead).
- *Row0Wait*: time that the encoder has to wait since it receives a frame to encode until its first row of CTUs is allowed to start compression. This is the latency introduced by reference frames being reconstructed and making filtered rows available.
- *Wall time*: difference between when the first CTU is ready to be compressed and the entire frame is output to the coded stream.
- *Ref Wait Wall*:difference between when the first and the last reference row become available.
- *Total CTU time*: the total time spent by working threads in compression and filtering operations of the CTUs of a given frame.
- *Stall Time*: the total time spent with zero working threads, i.e, no compression operation was performed.

To evaluate the quality of the encoded frames and sub-frames (smaller FoV) the Peak Signal-to-Noise Ratio (PSNR) is used, both at the frame and video-level. The coded frame size was also taken into consideration, as shown in the next section.

IV. Results and Analysis

In this section, the results of the simulation study are presented and discussed in detail. This analysis is organised in three parts: (i) analysis of the encoding times, (ii) analysis of compression results, i.e., coded frame size, versus encoding times and (iii) overall performance evaluation using rate-distortion results.

A. Evaluation of encoding time

The objective of these experiments is to evaluate whether the processing time (i.e., computational complexity) required by single encoding of full-FoV UHD panoramic video is equal to overall multi-encoding time of several sub-video sequences, each one representing a smaller FoV of the same full-FoV UHD panoramic video. To this aim, the results obtained for the time-related variables described in the previous section are compared for different presets and CRFs

The first comparison is between the average encoding times of each frame. For the sub-video the encoding times of each FoV were added together in order to directly compare to the full-FoV video. Figure 2 contains the results of sequence

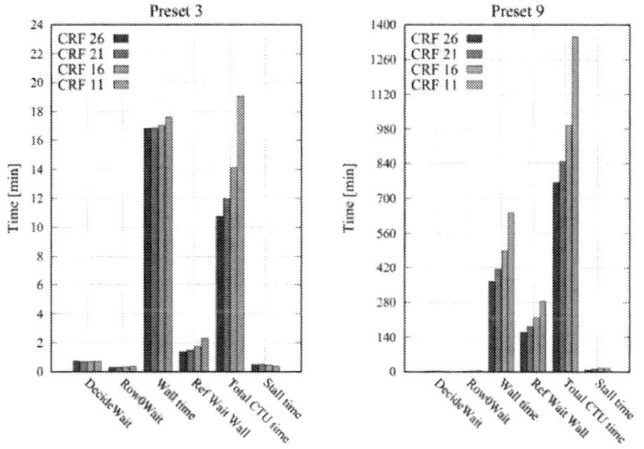

Figure 3. Encoding times for ReadySteadyGo sequence using 10 FoVs.

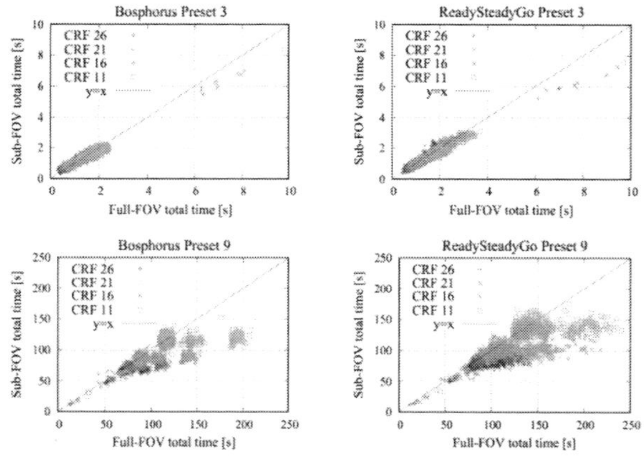

Figure 4. Total encoding time of each frame for full-FoV versus the limited sub-video encoding with 10 FoVs for the Preset 3 and 9.

ReadySteadyGo, which has a very high motion and Bosphorus, which has much lower motion (see TI in Table I), for the Presets 3 and 9 and CRF 21. Results reveal that the overall measured times add up to similar values of the single encoding of full-FoV. This can be seen by similar value of the *Wall time* which represents the time difference occurred during the frame encoding process.

Comparing results from both sequences in Figure 2, on the one hand the sequence with higher motion (i.e., ReadySteadyGo) shows higher variations in the encoding times, specially for encoding the whole frame with variations up to 700 minutes (50% increase). On the other hand, the results from Bosphorus are roughly similar with variations up to 7 minutes (25% increase). This indicates that in panoramic video with low motion content, the wide FoV can be divided into smaller FoV captured from several cameras and encoded across multiple processors with lower computational resources. In this case the overall processing requirements can be distributed across multiple processors without increasing the total encoding time. In the case of higher motion video, the encoding time variations show that the overall encoding time of multiple small FoV sequences is greater than encoding the same sequence with a single encoder for the full-FoV. This means that the encoding time of small FoV sequences cannot be estimated from the total encoding time of full-FoV sequences by simply dividing the full-FoV encoding time by the FoV splitting factor of the acquisition system. This also indicates that TI (Table I) can be a useful parameter to include in a processing time estimation model of split video.

The results of Figure 2 that in the Preset 9 (slower preset) the *Total CTU time* is higher than the *Wall time*. One should note that the former corresponds to the processing time and the latter to the elapsed time. Therefore, these results reveal that in slower presets the encoder takes more advantage of the parallel processing features, incurring in higher processing time in a short time period. Figure 3 shows the encoding times for different CRFs and fixed presets of 3 and 9. In this case a FoV width of 384 pixels was used, corresponding to a partitioning factor of 10. Results confirm the expected behaviour that the processing time increases with the increase in quality, however this is less noticeable for faster presets (e.g., Preset 3).

In order to show the relation between the encoding time of

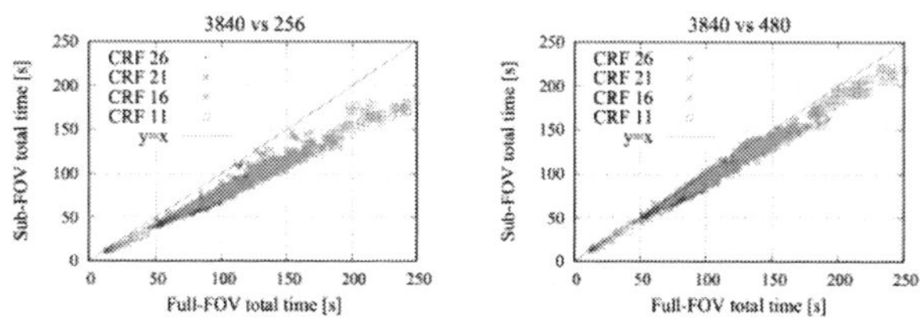

Figure 5. Total encoding time of each frame for full-FoV versus the narrow FoV encoding for the ReadySteadyGo sequence and the Preset 9.

full-FoV against multiple smaller FoV, Figure 4 shows a scatter plot of all results from different sequences. The horizontal axis corresponds to the encoding time of full-FoV while the vertical axis represents multiple smaller FoVs using 10 partitions (FoV resolution: 384 × 2160 pixels). The sum of the FoV times is directly compared with the full-FoV video. Moreover, a diagonal line corresponding to $y = x$ is also represented to indicate the threshold from which the sub-FoV videos spend higher amount of encoding time than the reference case with full-FoV. These results reveal that quite linear correlation exists between the two encoding times, which is more noticeable for Preset 3 (faster than Preset 9). This indicates that the encoding times are not significantly affected by the video partitioning into sub-images. Moreover, it is also noticeable a faster preset can achieve a processing time reduction of approximately 25 times.

In the results of Figures 4 the points are most often bellow the diagonal line (i.e., $y = x$) revealing that the overall time produced by the sum of sub-image videos is slightly lower than the single image video. This trend can be observed in most tests using faster presets. However, when using slower presets the linear relationship is no longer observed. The reason is that the coding order of I, P and B slices for faster presets is somehow fixed and does not deviate much from a certain pattern, while in higher presets this predictable pattern does not exist, making this direct frame-by-frame comparison not fully valid.

To overcome such limitation, another set of tests were made with fixed encoding slice order. The results are shown in

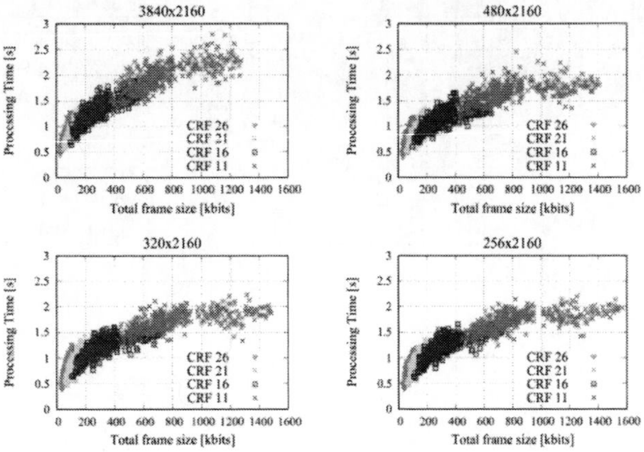

Figure 6. Relation between the processing time and the total frame size for different FoV partitioning sizes and Preset 3.

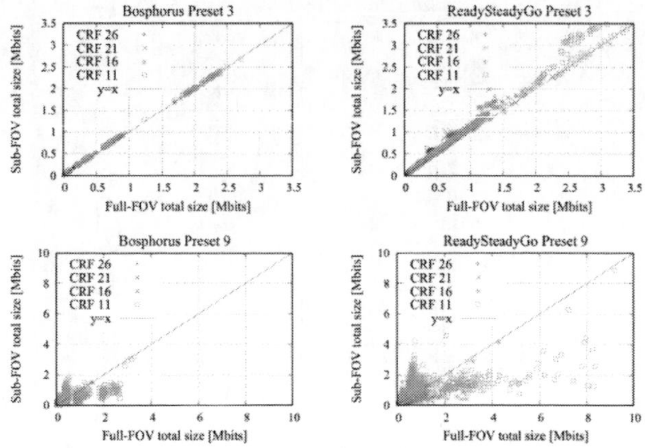

Figure 7. Total frame size for full-FoV versus the limited sub-video encoding with 10 FoVs for the Preset 3 and 9.

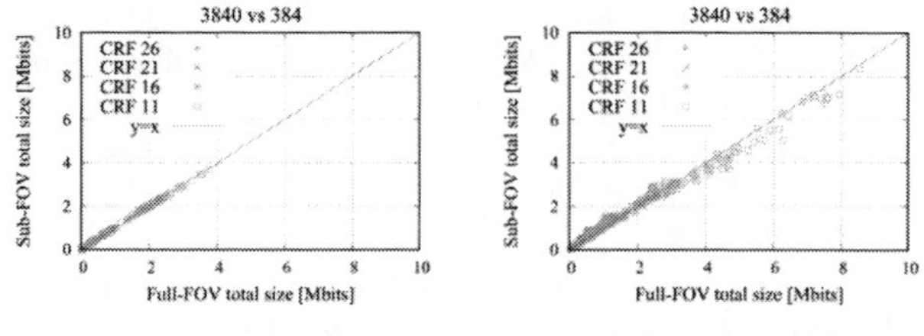

Figure 8. Total frame size for full-FoV versus the narrow FoV encoding for the ReadySteadyGo sequence and Preset 9 for different CRF.

Figure 5, where one can observe that the linear correlation is now restored. There is also a pattern that can be seen in these results, indicating that for higher number of FoV partitions a lower total processing time is required to encode the full video. This pattern is also more noticeable in slower presets. This is due to the fact that each slice is independently encoded from the others, therefore, less processing time is consumed with prediction methods, resulting in smaller encoding times.

B. Coded frame size evaluation

1) Frame size versus encoding time: The relationship between the size of coded frames and corresponding encoding time was also evaluated. To this aim, tests were made in order to find whether there was a relation between the size of the compressed frames and their encoding times. Since the coded I-,P- and B-Slices are not consistent between them, only the results for B-Slices are analysed.

Figure 6 shows the relation between the encoding time and the size of the coded frame in the case of the ReadySteadyGo sequence. The results correspond to the Preset 3 and each CRF is illustrated with a different colour. These results correspond to both the full-FoV coding and sub-video coding (i.e., smaller FoV). Results reveal that video frames which require higher amount of coded bits normally take longer time to be processed. This is due to the fact that more coding modes are tested until an efficient rate-distortion trade-off is achieved. Moreover, these results confirm that decreasing the CRF (i.e., lowering the QP) leads to higher encoding time. The linear regression of the results shown in Figure 6, show a solid linear relation with the number of bits from each frame, with R^2 varying between 0.80 and 0.99 for all presets and CRFs combinations.

2) Coded frame size comparison: Moreover, the direct comparison of coded frame size between the full-FoV video and multiple FoV videos was analysed. As before, to compare with the full-FoV case the sum of the coded frame size of each sub-video was used. Figure 7 shows the comparison between the size of each full-FoV frame with the sum of the twelve 320×2160 FoV partitions, all encoded with Preset 3 and CRF 16. The diagonal line ($y = x$) is also shown. Results show that for a faster configuration, i.e., Preset 3, the overall size produced by the sum of all multiple FoV videos is slightly higher than the full-FoV video, as most points are above the diagonal line. However, in the case of Preset 9 there is not a clear relation between the total size of bitstreams, thus it is not possible to accurately determine which approach leads to smaller bitstream.

In regard to Figure 4, one can see that for Preset 9 there is not a linear relationship between the size of coded frames when using full and sub-image encoding. This is due the slice coding order selected by the encoder. Moreover, as shown in previous results, fixing the slice coding order results in a linear relation between bitstream size in both cases. This is shown in the results of Figure 8.

C. Coding efficiency evaluation

1) Rate-distortion analysis: The coding efficiency is evaluated by comparing the average PSNR and bitrate, for different FoV sizes. Figure 9 shows the quality obtained for different bitrates, by varying the CRF. Results in this figure reveal that for the same bitrate, increasing the number of FoV partitions results in lower average video quality, which is more noticeable for the sequence with higher motion (i.e., ReadySteadyGo sequence). However, for a sequence with lower motion the quality decreasing is less significant, revealing that this encoding approach does not have great impact in the overall performance. Moreover, one can notice that by decreasing the number of FoV partitions the coding efficiency increase, revealing that a trade-off between coding efficiency and number

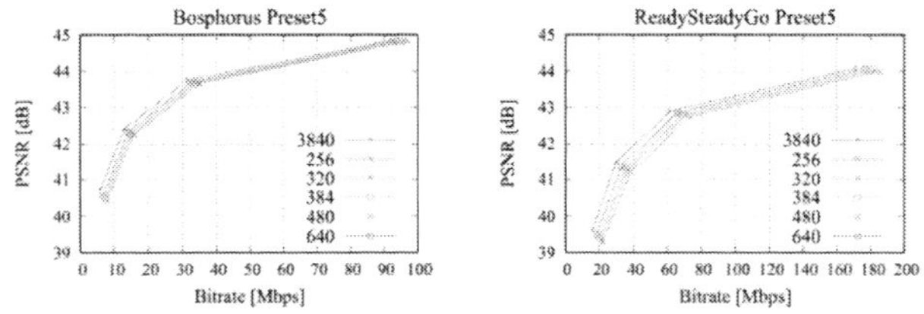

Figure 9. Rate-distortion results for the preset 5 and different FoV partition sizes – horizontal axis: bitrate (kbits/s); vertical axis: average PSNR (dB).

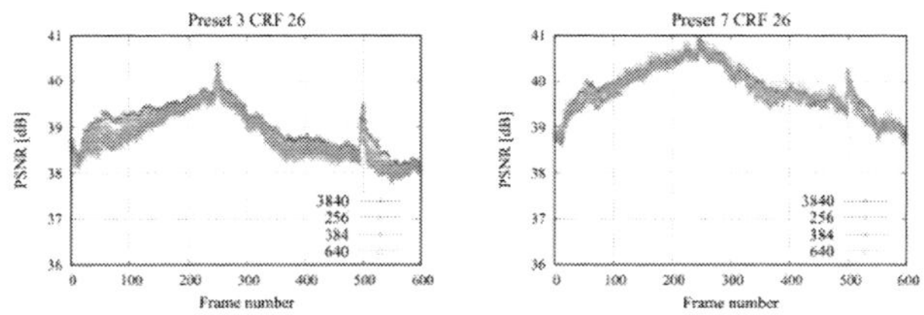

Figure 10. Average frame-by-frame quality for the ReadySeadyGo sequence and different FoV partition sizes.

of processing cores can be obtained for different application requirements.

2) Quality comparison: Finally, the overall quality obtained for the full-FoV and sub-image video sequences is evaluated using the PSNR metric. Figure 10 shows the PSNR results for each frame using different FoV partitions with presets 3 and 7. The results show that for the same preset and CRF the overall quality does not significantly change between partitions. Although there is not a clear best option when comparing the full-FoV with the average of all sub-videos. Such overall behaviour is similar for all the tests carried out in these simulations.

V. CONCLUSION

In this work, the performance of encoding UHD panoramic video as several sub-sequences of smaller FoVs was evaluated for multi-encoding systems with multiple independent processors. The simulation study was based on splitting the full-FoV UHD panoramic scene into various smaller FoVs and encode each of them in a single encoding processor. The rate-distortion performance, as well as the computational complexity was evaluated in comparison with conventional coding of a single frame with full-FoV per processor. The results show that the rate-distortion performance of multi-processor systems is quite similar to single processor ones, which allows to distribute the huge computational requirements of HEVC encoding across several low-cost processors. Therefore, this simulation study provides relevant insights on future research directions and allow efficient development of UHD panoramic video acquisition and coding systems using multiple cameras and processors with reduced computational resources. The results are particularly useful in the design of wide FoV multi-camera rigs, such as those used to capture 360-degree video. Overall the paper demonstrates that the smaller FoV captured by each camera can be independently encoded using low-cost processors and then sent to central unit for further processing, without incurring additional loss of performance in comparison with a single encoder system.

ACKNOWLEDGEMENTS

This work was funded by Instituto de Telecomunicações through Fundação para a Ciencia e Tecnologia, Portugal through the projects: ACode180Video UID/EEA/50008/2019 and ARoundVision PTDC/EEI-COM/30652/2017 (SAICT-45-2017-POCI-01-0145-FEDER-030652)

REFERENCES

[1] G. Correa, P. Assuncao, L. Agostini, and L. S. da Cruz, "Performance and computational complexity assessment of high-efficiency video encoders," IEEE Transactions on Circuits and Systems for Video Technology, vol. 22, no. 12, Dec. 2012, pp. 1899–1909.

[2] ISO/IEC JTC1 ITU-T, "High efficiency video coding, ITU-T rec. H.265 and ISO/IEC 23008-2," ITU-T/ISO, Standard, Feb. 2018.

[3] R. Skupin, Y. Sanchez, Y. . Wang, M. M. Hannuksela, J. Boyce, and M. Wien, "Standardization status of 360 degree video coding and delivery," in IEEE Visual Communications and Image Processing (VCIP), Dec. 2017, pp. 1–4.

[4] A. Mazumdar, T. Moreau, S. Kim, M. Cowan, A. Alaghi, L. Ceze, M. Oskin, and V. Sathe, "Exploring computation-communication tradeoffs in camera systems," in IEEE International Symposium on Workload Characterization (IISWC), Oct. 2017, pp. 177–186.

[5] J. Duarte and P. Assuncao, "Low-complexity acquisition of 180-degree panoramic video using early data reduction," in IEEE International Conference on Smart Technologies (EUROCON 2019), Jul. 2019, pp. 1–4.

[6] C. Herglotz, D. Springer, and A. Kaup, "Modeling the energy consumption of HEVC P- and B-frame decoding," in IEEE International Conference on Image Processing (ICIP), Oct. 2014, pp. 3661–3665.

[7] A. Gürhanlı, C. Chung, P. Chen, and S.-H. Hung, "Coarse grain parallelization of H.264 video decoder and memory bottleneck in multi-core architectures," International Journal of Computer Theory and Engineering, vol. 3, no. 12, Jan. 2011, pp. 375–381.

[8] H. Migallón, J. Hernández-Losada, G. Cebrián-Márquez, P. Piñol, J. Martínez, O. López-Granado, and M. Malumbres, "Synchronous and asynchronous HEVC parallel encoder versions based on a GOP approach," Advances in Engineering Software, vol. 101, 2016, pp. 37–49.

[9] K. Misra, A. Segall, M. Horowitz, S. Xu, A. Fuldseth, and M. Zhou, "An overview of tiles in HEVC," IEEE Journal of Selected Topics in Signal Processing, vol. 7, no. 6, Dec. 2013, pp. 969–977.

[10] R. Rodrguez-Snchez and E. S. Quintana-Ort, "Tiles-and WPP-based HEVC decoding on asymmetric multi-core processors," in IEEE Third International Conference on Multimedia Big Data (BigMM), Apr. 2017, pp. 299–302.

[11] K. Chen, J. Sun, Y. Duan, and Z. Guo, "A novel wavefront-based high parallel solution for HEVC encoding," IEEE Transactions on Circuits and Systems for Video Technology, vol. 26, no. 1, Jan. 2016, pp. 181–194.

[12] H. K. Zrida, A. Jemai, A. C. Ammari, and M. Abid, "High level H.264/AVC video encoder parallelization for multiprocessor implementation," in Design, Automation Test in Europe Conference Exhibition, Apr. 2009, pp. 940–945.

[13] C. G. Gurler, A. Aksay, G. B. Akar, and A. M. Tekalp, "Multithreaded architectures and benchmark tests for real-time multi-view video decoding," in IEEE International Conference on Multimedia and Expo (ICME), Jun. 2009, pp. 237–240.

[14] x265 HEVC Encoder / H.265 Video Codec. [Online]. Available: http://x265.org (Retrieved: July 17, 2019)

[15] Ultra Video Group test sequences. [Online]. Available: http://ultravideo.cs.tut.fi/ (Retrieved: July 17, 2019)

[16] ITU-T, "Recommendation P.910, Subjective video quality assessment methods for multimedia applications."

[17] x265 HEVC encoder preset. [Online]. Available: https://x265.readthedocs.io/en/default/presets.html (Retrieved: July 17, 2019)

Approximate Analytical Model for Queued Handover Requests in Cellular Networks

Vicente Casares-Giner, Jorge Martinez-Bauset
Instituto Universitario de Tecnologas de la Informacin y Comunicaciones
Universitat Politcnica de Valncia
Email: vcasares@itaca.upv.es, jmartinez@itaca.upv.es

***Abstract*—An approximate analytical model to analyse the performance of the handover process in cellular networks is proposed, where new and handover calls that arrive when insufficient free resources are available are queued instead of being lost. The approximation is based on the aggregation of states of the double infinite continuous-time Markov chain that models the system, and exhibits an excellent accuracy and low computational cost. The approximate model might be of interest to the next-generation of 5G mobile networks that must be engineered to achieve high QoS and extremely low latencies.**

***Index Terms*—Guard Channel Algorithm (GCA); handover; priority; forced termination; Quasi Birth Death (QBD) process.**

I. INTRODUCTION

Handover algorithms are of paramount importance in wireless cellular networks, and suitable analytical models are needed to evaluate their performance. From the user equipment (UE) point of view, it is less desirable the interruption of a call in progress than the blocking of a new one. The most commonly deployed strategy to achieve this Quality of Service (QoS) objective has been to assign higher priority to calls in progress than to the newly arriving ones.

One of the most celebrated prioritization schemes is the Guard Channel Algorithm (GCA) [1]. Let C be the total number of Resource Units (RU) available at an LTE eNodeB (eNB). The meaning of a unit of resource depends on the specific implementation of the radio interface. Let $C_h \leq C$ the number of guard RUs. Then, new and handover calls are admitted when the number of free RUs is larger than C_h. However, when the number of free RUs is equal to C_h, or less, only handover calls are admitted, while new calls are blocked. Clearly, when all C RU are occupied, both new and handover requested calls are blocked. Note that there is no prioritization when $C_h = 0$. It is worth pointing out that the GCA has been proposed in other wireless networks, such as trunking systems in which interconnect calls have priority over dispatch calls [2].

The problem of prioritization of handover calls over new one has been commonly treated in the context of admission control in cellular networks. Table I summarizes the four main schemes that have received attention in the literature. In the *loss-loss* scheme, both new and handover requests that arrive when not enough free RU are available, will terminate being lost.

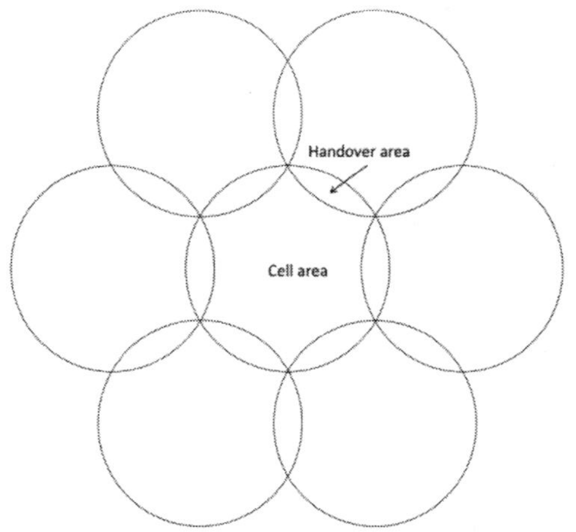

Fig. 1. Cell area and handover area.

In the *loss-delay* scheme, new calls might be blocked, but instead of blocking handover requests, they are placed in a waiting queue of capacity Q_h until enough RU become available. The time handover requests are maintained in the queue is mainly a function of two parameters: i) the residence time of the UE in the handover area, i.e., the overlapping area between the current serving cell and the new one; ii) the speed of the UE. Please refer to Fig. 1. This scheme has been analyzed in [3] with the GCA and the first-in-first-out (FIFO) service queue discipline for the queued handover requests. A later study in [4] extended the work in [3] by considering that a call might terminate while waiting in queue.

In the third scheme, the *delay-loss* one, handover requests might be blocked, but instead of blocking new requests, they are placed in a waiting queue of capacity Q_f, until enough free RU become available. In this case, the time new requests are

TABLE I
TREATMENT OF CALLS OR SESSIONS.

Scheme	New, (f)	handovers, (h)	Queue size, Q_*
1	Loss	Loss	$(Q_f = 0, Q_h = 0)$
2	Loss	Delay	$(Q_f = 0, Q_h > 0)$
3	Delay	Loss	$(Q_f > 0, Q_h = 0)$
4	Delay	Delay	$(Q_f > 0, Q_h > 0)$

maintained in the queue is mainly a function on the residual sojourn time in the non-overlapping area of the cell. Such scheme has been analysed in [1], and revisited in [5], where the system was modeled as a Quasi Birth and Death (QBD) Markov process and basic principles of the M/G/1 system were used to analyse the queuing model [6].

Finally, in the *delay-delay* scheme, both, new and handover requests, are queued when insufficient RU are available upon arrival. An exhaustive analysis of this fourth model is provided in [4] when both Q_f and Q_h are finite.

The interest of the *delay-loss* scheme is based on the fact that, in general, UEs spend a short time in the handover area. This might be due to small overlapping areas, UEs speed or both. In any case, the time spent by a UE in the handover area might be negligible when compared to the time spent in the non-overlapping area of the cell. However, the next-generation of 5G cloud-enabled services are being engineered to achieve high QoS and latencies as small as 1 ms. In such network operation scenarios, it is gaining a renewed interest the performance evaluation of handover schemes that might place handover requests in a queue for short periods of time.

An approximate analytical model to evaluate the *delay-delay* scheme is proposed, where the time evolution of the number of new and handover calls in the system is modeled by a double infinite continuous-time Markov chain (CTMC), that has the form of a QBD process. The QBD process turns out to be non-homogeneous in both dimensions, and therefore its solution is computationally expensive. The approximate analytical model is based on the aggregation of states of the CTMC, and exhibits an excellent accuracy and low computational cost. The original QBD process is in this way converted into an equivalent finite QBD, for which different efficient solution algorithms have been proposed.

Although in this paper a brief description of the approximation method and a preliminary study of the accuracy achieved is given, our interest is to extend the study and apply it to the analysis of the handover procedure in 5G cellular networks. In particular, to analyse the impact that different network features, such as size of the cell overlapping areas, UEs speed, density of small cells, etc, might have on the QoS perceived by the UEs, when both new and handover requests might get queued at eNB.

The paper is structured as follows. Section II defines the Markovian hypothesis for the queue models. Section III deals with a detailed qualitative description of the scheme analyzed in our work. The development of the analytical approach to determine the stationary distribution of the CTMC and the main performance parameters are presented in Sections IV and V, respectively. A cellular scenario is presented in Section VI, and the corresponding results are reported in Section VII. Conclusions and future work in progress are reported in Section VIII.

II. Makovian hypothesis

For model tractability, it is assumed that new and handover requests arrive following a Poisson process with rates λ_f and λ_h, respectively. This modeling approach has been widely debated and accepted in the literature [7], [8], [9]. In the same way, it is assumed that call or session duration, cell residence time, and residence time in the handover area, are exponentially distributed random variables with rates μ_M, μ_R and μ_F, respectively. Due to the memory-less property, the RU holding times are again exponentially distributed, with rates $\mu_H = \mu_M + \mu_R$ when the UE resides in the cell area, and $\mu_Q = \mu_M + \mu_F$ when it resides in the handover area. Obviously $\mu_R < \mu_F$ so $\mu_H < \mu_Q$. Note that in most of previous works it has been assumed that $\mu_Q \approx \mu_F$. Then, the call was not able to terminate while residing in the handover area. This limitation was overcome in the model proposed in [4], where, for the first time and to our best knowledge, the authors consider that the call can finish in the handover area, i.e., $\mu_Q = \mu_M + \mu_F$. Finally, note that according to [10] and [11], the mean residence time in the handover area, $1/\mu_F$, can be around 5-10 seconds, which is much shorter than the cell residence time $1/\mu_R$, or to the call duration $1/\mu_M$, that can be around 2 minutes on average.

III. Model of the delay-delay scheme

In this Section, we describe the model proposed for the scheme 4 of Table I. As described before, let C the total number of RUs of the eNB and C_h the number of guard RUs. Sessions or calls occupy a singe RU in the eNB while being served. Two types of requests are offered to the eNB, new (fresh) and handover calls requests. A new call originated in a given cell is admitted if more than C_h free RUs are found upon arrival. Otherwise, the fresh call is placed in a queue of infinite capacity, and remains in that queue while residing in the cell area. No impatience is assumed for the calls in the queue. A handover request is admitted if at least one free RU is found upon arrival. Otherwise, it joins a queue of infinite capacity and remains in that queue until the UE abandons the handover area, or until the call ends, whichever occurs first.

The system is modelled as a 2-D Markov process of infinite size in both dimensions, as shown in Fig. 2. The system state is defined by the tuple (i,j), $i,j = 0,1,2,\ldots\infty$, where $\min(i,C)$ define the number of calls in progress in the cell, $\max(i-C,0)$ the number of handover requests in the queue, and j the number of new (fresh) calls in the queue.

Our model is an extension of the one studied in [1] and [5] in two aspects. First, queued fresh calls are allowed to leave the queue when they leave the cell area. In this case, the set up request will be rejected, and it will not be transferred to any neighboring cell. Although the subscriber might retry the call after a random period, this behavior has not been considered in the current model. Second, different to the treatment in [5], we allow that a handover request that joins the queue remains in it until the call in progress ends, or until the UE leaves the handover area, whichever occurs first.

Parallel to [5], when visiting state (i,j) we say that the process is at phase i and at level j. Two key observations. First, for any phase $i > C_s = C - C_h$, we realize that transition between phases are independent of the arrival rate of new calls

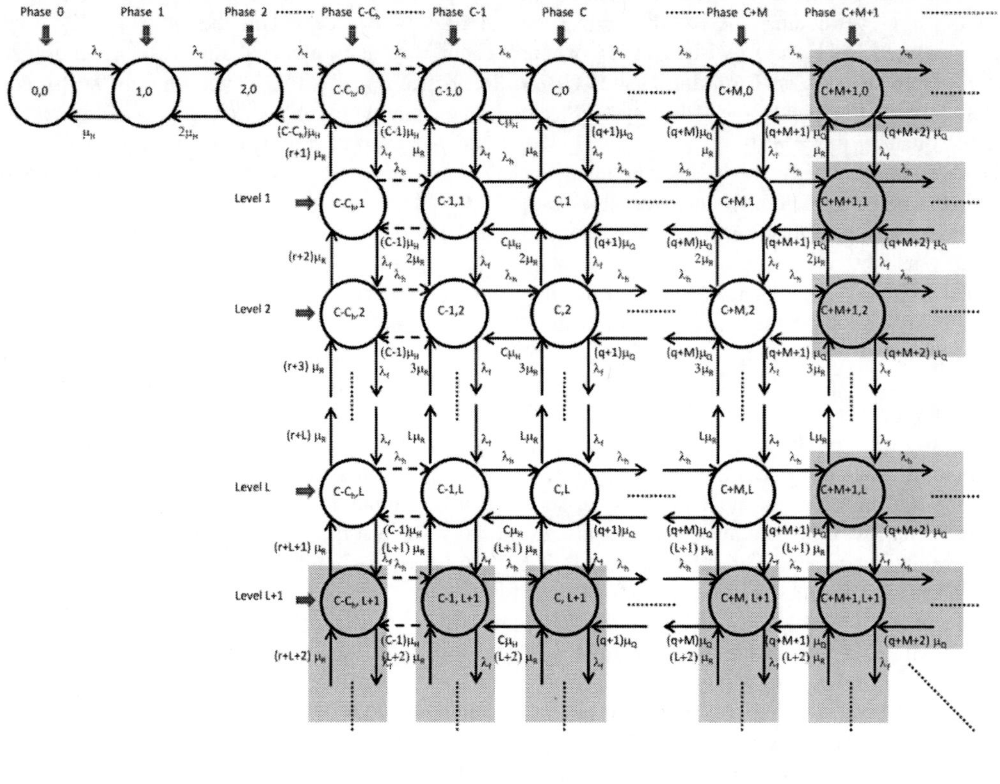

Fig. 2. State transition diagram of the 2D CTMC for the delay-delay model.

λ_f. Second, for any level $j > 0$ we realize that transitions between levels are independent of the arrival rate of handover requests λ_h. Also, note that for $i \geq C$, the number of handover requests in the handover queue increases by one unit when a transition from phase i to phase $i+1$ occurs. In the same way, for $j \geq 0$, a transition from level j to level $j+1$ makes the number of new requests in its queue to increase by one unit. Finally, note also that a transition form level j to level $j-1$ that happens when the system is in phase $C - C_h$, leads to the reduction of the number of new calls in its queue by one unit.

In the next Section, we describe the approximate model. As mentioned before, is based on the aggregation of sets of states of the 2D Markov process [12].

IV. State aggregation approach.

First, we focus on the set of states at level $j \geq 0$, and which phases meet $i \geq C$, i.e., states in which the handover queue is not empty. This infinite set of states recall us a similar set of states in a $M/M/\infty$ queue. This infinite set of states recall us a similar set of states in a $M/M/\infty$ queue. Then, we evaluate the mean value of the first passage time from state $C+M+1$ to state $C+M$ and approximate this infinite set of states by a single (aggregated) state for which the service (exiting) rate equals the inverse of the mentioned mean value.

Second, we focus on the set of states at a fixed phase $i \geq C_s$, and which levels meet $j > 0$, i.e., states in which the queue of new calls is not empty. The aggregation procedure turns out to be similar to the one described above, with the exception that two sets of states must be taken into account. The first one is the set with phase $i = C_s = C - C_h$, while the second is with phase $i > C_s$. Clearly, aggregating a set of states into a single one is an approximation, where only the first moment of the first passage time is being taken into account.

A. First passage time from phase $C+M+1$ to phase $C+M$

An upper and lower bound for the mean value of the first passage time from phase $C+M+1$ to phase $C+M$, $M > 0$, is derived. This mean value is denoted as $\bar{t}_{ph}(\lambda_h, \mu_Q, q, M)$ where $q = C\mu_H/\mu_Q$. Please refer to Table II for details. The procedure is as follows. From Fig. 2 the set of states with phase $i \geq C$ and level $j = 0$, define a birth-death process, as

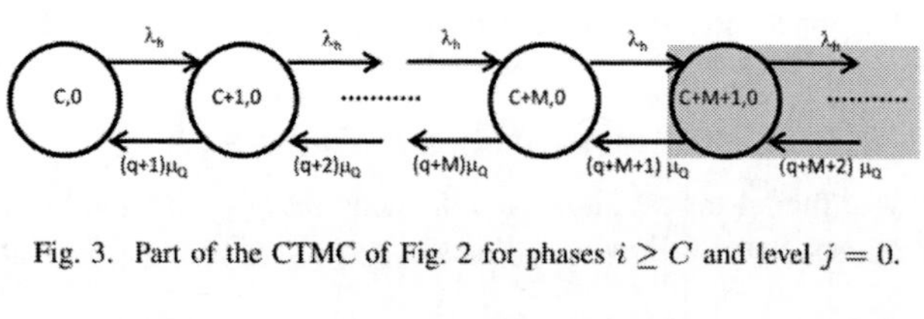

Fig. 3. Part of the CTMC of Fig. 2 for phases $i \geq C$ and level $j = 0$.

TABLE II
MAIN PARAMETERS

Capacity (RUs)	Definition
$C = C_s + C_h$	# of RUs in the cell.
C_s	# of RUs shared (fresh or new and handovers).
C_h	# of RUs reserved for handovers.
Rate (e.r.v.)	Definition
λ_f	Rate of offered fresh (new) calls
λ_h	Rate of offered handover calls
$\lambda_t = \lambda_f + \lambda_h$	Total arrival rate
γ_f	Admitted fresh (new) calls
γ_h	Admitted handover calls
$\gamma_t = \gamma_f + \gamma_h$	Total rate of admitted calls.
μ_M	Call (message) departure rate
μ_R	UE residence time in the cell area
$\mu_H = \mu_M + \mu_R$	RU occupancy in the cell
μ_F	UE residence time in the handover area
$\mu_Q = \mu_M + \mu_F$	RU occupancy in the handover area
$q = C\mu_H/\mu_Q$	$q_f = \lfloor q \rfloor, \quad q_c = \lceil q \rceil$
$r = C_s\mu_H/\mu_R$	$r_f = \lfloor r \rfloor, \quad r_c = \lceil r \rceil$
Erlangs	Traffic
$A_{os} = \lambda_f/\mu_M$	Offered new traffic -session, call or message-.
$A_f = \lambda_f/\mu_H$	Offered traffic at cell level -RU-.
$A_h = \lambda_h/\mu_H$	Handover requested traffic at cell level -RU-
$A_t = A_f + A_h$	Total offered traffic at cell level -RU-.
$A_R = \lambda_f/\mu_R$	"Unattended" new traffic in the queue.
$A_Q = \lambda_h/\mu_Q$	Ongoing handover traffic in the queue.
$A_F = \lambda_h/\mu_F$	"Unattended" handover traffic in the queue.
Probability	Definition
$P_{sc} = \mu_M/\mu_H$	Call ends in the cell.
$P_{hd} = \mu_R/\mu_H$	Request for a handover.
$P_{sh} = \mu_M/\mu_Q$	Call ends in the handover area.
P_B	Blocking of new (fresh) calls.
P_{fh}	Failure of handover request.
P_{FT}	Forced termination.
P_{NC}	Unencumbered call.

shown in Fig. 3. Omitting the level sub-index in Fig. 3, the transition rates and the steady state probabilities are given by,

$$\begin{aligned} \lambda_i &= \lambda_h; \quad i \geq C \\ \mu_i &= (q + i - C)\mu_Q; \quad i \geq C+1. \end{aligned} \tag{1}$$

$$P_{C+i} = \begin{cases} P_C = \left[1 + \sum_{k=1}^{\infty} \frac{A_Q^k}{\prod_{n=1}^{k}(q+n)}\right]^{-1}; & i = 0 \\ \frac{A_Q^i}{\prod_{n=1}^{i}(q+n)} P_C; & i \geq 1 \end{cases} \tag{2}$$

with $A_Q = \lambda_h/\mu_Q$.

Following Appendix A in [13], we can derive the mean value of the first passage time from phase $C + M$ to phase $C + M + 1$. Its mean value, denoted as $\overline{\tau}_{ph}(\lambda_h, \mu_Q, q, M)$, can be written as,

$$\overline{\tau}_{ph}(\lambda_h, \mu_Q, q, M)\lambda_h = \left[1 + \sum_{k=1}^{M} \frac{A_Q^k}{\prod_{n=1}^{k}(q+M+n)}\right]\left[\frac{A_Q^M}{\prod_{n=1}^{M}(q+M+n)}\right]^{-1} \tag{3}$$

Finally, it is straightforward to see that $\overline{t}_{ph}(\lambda_h, \mu_Q, q, M)$, the mean value of the first passage time from phase $C+M+1$ to phase $C + M$ can be written, after some simple algebra,

$$\overline{t}_{ph}(\lambda_h, \mu_Q, q, M) = \overline{\tau}_{ph}(\lambda_h, \mu_Q, q, M)\frac{1 - \sum_{k=C}^{C+M} P_k}{\sum_{k=C}^{C+M} P_k} = \frac{1}{\lambda_h}\sum_{k=1}^{\infty} \frac{A_Q^k}{\prod_{n=1}^{k}(q+M+n)} \tag{4}$$

where P_k are the steady state probabilities given in (2). In addition, it can be verified that,

$$\overline{t}_{ph}(\lambda_h, \mu_Q, q, M) = \frac{1 + \lambda_h \overline{t}_{ph}(\lambda_h, \mu_Q, q, M+1)}{(q+M+1)\mu_Q} \tag{5}$$

From now, unless ambiguity does not allow it, we will use a short notation, i.e., $\overline{t}_{ph} = \overline{t}_{ph}(\lambda_h, \mu_Q, q, M, T_h)$. Then, for a suitable threshold $T_h \geq 1$, the following lower (lw) and upper (up) bounds can be written as,

$$\overline{t}_{ph,lw} = \frac{1}{\lambda_h}\sum_{k=1}^{T_h} \frac{A_Q^k}{\prod_{n=1}^{k}(q+M+n)} \tag{6}$$

$$\overline{t}_{ph,up} = \overline{t}_{ph,lw} + \frac{1}{\lambda_h}\frac{A_Q^{T_h}}{\prod_{n=1}^{T_h}(q+M+n)}\frac{A_Q}{q+M+T_h-A_Q} \tag{7}$$

Note that $\overline{t}_{ph,lw}$ is obtained by truncating up to the first T_h elements the infinite sum in (4). This approximation defines a lower bound to (4). To obtain $\overline{t}_{ph,up}$ we set μ_k constant at $\mu_k = (C+M+T_h)\mu_Q$ for $k > C+M+T_h$. As $(q+k-C) > (q+M+T_h)$ for $k > C+M+T_h$, this approximations sets an upper bound to (4). The infinite terms $k > C+M+T_h$ in (4) define a geometric progression with ratio $r_{ph} = A_Q/(q+M+T_h)$ that can be added, provided that $r_{ph} < 1$.

B. First passage time from level $L+1$ to level L

As in previous sub-Section IV-A, for a given phase $i \geq C_s = C - C_h$, we analyse the aggregation of states located at level $L+1$, $L > 0$. Let $\bar{t}_{le}(\lambda_f, \mu_R, r, L; i)$ denote the mean value of the first passage time from level $L+1$ to level L, where $r = C_s \mu_H / \mu_R$. Please refer to Table II for details. By inspection of Fig. 2, two different sets of states are identified. First, when the phase is $i = C_s$, left side of Fig. 4. Second, when the phase is $i > C_s$, right side of Fig. 4. For a level $j > L$, the transition rates between levels are given by,

$$\begin{aligned} \lambda_j &= \lambda_f; \quad j \geq 0 \\ \mu_j &= (r\delta_{i,C_s} + j)\mu_R; \quad j \geq 1 \end{aligned} \tag{8}$$

where δ_{i,C_s} is the Kronecker delta. Parallel to (4) we can write, being $A_R = \lambda_f / \mu_R$,

$$\bar{t}_{le}(\lambda_f, \mu_R, r, L; i) = \frac{1}{\lambda_f} \sum_{k=1}^{\infty} \frac{A_R^k}{\prod_{n=1}^{k} (r\delta_{i,C_s} + L + n)} \tag{9}$$

A simple inspection to the state transition diagrams in Fig. 4 reveals that $\bar{t}_{le}(\lambda_f, \mu_R, r, L; i = C_s,) < \bar{t}_{le}(\lambda_f, \mu_R, r, L; i > C_s)$.

For clarity, we use the notation $\bar{t}_{le}(i) = \bar{t}_{le}(\lambda_f, \mu_R, r, L; i)$, unless otherwise specified. Using the same arguments as we did for (6)-(7), and given a suitable threshold $T_f \geq 0$, the lower and upper bounds for $\bar{t}_{le}(i)$ are given by,

$$\bar{t}_{le,lw}(i) = \frac{1}{\lambda_f} \sum_{k=1}^{T_f} \frac{A_R^k}{\prod_{n=1}^{k} (r\delta_{i,C_s} + L + n)} \tag{10}$$

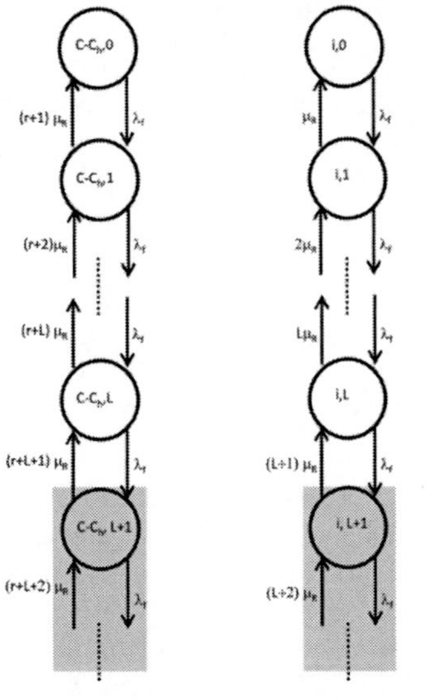

Fig. 4. Part of the CTMC of Fig. 2 for level $j \geq 0$ and phases $i = C_s = C - C_h$ (left); $i > C_s$ (right).

$$\begin{aligned} \bar{t}_{le,up}(i) &= \bar{t}_{le,lw}(i) + \\ &= \frac{1}{\lambda_f} \frac{A_R^{T_f}}{\prod_{n=1}^{T_f} (r\delta_{i,C_s} + L + n)} \frac{A_R}{r\delta_{i,C_s} + L + T_f - A_R} \end{aligned} \tag{11}$$

provided that $r_{le} = A_R / (\delta_{i,C_s} + L + T_f) < 1$. Note that the most restrictive case in the last inequality occurs when $i > C_s$, where $A_R < L + T_f$ must be fulfilled.

C. Steady state probabilities

Following the state aggregation process described in Section IV-A and Section IV-B, the original QBD process is converted into an equivalent finite QBD, for which different efficient solution algorithms have been proposed. The interested reader might refer to [14], or Chapter 10 in [15], for details of the algorithms used to solve the finite QBD process. Let $P_{i,j}$ and $\tilde{P}_{i,j}$ denote the exact and approximate steady state probabilities of the finite QBD, respectively. Clearly, $\tilde{P}_{i,j}$ can be evaluated for the four aggregation approaches shown in Table III.

TABLE III
FOUR APPROACHES FOR SCHEME 4 OF TABLE I

Approaches	Phase (level j independent)	Level (phase i dependent)
1: (6)-(10)	$\bar{t}_{ph,lw}(\lambda_h, \mu_Q, q, M, T_h)$	$\bar{t}_{le,lw}(\lambda_f, \mu_R, r, L, T_f; i)$
2: (6)-(11)	$\bar{t}_{ph,lw}(\lambda_h, \mu_Q, q, M, T_h)$	$\bar{t}_{le,up}(\lambda_f, \mu_R, r, L, T_f; i)$
3: (7)-(10)	$\bar{t}_{ph,up}(\lambda_h, \mu_Q, q, M, T_h)$	$\bar{t}_{le,lw}(\lambda_f, \mu_R, r, L, T_f; i)$
4: (7)-(11)	$\bar{t}_{ph,up}(\lambda_h, \mu_Q, q, M, T_h)$	$\bar{t}_{le,up}(\lambda_f, \mu_R, r, L, T_f; i)$

V. PERFORMANCE PARAMETERS

The performance parameter evaluated in this study are: i) the blocking probability of a new (fresh) call, ii) the handover failure probability, iii) the forced termination probability of an initiated call, and iv) the non-completed call probability. These parameter depend on $P_{i,j}$ through the analytical expressions defined in the next Subsections.

A. The blocking probability of new calls

Upon arrival, if a new (fresh) call finds $C_s = C - C_h$ RUs occupied, or more, it joins the queue. The call is finally blocked when the UE leaves the area of the serving cell. Then,

$$P_B = \frac{1}{\lambda_f} \sum_{i=C_s}^{\infty} \sum_{j=0}^{\infty} j \mu_R P_{i,j} = \frac{1}{A_R} \sum_{i=C_s}^{\infty} \sum_{j=0}^{\infty} j P_{i,j} \tag{12}$$

To evaluate (12) we use the probabilities $\tilde{P}_{i,j}$, obtained in Section IV-C, that is,

$$\begin{aligned} &P_{B,lw} \approx \\ &\sum_{i=C_s}^{C+M+1} \sum_{j=0}^{L} j \frac{\tilde{P}_{i,j}}{A_R} + \sum_{i=C_s}^{C+M+1} \varsigma_{i,C_s} \frac{\mu_{le}(i)}{\lambda_f} \tilde{P}_{i,L+1} \end{aligned} \tag{13}$$

where, $\mu_{le}(i) = 1/\bar{t}_{le}(i)$ from (9), $\zeta_{i,C_s} = 1 - \delta_{i,C_s} r/(r + L + 1)$ and $A_R = \lambda_f/\mu_R$.

When the phase is $i = C_s$, $\zeta_{C_s,C_s} = (L+1)/(r+L+1)$ can be interpreted as the fraction of transitions $(C_s, L+1) \to (C_s, L)$ that represent the blocking of new (fresh) calls. Note that the transition $(C_s, L+1) \to (C_s, L)$ might also occur when a call terminates successfully and a queued new call occupies the freed RU. When the phase is $i > C_s$, then $\zeta_{i,C_s} = 1$, which means that each transition $(i, L+1) \to (i, L)$ reflects the lost of one new call.

$P_{B,lw}$ is a low bond as it only considers the blocking of new calls due to UEs abandoning the cell service area. An upper bound can be defined when, in addition, we consider the blocking of new calls that arrive at states $(i, L+1)$, $i \geq C_s$.

$$P_{B,up} \approx P_{B,lw} + \sum_{i=C_s}^{C+M+1} \tilde{P}_{i,L+1}. \tag{14}$$

We remark that, when evaluating $P_{B,lw}$, from (13), we use $\mu_{le,lw}(i) = 1/\bar{t}_{le,up}(i) \leq 1/\bar{t}_{le}(i) = \mu_{le}(i)$ given in (10), and when evaluating $P_{B,up}$, from (14), we use $\mu_{le,up}(i) = 1/\bar{t}_{le,lw}(i) \geq 1/\bar{t}_{le}(i) = \mu_{le}(i)$, given at (11).

B. Probability of a handover attempt failure

The probability of a handover attempt failure, P_{fh}, can be expressed as the quotient between the rate of failure handovers and the rate of handover attempts,

$$P_{fh} = \frac{1}{\lambda_h} \sum_{i=C}^{\infty} \sum_{j=0}^{\infty} (i - C)\mu_F P_{i,j} \tag{15}$$

As before, to evaluate (15) we use the probabilities $\tilde{P}_{i,j}$ of the finite QBD process,

$$P_{fh,lw} \approx \sum_{i=C}^{C+M} \sum_{j=0}^{L+1} (i - C)\frac{\tilde{P}_{i,j}}{A_F} + \sum_{j=0}^{L+1} \frac{\mu_{ph}}{\lambda_h} \tilde{P}_{C+M+1,j} \tag{16}$$

where $\mu_{ph} = 1/\bar{t}_{ph}$ from (4) and $A_F = \lambda_h/\mu_F$.

Using the same arguments as in (13), we consider (16) as the lower bound for P_{fh}. Also, in a parallel way to (14), the upper bound for P_{fh} is define as,

$$P_{fh,up} \approx P_{fh,lw} + \sum_{j=0}^{L+1} \tilde{P}_{C+M+1,j} \tag{17}$$

When evaluating $P_{fh,lw}$, expression (16), we use $\mu_{ph,lw} = 1/\bar{t}_{ph,up} \leq 1/\bar{t}_{ph} = \mu_{ph}$, from (6), and when evaluating $P_{fh,up}$, expression (17), we use $\mu_{ph,up} = 1/\bar{t}_{ph,lw} \geq 1/\bar{t}_{ph} = \mu_{ph}$, from (7).

C. Forced termination probability

Based on previous result for P_{fh}, the forced-termination probability P_{FT} can be evaluated as follows [3],

$$P_{FT} = P_{hd} \sum_{k=1}^{\infty} [(1 - P_{fh})P_{hd}]^{k-1} P_{fh} = \frac{P_{hd}P_{fh}}{1 - (1 - P_{fh})P_{hd}} \tag{18}$$

where P_{hd} is the probability of handover demand or attempt, and it is given by $P_{hd} = \mu_R/(\mu_R + \mu_M)$.

Using previous results of (16) (17), P_{FT} can be approximated as follows,

$$P_{FT,lw} = \frac{P_{hd}P_{fh;lw}}{1 - (1 - P_{fh,up})P_{hd}} \tag{19}$$

$$P_{FT,up} = \frac{P_{hd}P_{fh;up}}{1 - (1 - P_{fh,lw})P_{hd}} \tag{20}$$

D. Call non-completion probability

The new call blocking probability P_B, and the forced-termination probability P_{FT} can be combined to define the probability that a call does not terminate successfully, i.e., the non-completion probability,

$$P_{NC} = P_B + (1 - P_B)P_{FT} \tag{21}$$

As before, the lower and upper bounds for P_{NC} are defined as,

$$P_{NC,lw} = P_{B,lw} + (1 - P_{B,up})P_{FT,lw} \tag{22}$$

$$P_{NC,up} = P_{B,up} + (1 - P_{B,lw})P_{FT,up} \tag{23}$$

VI. Cellular Scenario. Flow Equations

The objective of this section is to determine a realistic value for λ_h in a conventional cellular scenario with multiple cells. As in [8], we assume regular tessellation of the 2D cellular area, cells of equal size, and uniform spatial distribution of UEs. We also assume that handover requests arrive following a Poisson process with rate λ_h. Basically, λ_h depends on the mobility of the UE, and must meet the following flow equations. Let $\gamma_{c,in}$ be the rate of calls in progress in a tagged cell. $\gamma_{c,in}$ has two terms, the rate of new calls that are admitted, i.e., $\lambda_{f,in}(1 - P_{B,in})$, and the rate of handover requests arriving from neighboring cells that are admitted, $\gamma_{c,out}P_{hd,out}(1 - P_{fh,in})$. Then,

$$\gamma_{c,in} = \lambda_{f,in}(1 - P_{B,in}) + \gamma_{c,out}P_{hd,out}(1 - P_{fh,in}) \tag{24}$$

In equilibrium we have $\gamma_c = \gamma_{c,in} = \gamma_{c,out}$; $\lambda_f = \lambda_{f,in} = \lambda_{f,out}$; $P_{hd} = P_{hd,in} = P_{hd,out}$; $P_B = P_{B,in} = P_{B,out}$ and $P_{fh} = P_{fh,in} = P_{fh,out}$. Solving (24) for γ_c, hence for λ_h,

$$\lambda_h = \gamma_c P_{hd} = \frac{\lambda_f(1 - P_B)}{1 - P_{hd}(1 - P_{fh})} P_{hd} \tag{25}$$

TABLE IV
BOUNDS FOR $\bar{t}_{ph}(\lambda_h, \mu_Q, q, M, T_h)$, (6) AND (7); NORMALIZED TO $1/\lambda_h = 1/3.5$ WITH $A_Q = 0.70$, $C = 8$, $q = 3.2$,

	$\bar{t}_{ph}$	$T_h = 1$	2	3	4	5
$M=$	*up*	0.1555	0.1517	0.1514	0.1514	0.0432
1	*lw*	0.1346	0.1498	0.1512	0.1514	0.0432
	relative gap	0.1555	0.0129	0.0010	0.0000	0.0000
	r_{ph}	0.1346	0.1129	0.0972	0.0853	0.0432
	up	0.1272	0.1250	0.1249	0.1248	0.1248
2	*lw*	0.1129	0.1238	0.1248	0.1248	0.1248
	relative gap	0.1272	0.0095	0.0007	0.0000	0.0000
	r_{ph}	0.0853	0.0972	0.0853	0.0760	0.0686
	up	0.1076	0.1062	0.1062	0.1061	0.1061
3	*lw*	0.0972	0.1055	0.1061	0.1061	0.1061
	relative gap	0.1076	0.0073	0.0004	0.0000	0.0000
	r_{ph}	0.0972	0.0853	0.0760	0.0686	0.0625
	up	0.0933	0.0923	0.0923	0.0923	0.0923
4	*lw*	0.0853	0.0918	0.0923	0.0923	0.0923
	relative gap	0.0933	0.0058	0.0000	0.0000	0.0000
	r_{ph}	0.0853	0.0760	0.0686	0.0625	0.0573
	up	0.0823	0.0816	0.0816	0.0816	0.0816
5	*lw*	0.0760	0.0813	0.0816	0.0816	0.0816
	relative gap	0.0823	0.0047	0.0000	0.0000	0.0000
	r_{ph}	0.0760	0.0686	0.0625	0.0573	0.0530

TABLE V
BOUNDS FOR $\bar{t}_{le}(\lambda_f, \mu_R, r, L; i)$, FOR PHASE $i > C_s$, (10) AND (11); NORMALIZED TO $1/\lambda_f = 1/7$, WITH $A_R = 7.00$, $C = 8$, $C_h = 1$,$r =$

	$\bar{t}_{le}$	$T_f = 7$	8	9	10	11
L=	*up*	2.7023	2.6964	2.6942	2.6935	2.6932
7	*lw*	2.6547	2.6769	2.6867	2.6907	2.6922
	relative gap	0.0179	0.0058	0.0028	0.0010	0.0003
	r_{le}	0.5000	0.4666	0.4375	0.4117	0.3888
	up	2.0816	2.0791	2.0783	2.0780	2.0779
8	*lw*	2.0594	0.0705	2.0751	2.0768	2.0775
	relative gap	0.0107	0.0041	0.0015	0.0005	0.0001
	r_{le}	0.4666	0.4375	0.4177	0.3888	0.3684
	up	1.6732	1.6721	1.6717	1.6716	1.6715
9	*lw*	1.6621	1.6679	0.6702	1.6711	1.6714
	relative gap	0.0066	0.0024	0.0008	0.0002	0.0001
	r_{le}	0.4375	0.4117	0.3888	0.3684	0.3500
	up	1.3887	1.3881	1.3880	1.3879	1.3879
10	*lw*	1.3828	1.3861	1.3873	1.3877	1.3878
	relative gap	0.0042	0.0015	0.0008	0.0001	0.0000
	r_{le}	0.4117	0.3888	0.3684	0.3500	0.3333
	up	1.1814	1.1811	1.1810	1.1810	1.1810
11	*lw*	1.1781	1.1800	1.1807	1.1809	1.1810
	relative gap	0.0027	0.0009	0.0003	0.0000	0.0000
	r_{le}	0.3888	0.3684	0.3500	0.3333	0.3181

The rate λ_h in equation (25) (see also (17) in [16]), together with the steady state probabilities, $\tilde{P}_{i,j}$, define a fixed-point equation [17] [18]. To solve it, we set initially $\lambda_h \approx \lambda_f P_{hd}$ and the corresponding $\tilde{P}_{i,j}$ are obtained by solving the QBD process. A new λ_h is obtained from (25) and the iteration process is repeated until the difference between the probabilities $\tilde{P}_{i,j}$ of two consecutive iterations is less than a certain threshold.

The mobility rates μ_R and μ_F can been derived according to the fluid flow model, equations (12), (13) in [19]. Then,

$$\mu_x = \frac{E(v)L_x}{\pi A_x}; \quad x = R, F \tag{26}$$

where $E(v)$ is the expected velocity of the UE and L (A) the perimeter (the area) of the coverage area, R for the cell area and F for the handover area, see Fig. 1. From the geometry of that figure and denoting by R_c the radius of the circle, it can be shown that $\mu_R = 2(3\sqrt{3} - \pi)^{-1}E(v)/R_c \approx 0.9734E(v)/R_c$ and $\mu_F = 2(\pi - 3\sqrt{3}/2)^{-1}E(v)/R_c \approx 3.6797E(v)/R_c$. Then, $\mu_F/\mu_R \approx 3.7801$.

VII. RESULTS

A reference evaluation scenario is define with the following parameters: $C = 8$, $C_h = 1$, $\mu_M = 1$, $\mu_R = 1$ and $\mu_F = 4$.

Table IV shows the accuracy of the proposed lower and upper bounds for $\bar{t}_{ph}$ (phase). Results have been obtained for $\lambda_h = 3.5$, that makes $A_Q = \lambda_h/\mu_Q = 0.7$ Erlangs, and $q = C\mu_H/\mu_Q = 3.2$. The accuracy is measured in terms of the *relative gap* $= (up - lw)/lw$, i.e., the relative difference between both bounds. Note that taking the upper bound as a reference would not change the results. Observe that the *relative gap* decreases faster by increasing T_h than by increasing M.

Table V shows the accuracy of the proposed lower and upper bounds for $\bar{t}_{le}$ (level). Results have been obtained for $\lambda_f = 7$, that makes $A_R = \lambda_f/\mu_R = 7$ Erlangs, and $r = C_s\mu_H/\mu_R = 7$. As with the phase, note that *relative gap* decreases faster by increasing T_f than by increasing L.

Observe that the *relative gap* is below 10^{-4} when $r_{ph} = A_Q/(q + M + T_h) \leq 0.06$ in table IV, and when $r_{le} = A_R/(L + T_f) \leq 0.33$ in table V, approximately. A sensibility study of the impact that M, T_h, L and T_f have on the accuracy of the approximation is left for future work.

Figure 5 and Fig. 6 show the evolution of the main performance parameters studied with the load in a realistic scenario. The scenario is composed of multiple cells, and the cell under study is characterized by $C = 80$ RU. The approximate stationary distributions are obtained for $r_{ph} < 0.01$ and $r_{le} < 0.1$, that are more restrictive than those suggested above by inspection of Table IV and Table V. Note that in a multicell scenario, the fluid flow equation (25) most be solved iteratively using the fixed-point equation. As can be observed, the Guard Channel Algorithm is rather efficient, as the handover attempt failure and the forced termination probabilities decrease quite rapidly when the number of guard RUs changes from $C_h = 1$ to $C_h = 2$, while the non-completion probability keeps approximately invariant. However, the blocking probability of new (fresh) calls increases with C_h, as expected.

VIII. CONCLUSION AND FUTURE WORK

We study a cellular system where new and handover calls that arrive when insufficient free resources are available are queued instead of being lost. The time evolution of the number of new and handover calls in the system is modeled by a double infinite continuous-time Markov chain (CTMC), that has the form of a QBD process. As the solution of the QBD process is computationally expensive, we propose an

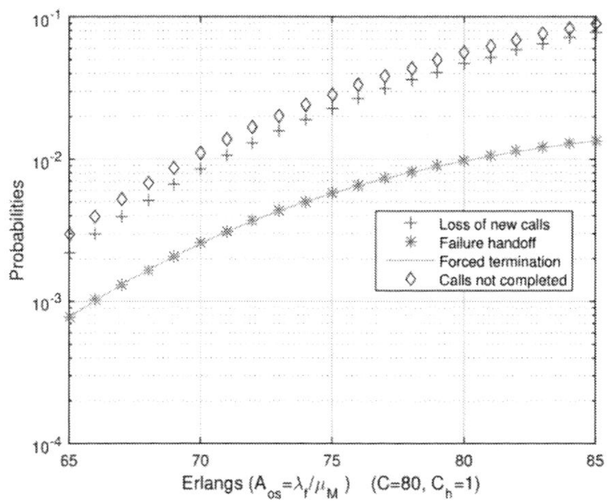

Fig. 5. Main parameters for $C = 80$, $C_h = 1$. P_B (13)-(14); P_{fh}, (16)-(17); P_{FT}, (19)-(20); P_{NC}, (22)-(23).

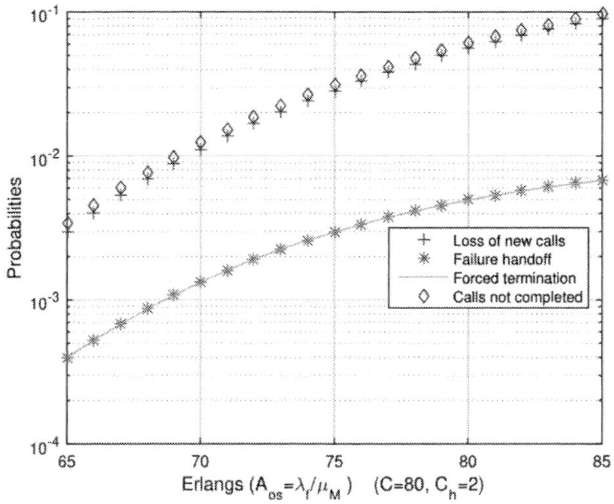

Fig. 6. Main parameters for $C = 80$, $C_h = 2$. P_B (13)-(14); P_{fh}, (16)-(17); P_{FT}, (19)-(20); P_{NC}, (22)-(23).

approximate analytical model based on the aggregation of states of the CTMC.

The approximation shows a very good accuracy and low computational cost. It is applicable to current 4G and forthcoming systems 5G systems. We plan to extend the study to analyze heterogeneous scenarios where femtocells and macrocells coexist, and where the corresponding CTMC that models the system behavior has a huge amount of states. We believe that the state aggregation technique is a powerful tool that makes the analysis of highly complex systems feasible.

Acknowledgment

This work is part of the project PGC2018-094151-B-I00. The authors would like to thank the financial support received from *Ministerio de Ciencia, Innovacin y Universidades (MCIU)*, from *Agencia Estatal de Investigacin (AEI)* and from *Fondo Europeo de Desarrollo Regional (FEDER)* (MCIU/AEI/FEDER.UE).

References

[1] R. Guerin, "Queueing-blocking system with two arrival streams and guard channels," *IEEE Transactions on Communications*, vol. 36, no. 2, pp. 153–163, 1988.

[2] V. Casares-Giner, "Integration of dispatch and interconnect traffic in a land mobile trunking system. waiting time distributions," *Telecommunication Systems*, vol. 16, no. 3-4, pp. 539–554, 2001.

[3] D. Hong and S. S. Rappaport, "Traffic model and performance analysis for cellular mobile radio telephone systems with prioritized and nonprioritized handoff procedures," *IEEE Transactions on Vehicular Technology*, vol. 35, no. 3, pp. 77–92, 1986.

[4] C.-J. Chang, T.-T. Su, and Y.-Y. Chiang, "Analysis of a cutoff priority cellular radio system with finite queueing and reneging/dropping," *IEEE/ACM Transactions on Networking*, vol. 2, no. 2, pp. 166–175, 1994.

[5] J. N. Daigle and N. Jain, "A queueing system with two arrival streams and reserved servers with application to cellular telephone," in *IEEE INFOCOM'92*, 1992, pp. 2161–2167.

[6] M. F. Neuts, *Matrix-geometric solutions in stochastic models: an algorithmic approach.* Johns Hopkins University, Baltimore, 1981.

[7] E. Chlebus and W. Ludwin, "Is handoff traffic really Poissonian?" in *Proceedings of ICUPC'95-4th IEEE International Conference on Universal Personal Communications*, 1995, pp. 348–353.

[8] P. V. Orlik and S. S. Rappaport, "On the handoff arrival process in cellular communications," *Wireless Networks*, vol. 7, no. 2, pp. 147–157, 2001.

[9] V. Casares-Giner, J. Martinez-Bauset, and X. Ge, "Performance model for two-tier mobile wireless networks with macrocells and small cells," *Wireless Networks*, vol. 24, no. 4, pp. 1327–1342, 2018.

[10] C. Jedrzycki and V. C. Leung, "Probability distribution of channel holding time in cellular telephony systems," in *Proceedings of Vehicular Technology Conference-VTC*, vol. 1. IEEE, 1996, pp. 247–251.

[11] F. Barceló and J. Jordán, "Channel holding time distribution in public telephony systems (PAMR and PCS)," *IEEE Transactions on Vehicular Technology*, vol. 49, no. 5, pp. 1615–1625, 2000.

[12] V. Casares-Giner, L. Tello-Oquendo, V. Pla, and J. Martinez-Bauset, "A queueing system with two arrival streams and reserved servers with application to cellular telephone," in *XIII Jornadas de Ingeniera Telemtica, JITEL 2017, Ed. Universitat Politècnica de València*, 2017.

[13] V. C. Giner, "Variable bit rate voice using hysteresis thresholds," *Telecommunication Systems*, vol. 17, no. 1-2, pp. 31–62, 2001.

[14] D. Gaver, P. Jacobs, and G. Latouche, "Finite birth-and-death models in randomly changing environments," *Adv. App. Prob.*, vol. 16, no. 4, pp. 715–731, 1984.

[15] G. Latouche and V. Ramaswami, *Introduction to matrix analytic methods in stochastic modeling.* ASA-SIAM, 1999.

[16] D. Hong and S. S. Rappaport, "Priority oriented channel access for cellular systems serving vehicular and portable radio telephones," *IEE Proceedings I (Communications, Speech and Vision)*, vol. 136, no. 5, pp. 339–346, 1989.

[17] D. McMillan, "Traffic modelling and analysis for cellular mobile networks," in *Teletraffic and Datatraffic in a Period of Change.* North-Holland, 1991, pp. 627–632.

[18] F. Kelly, "Fixed point models of loss networks," *J. Austral. Math. Soc. Ser. B*, vol. 31, no. 2, pp. 204–218, 1989.

[19] V. Casares-Giner, V. Pla, and P. Escalle-García, "Mobility models for mobility management," in *Network performance engineering.* Springer-Verlag, 2011, pp. 716–745.

Contextualization of the Trialability Concept in the SaaS Model for Mobile and Ubiquitous Environment Deployed in Public Cloud

Possibilities, limitations, mitigations, cost and, measures for mobile SaaS (free trial) potential adopters

Giuseppe Ercolani
Università degli Studi della Tuscia - Ufficio di Staff del Direttore Generale Prof. Vincenzo Sforza
Viterbo, Italy
e-mail: ercolani@unitus.it; giuseppe.ercolani@um.es

Jose Vicente Rodriguez Muñoz
Universidad de Murcia - Facultad de Comunicación y Documentación - Campus Universitario de Espinardo
Murcia, Spain
e-mail: jovi@um.es

Abstract—**In this research a generic commercial Software as a Service (SaaS) product offered in the mobile marketplace and deployed in a public cloud is analyzed in order to: (i) identify the possibilities and limitations of the "free to try" version in cloud computing environment; (ii) highlight the cost of the free trial; (iii) determine the correspondence between the "free to try" version and the one available after an onerous subscription contract; (iv) make reference to a series of metrics for measuring the intention to use the application, its effective and real use of available resources. The paper aims to facilitate an educated informed adoption (or rejection) with respect to a mobile SaaS commercial product deployed in public cloud, during the free trialability period, evaluating the SaaS characteristics and functionalities jointly with some perceptions and measures which could arise from its active use, inspection and consideration.**

Keywords-Trialability; SaaS; Software as a Service; SaaS Trialability Cost; SaaS Trialability Factor; Potential Adoption Index.

I. INTRODUCTION

The vast availability of mobile software applications exploitable in ubiquitous environment together with the accessibility of public shared information/opinions on the functionality from earliest adopters (with the rate of downloads) is normally utilized as the first hint for later adopters in the selection of an application.

Cloud Computing (CC)[1] is defined from the National Institute of Standards and Technology (NIST) as a *"model for enabling ubiquitous, convenient, on-demand network access..."*

The availability of specialized platforms for the distribution of mobile software products through the Internet (marketplace) allows the identification of different ubiquitous products offered through a public offer.

The functionalities offered by search engines allow an easy identification of potentially valid products for mobile and ubiquitous environment under different types of platforms (e.g., Windows, iOS, Android, etc.). Information and opinions on the software product, the producer, the developer, the facilities are normally publicly accessible, as well as the indication of the provider's website. The possibility of free testing ("free to try") is usually offered on products in the commercial mobile market. They can be downloaded directly from one or more websites free of charge (marketplace, supplier site, etc.).

The free trial period, under certain condition explicated in this research, could be used to prove and investigate the characteristics of CC application and how the SaaS provider has implemented, incorporated or subcontracted them, within the public offer he advertises in the marketplace.

Fig. 1 represent a new and unpublished graphical visual model image of the complexity available and the necessary elements for a SaaS application to be considered as cloud: (i) Quadrant I represents the horizontal layer of the CC service models; (ii) quadrant II the vertical layer of the CC essential characteristics; (iii) quadrant III the CC deployment models layer (community has been omitted for legibility) and, (iv) quadrant IV visualizes all possible combinations of all previous layers.

The authors underline that, as in Fig. 1, all the defined CC essential characteristics [1] should be present or at least contractually available in all underlying CC service models.

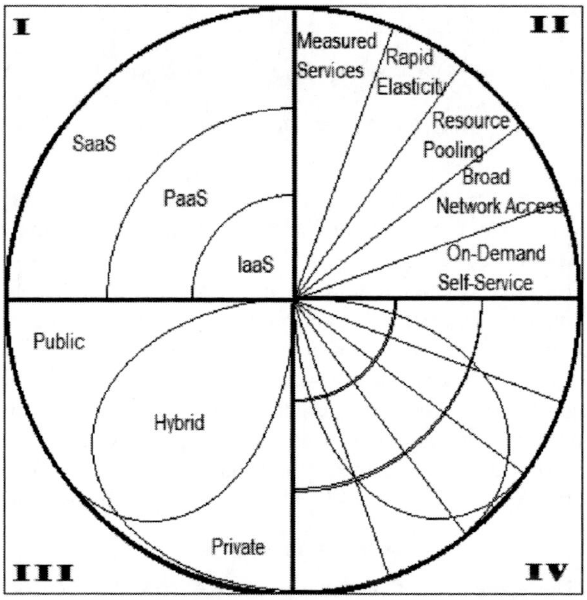

Figure 1. Graphical visual model image of complexity available and needed for a SaaS to be pondered as Cloud Computing application. Source: Drawn up using The NIST Definition of Cloud Computing [1].

Quite often, for marketing reasons and without considering the verticality of CC essential characteristics, the web-based applications advertised as cloud computing solution are identified as "cloud washing" [2], [3].

It is possible to speculate that Software as a Service (SaaS) products for mobile devices that are actively tested before engaging in an onerous contract offer a lower risk and error assessment than those that cannot be proven in advance (before the contract acceptance and payment). The use in probation: (i) can generate perceptions and/or preventive verifications deriving, even if only, from a limited basis usage and (ii) dependent on the degree of aptitude and/or knowledge of the possible future adopter.

In this paper, the concept of trialability as *"the degree to which an innovation can be experienced on a limited basis ..."* [4] is contextualized in the technological scope of Cloud Computing (CC) [1] jointly with the prospect of a free trial period, more often than not, offered by the SaaS providers.

The trial period or trialability has been revealed as relevant for the adoption or selection of a SaaS product in [5]-[13].

The original concept of trialability [4] is analyzed, contextualized in the Cloud Computing paradigm [1] and presented here in explicit and elucidate details, not yet evidenced in any scientific literature to date.

The following new and original contributions are presented: (i) SaaS Trialability Factor (SaaS_TFct) and its related "Intention of Use" experiment; (ii) SaaS Trialability Cost (SaaS_TCst) and considerations; (iii) extended graphical representation, as part of the case study validation, for the Potential Adoption Index (PAI) [14].

The structure of the paper is as follows. In Section II, a free trialability analysis of a generic mobile SaaS application is presented under three sub-sections: (A) concurrent possibilities; (B) potential limitations, and (C) mitigation. In Section III, a descriptive computation of the SaaS Trialability Cost (SaaS_TCst) related to the adopting or rejection process through the SaaS free trial period is presented. A new concept of SaaS Trialability Factor (SaaS_TFct) is introduced in Section IV, in order to base the construction of a practical model for evaluating the intention (to continue) to use (or reject and dismiss) a SaaS application, after an active and monitored free trial period, by a single non-SaaS-expert user and some measurements. In Section V, the validate model Potential Adoption Index (PAI) is contextualized and briefly described, for the support of this research, adding new graphs outcome, ready for interpretation, resulting from the original case-study [14].

The aim of this work in progress research, with the definition in concept of trialability contextualized in the SaaS service model, is to allow in real conditions, even if on a limited basis: (i) to anticipate evaluations (ex-ante the onerous subscription contract) by potential interested adopters; (ii) to assist in an informed subscription (or the decommission) of a SaaS service contract through a reflective/formative approach within determined constraints, possibilities, knowledge and available resources while reconciling these decisions with relevant prior research.

II. Trialability Contextualization: Concurrent Possibilities, Potential Limitation and, Mitigation

In order to arrive to a detailed contextualization, the limitations of trialability concept, as proposed by Rogers [4] in the Diffusion of Innovation theory, is detailed exclusively in light of a generic SaaS mobile application "pay as you go" deployed in public clouds where the SaaS provider offers a free trial period, because it is possible to detect, through direct observation, the combined presence of concurrent possibilities, potential limitation, and mitigations.

A. *Concurrent possibilities*

- The SaaS product is offered to anyone through a global public offering (public cloud deployment model) in/and through the Web (broad network access characteristic);
- A user can unilaterally access and use the program autonomously (on-demand self-service characteristic) through the network (broad network access characteristic);
- The SaaS offered during the free period:
  - has the same technical and functional features of the purchased product in case of subscription agreement acceptance (the multitenancy future in SaaS does not allow, still, an easy implementation of functional differentiation and all users normally use the same application [15] and [16]; customizations should be done through configuration [17]);
  - can be used without any installation (web version), on any device that supports a web browser compatible with the SaaS software and/or can be installed and used on all mobile devices available (mobile version), compatible with the SaaS platform offered by the provider (Android, iOS, etc.), without any limitation in number (pay per use and not by physical device or per-seat license);
- The SaaS provider normally guarantees:
  - free versions upgrades/updates also during the free trial period (multitenancy future);
  - the possibility of unlimited use of the virtualized resources offered through the SaaS application (resource pooling and rapid elasticity characteristics);
  - full access (in same case limited) of all support services offered by the provider in the exclusive context of the SaaS application execution;
- Usually the SaaS application utilization is free of charge during the free period also for commercial use even in the case of business applications (e.g., invoicing, accounting, etc.).

B. Potential limitations

- The access to the SaaS program is possible only for a limited number of users (typically one), but all authorized users (typically one) can alternatively be connected via any of the compatible devices they have availability (mobile and/or web version);
- Virtualized resources provided could be limited during the trial period;
- Same technical or functional features of the SaaS product could be available only after the subscription agreement acceptance and the payment of a fee (e.g., add-ins, extended functionalities, etc.);
- Normally the use of the trial application is free only during a delimited timeframe (generally trial period could be 15-30 consecutive days from the initial user registration).

C. Mitigations

Moreover, it is possible to mitigate the above limitations with a self-administration possibility option to request in on-demand self-service mode, upon payment of a certain sum, calculable and calculated before accepting the contract, any number of users and/or resources and/or features offered by the provider, for an established minimum period of time (days, month, year, etc.) with the assurance of termination (even in advance but with possible penalties), through the same contractual terms and conditions previously known and already subscribed.

With the above, greater precision was sought, based on the same definition used in the field of scientific literature and still maintaining the original limitations proposed by Rogers [4] *"on a limited basis"*, with exclusive reference to the trialability only in the innovation context introduced by the Cloud Computing paradigm with commercial "pay as you go" SaaS application deployed in public cloud that offers a free trial period.

Note that SaaS product offered in the marketplace, because the CC on-demand self-service characteristic, are normally proposed as a unilateral closed public offer. The adopter has only the chance to opt-in only if (additional or alternative) options are offered (e.g. personalization of SLA, emergency plan, different IaaS provider, different levels of support, etc.), by the SaaS provider, during the contract subscription phase or after, altering or renovating, the original contract and solely in on-demand self-service mode.

In a more general and abstract level of interpretation, it is possible to sustain the thesis that a SaaS provider may create a sense of trust in a potential client by (just only) manifesting an intention to create it (free SaaS trialability or free trial with few and fixed formalities). This level of trust can so indirectly be experienced, by using and testing the SaaS application *"on a limited basis"* by the potential client and, eventually, with and through the provider support services and information offered upon request or published on the web.

III. SaaS Trialability Cost (SaaS_TCst)

The "free" trial actually has some hidden, but still identifiable and, evaluable costs for both the SaaS provider and the potential customer.

On the provider's side: (i) he offers the use of the SaaS program (intellectual creation) free of charge; (ii) he is responsible and accountable for the costs incurred in the virtualized environment used (or pays the subcontracted IaaS provider) and related support services; (iii) so that potential customers can experience the application's features in advance and "free" of any cost for their use during the trial period.

The potential client invests his time and, consequently, his money to evaluate the program.

In a very synthetic way and without pretending to present an exhaustive generic case, but in a clarifying way for our purpose, it can be pointed out that the most obvious elements when it comes to knowing the costs of a SaaS trial are here briefly mentioned. The SaaS Trialability Cost (SaaS_TCst) or the cost of the free application trial period should consider for the SaaS provider, the sum, during a limited timeframe, of:

- the temporary use of intellectual creation (or non-depreciation cost for a specific timeframe);
- the effective use of virtualized resources (IaaS and measured service – essential characteristic);
- the effective support/aids provided to the test user from the provider support service representatives;

for the potential customer, the sum of:

- the effective time of use of the SaaS (measured service – essential characteristic);
- learning time to use the program (e.g. Website inspection, self-learning, emails/calls to provider customer support);
- time for any further inspection and obtaining any necessary additional information (including waiting time for provider support issues reply and incidents resolution);

multiplied each one of the above, by the hourly cost dedicated to these activities. The total time is also a function of the physical and mental effort, considered as sufficient, by the user, for the evaluation of the SaaS product.

The in-depth analysis of the software test can, in this way, be adjusted for each potential customer, depending on the degree of interest or application requirements, in order to ensure: (i) a balance between the economic cost of the strategic choice; (ii) the time dedicated to the inspection/ learning/assessment activities and (iii) the physical and mental effort required for these activities. And all this, within a free timeframe limited by the SaaS application provider (SaaS Trialability period).

In other words, it can be said that the cost of a "free trial" of a SaaS program (or the SaaS_TCst) represents a measurable investment (hidden and for consideration) distributed among the parties (SaaS application provider and potential customer).

It is also possible to identify the value at margin (separation point between acceptance and repudiation), at a given moment in time, of a SaaS application for a generic user, deriving from the total utility generated equal to the cost of the physical and economic components necessary to allocate and execute the application on the mobile device, at a level of use considered by her/him to be minimally adequate and/or free of efforts.

For a detailed Total Cost of Ownership (TCO) approach of Cloud Computing services the proposed TCO method in [18], where a mathematical modeling of cost types is introduced along with a case study, could be used *mutatis mutandis* for additional rationale.

IV. SAAS TRIALABILITY FACTOR (SAAS_TFCT) AND "INTENTION OF USE" WITHIN MEASURED SERVICE CC CHARACTERISTICS FOR A SINGLE NON-SAAS-EXPERT USER

In paid SaaS programs that offer a trial period, it is possible to experiment free operational features *"on a limited basis"* without others human intervention (on-demand self-service characteristic) and autonomously under much more extensive conditions than any other forms of demo-software products that do not use Cloud Computing paradigm [1].

The degree that allows identifying the level of transparency, compliance and correspondence between the version that can be used after an onerous subscription contract and the free trial version is here defined as SaaS Trialability Factor (SaaS_TFct). The SaaS_TFct corresponds to 1:1 only if the limitation of the SaaS trial product is correlated and limited only to the number of granted users who can access simultaneously the application (minimum one user).

In this case, where SaaS_TFct is equal to 1:1 (SaaS_TFct = 1:1), the trial period is fully comparable, from the point of view of the systems, data, information, processes, functions and support to a SaaS application in live operation and under payment contract ("pay as you go" period) for at least a single user.

In fact, more often than not, SaaS providers offers: (i) the use of the SaaS application for trial; (ii) free of all the potential limitations (see Section II B) but not the number of users (normally one) and the time limit (established trialability period); and, (iii) at the same time, all available concurrent possibilities (see Section II A). Only when the three previous conditions are met the SaaS_TFct is equal to 1:1 (*"trialability on a virtually free full basis for at least one concurrent test-user during a no-cost time-period"*).

When the SaaS application has a SaaS_TFct = 1:1 it is possible to let the registered user to perform the desired tests while collecting additional data, in a controlled environment, in order to determine and measure the effective use of the application in terms of the amount of time and resources used (see the vertical layer of CC measured service essential characteristic in Quadrant IV of Fig. 1 crossing all underlying CC service models from SaaS to IaaS).

The CC Effective Use (CC_EU) can be captured (or logged) in automatic mode, when/if needed, for any registered user accessing the SaaS: (i) at application level (e.g., frequency of use, duration of use, nature of use, number of functions or features used, etc.); (ii) at virtualized hardware level (IaaS) (e.g., CPU used, memory allocated, hard drive space used or read/write, etc.); (iii) analytically and; (iv) in aggregate form for statistical purpose.

For any registered user, the SaaS provider in addition to "transactional use" (CC_EU at the application level), could collect additional data on "informational use" and "customer-service use" through his web site and with the same login credential already granted to the potential adopter during the trial period.

In order to experiment if is it possible, for a single non-SaaS-expert possible adopter, to take a preliminary informed adoption (or rejection) decision at individual-level, respect to a SaaS commercial product, inside a Business Environment Context (BEC), during the free trialability period through:

- a set of predefined data collection items in the form of a simple survey, administered (e.g. in a pop-up modality) to the specific trial user (e.g., triggered when he logs off the application), containing the measurement items for "Usefulness" (U) and "Perceived Ease of Use" (PEU), as described in "Appendix" of [19] without decompose the original model and maintaining the reflective/formative measurement, are here contextualized and reported from the original research, in Table I and Table II;
- a simplified algorithm (Fig. 2) named "SaaS Trialability Algorithm Simple Adoption Process in Business Environment Context for Single-User" (STASAP∩BECxSU) that describes the procedure and contains all essential elements for its coding;
- the code for a randomized STASAP∩BECxSU simulation algorithm using the B.A.S.I.C. programming language (Fig. 3);
- the results of a single run of the coded program STASAP∩BECxSU (Fig. 4);

are here offered in order to facilitate the reader to perform the live experiment in auto evaluation self-service mode of **any** BEC related mobile application she/he eventually has access to.

TABLE I. MEASUREMENT ITEMS FOR "USEFULNESS" (U) AND "PERCEIVED EASE OF USE" (PEU) AS PER THEORETICAL CONSTRUCT IN "APPENDIX" OF [19]

#	Question
1	Using (the SaaS solution) in my job would enable me to accomplish tasks more quickly.
2	Using (the SaaS solution) would improve my job performance.
3	Using (the SaaS solution) in my job would increase my productivity.
4	Using (the SaaS solution) would enhance my effectiveness on the job.
5	Using (the SaaS solution) would make it easier to do my job.
6	I would find (the SaaS solution) useful in my job.
7	Learning to operate (the SaaS solution) would be easy for me.
8	I would find it easy to get (the SaaS solution) to do what I want it to do.
9	My interaction with (the SaaS solution) would be clear and understandable.
10	I would find (the SaaS solution) to be flexible to interact with.
11	It would be easy for me to become skillful at using (the SaaS solution).
12	I would find (the SaaS solution) easy to use.

As soon as the collected information is inputted, it is possible to calculate the "Intention Of Use" (IOU) as the arithmetical average of all the single measurement items (as a sum of evaluation values for each U and PEU acquired, divided by 12).

TABLE II. MEASUREMENT SCALES FOR "USEFULNESS" (U) AND "PERCEIVED EASE OF USE" (PEU) AS PER THEORETICAL CONSTRUCT IN "APPENDIX" OF [19]

Evaluation values								
likely	1 - extremely	2 - quite	3 - slightly	4 - neither	5 - slightly	6 - quite	7 - extremely	unlikely

If is it possible to repeat the above measurements at a specific point in time (in the original research [19], after the first hour introduction and, then, after 14 weeks), during the trial period, a differential could be highlighted that would lead to a reasoned acceptance or refusal (depending also on time, methods and resources used in the SaaS tests or the collected CC_EU related measures) making also possible scoreboard the review progression in each of Perceived Ease of Use (PEU) and Usefulness (U) measures.

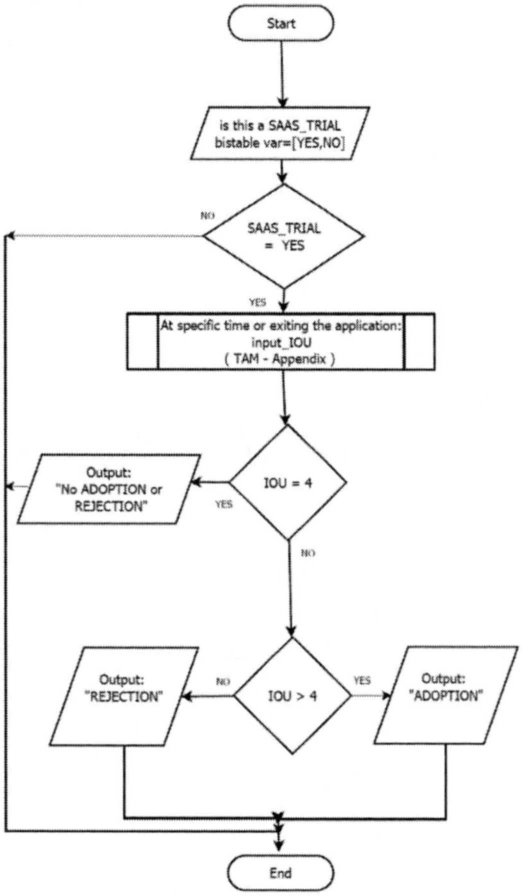

Figure 2. "SaaS Trialability Algorithm Simple Adoption Process in Business Environment Context for Single-User" (STASAP∩BECxSU)

Although the emerging trends of use of big data and powerful analytics place a new emphasis on the use of business intelligence as a source of competitive success, the here proposed experiment, and its calculated result can already provide a clarifying and useful solution (the calculated IOU).

In fact, if the average of IOU is > 4 the probable adopter is prone to adopt the SaaS application; if IOU < 4 the probable adopter, at this point in time, is willing to reject the application for her/his personal use in her/his BEC.

```
10 REM save"SAASAP_BC_SU
15 CLS: RANDOMIZE VAL(MID$(TIME$,7,2)):DIM IOU(100, 12)
20 I=1
30 IOU=0:PRINT "Collecting data for INTENTION TO USE: " :FOR X=1 TO 12:IOU(I,X)=
INT(RND*7+1):PRINT "The answer to Q";X;"is "; IOU(I,X):IOU=IOU+IOU(I,X):NEXT X:I
OU=IOU/12:PRINT: PRINT"*** The last calculated IOU average value = "; IOU:REM **
 randomized IOU
50 TRIAL=0:PRINT "Do you want to TRY more the SaaS application? 0=NO;1=SI";: INP
UT TRIAL:IF TRIAL = 0 THEN GOTO 1000 ELSE PRINT "Please USE again the Applicatio
n and then answer the proposed questions!"
60 REM ******************** gosub Subroutine GET_USEd  *****
100 GOTO 30
1000 PRINT "The computated FINAL decision is: ";:IF IOU = 4 THEN PRINT "Non deci
sion" : GOTO 2000
1010 IF IOU > 4 THEN PRINT "ADOPTION" ELSE PRINT "REJECTION"
2000 END
Ok
```

Figure 3. Coding of SaaS Trialability Algorithm Simple Adoption Process in Business Environment Context for Single-User (STASAP∩BECxSU)

```
Collecting data for INTENTION TO USE:
The answer to Q 1 is  7
The answer to Q 2 is  7
The answer to Q 3 is  5
The answer to Q 4 is  2
The answer to Q 5 is  2
The answer to Q 6 is  3
The answer to Q 7 is  6
The answer to Q 8 is  6
The answer to Q 9 is  1
The answer to Q 10 is  1
The answer to Q 11 is  5
The answer to Q 12 is  5

*** The last calculated IOU average value =  4.166667
Do you want to TRY more the SaaS application? 0=NO;1=SI? 1_
Please USE again the Application and then answer the proposed questions!
Collecting data for INTENTION TO USE:
The answer to Q 1 is  5
The answer to Q 2 is  3
The answer to Q 3 is  3
The answer to Q 4 is  7
The answer to Q 5 is  3
The answer to Q 6 is  3
The answer to Q 7 is  7
The answer to Q 8 is  1
The answer to Q 9 is  2
The answer to Q 10 is  1
The answer to Q 11 is  2
The answer to Q 12 is  2

*** The last calculated IOU average value =  3.25
Do you want to TRY more the SaaS application? 0=NO;1=SI? 0
The computated FINAL decision is: REJECTION
Ok
```

Figure 4. A single run of the program SaaS Trialability Algorithm Simple Adoption Process in Business Context Environment for Single-User STASAP∩BECxSU at two different points in time during the tests with the motivated final decision of rejection (final value = 3.25 < of 4).

In order to analyze and, eventually correlate in more detail, the final (rejection or acceptance) of IOU (calculated with the experimented STASAP∩BECxSU), the End-User Computing Satisfaction (EUCS) [20], experienced during the trial, could also be collected and examined (through the proposed measurement items and scale) with respect to Content (C), Accuracy (A), Format (F), Ease of use (E) and Timeliness (T) constructs as spelled out at p. 268 in [20], using the same tactic previously described for the STASAP∩BECxSU. Alternatively to the latter, collected /able CC_EU measures as: number of functions or/and features used (C_i); duration of each use ($T_{j,i}$); response time ($T_{j,i}$); output produced ($F_{j,i}$); any error reported by the application and/or the end-user (E_i and/or A_i); etc.; could be utilized/analyzed and/or integrated with the eventually available EUCS measures.

V. Potential Adoption Index (PAI)

In more complex BEC, where the strategic decision (in adopting a SaaS product deployed in public cloud) can be supported and integrated by an objective quality technical evaluation, the use of the Potential Adoption Index (PAI) described in pp. 145-160 in [14] and, also reported here, in Fig. 5, can be considered (in addition to STASAP∩BECxSU experiment) opportune.

The idea of the PAI has his foundation in [21], where (in Fig. 2, p. 186) the authors proposed, in the suggested research agenda section, the business-technology framework to refer to different views of correlated Cloud Computing scientific research aspects (on business - technology axis).

A PAI preliminary model was developed and subsequently presented in [22] and [23].

If the *trialability on a virtually free full basis for at least one concurrent test-user during a no-cost time-period* (SaaS_TFct = 1:1), is offered by the SaaS provider, it can be used, at an already explained cost (SaaS_TCst), to acquire all the necessary evaluations for the elements incorporated in the PAI model.

The validated PAI model [14]: (i) is generic because can refer to any BEC oriented SaaS deployed in public cloud; (ii) it has been created to assist and support "Decision-Maker not Technically expert in CC" (DMnTeCC), in the adoption decisions of the most apt SaaS product (available on the marketplace).

The single PAI resultant value is represented in numeric form (values range between 1 and 4) in which the two evaluations (business and technology) of all the specific constituent elements, converge in a weighted means, in the result: (i) relative importance of the DMnTeCC; (ii) quality-related to objectively verifiable elements of the services offered (or potentially available) and their modalities.

The 58 constituent selected attribute-elements are, in the PAI model, grouped by: (i) CC essential characteristics as in [1]; (ii) benefits and concerns as proposed in [24].

Each selected element or attribute is (i) uniquely identifiable; (ii) it is characteristic; (iii) it is evaluable by importance and quality; (iv) it is verifiable or testable and; (v) assigned to one or more representative groups or subgroups.

Potential Adoption Index (PAI)

				WEIGHT	% WEIGHT	RATING	WEIGHT% * RATING
				WEIGHT: Level of interest for the item to consider: 1-NO important; 10 VERY important	WEIGHT %: reduction in percentage (%) over total evaluations (Σ Weight)	RATING: Technical evaluation of the product when addressing the specific aspect considered: 1 poor; 4 best that can be found	WEIGHT % * RATING: Numerical multiplication of importance (Weight%) by technical evaluation (Rating)
Benefits	Essential Characteristic		On-demand self-service				
			Broad network access				
			Resource pooling				
			Rapid elasticity				
			Measured service				
	Deployment		ease to setup				
			ease to maintain				
			speed - implementation time				
	Financial	Cost - structuring of payment	contract payment terms (monthly...)				
			change of subscription fee (end of				
			penalty on early termination				
			data return on subscription cancel				
			cost scalability (per user, group)				
		pay-for-use	Total cost per year				
		Cost savings	small capital expense				
			convert capex to opex				
		Customer support - other services	provide user training				
			training charges fee				
			self support /documentation				
			customer support by phone				
			customer support by email				
			customer support web-ticket				
			Client manager (primary contact)				
			business consulting				
	Functional	up to date	planned frequency				
			policy to notify update/upgrade				
		Future expansion - evolution	expansion (new modules deployment)				
			evolution				
Concerns	Alignment	Integration	existing formats, interface, structured data				
			operating system compatibility				
			mobile compatibility				
			browser compatibility				
		Configurability - customization	customization / functional				
			configurability / technical				
		Availability	redundancy in data				
			redundancy in services				
			uptime/downtime requirement (99,9%)				
		Performance	network bandwidth usage/available				
			response time-reactivity (latency)				
			off-line functionality (if any)				
	Management and control of data and services	Data Security	Authentication (ie. User+psw)				
			secure protocol				
			security certification (ES. ISO 27001				
			encription option				
			security records - Logging and Monitoring				
		Data relocation - Lock-in	fast data portability				
			secure data portability				
			simple data portability				
		Data loss	backups/recovery				
			recover on client request				
			disaster plan				
	Legal		Legal protection -Liability-Out of business				
			Data disclosure - auditability				
			Legislation of reference				
			Data confidentiality - privacy				
			Data ownership - Data property				
			Location of the information - Data location				
			SLAs negotiation or customization				
							Σ

Figure 5. Model for the quantitative data acquisition for the PAI calculation. Source: [14] pp. 145-160.

The technical quality assessment is carried out from a SaaS-Specialized-Technical-EXPERT (SSTE) on an objective basis, made justifiably (susceptible to verification and adequately modifiable) and, using a pre-established discrete fixed scale of integer values (min. 1, max. 4) on an average of 2.5 (valorization not available as evaluation value) as pp. 161-177 in [14].

Different technical assessments values, on the same SaaS product, may depend on the experience of the SSTE evaluator, the objectivity of the evaluation and, the reproducibility of the measurement or/and its motivated justification.

The evaluation of the importance of each element is made by the DMnTeCC, with values that can be chosen from a preselected scale (usually between 1 and 10), even if this scale is modifiable during the assessment stage (retrofitted in the model, using % of the original Weight acquired in the case study protocol).

Each evaluable element in the PAI model obtains a discrete calculated numerical representation (Weight % * Rating) on: (i) the relative importance for the DMnTeCC (Weight %) and; (ii) quality of the SaaS product for the SSTE (Rating); (iii) in a specific BEC.

The PAI value synthesizes, in an aggregate and final result, the potential of the analyzed SaaS product with respect to the importance/quality attributes values in a specific BEC and, it provides a correct indication in itself, as a result of an agglomerated calculation (Σ of all Weight% * Rating).

The final value of the PAI is able to synthesize a positive potential (for a value greater than 2.5) or negative potential (for a value less than 2.5) between CC essential characteristics, benefits and concerns in relation to the SaaS program and its adoption in a BEC and, still maintains its connotation in terms of importance originally expressed by the DMnTeCC (Weight %).

The computation of the PAI is simple, although it incorporates clearly identified available levels of knowledge of the SSTE and, the explicit DMnTeCC will.

The potential of the PAI model depends exclusively on: (i) the consistency of the model; (ii) the underlying definitions and categorizations; (iii) the selected incorporated component elements; and, (ii) of its controlled use both in professional practice and in academic settings.

A detailed graphic analysis, that keeps in mind the DMnTeCC importance's and technical qualities (carried out from an SSTE), could be performed following the PAI data collection schema in order to visualize all the available information.

It is useful, now, to graphically address the relevance of the Potential Adoption Index (PAI) using, with a chart analysis, the set of evaluations within a Cartesian axis system, which refers to the dimensions of the importance of the DMnTeCC (axis of the ordinates) and the judgments on technical quality expressed from a SSTE (axis of the abscissa) as in Fig. 6, 7, 8 and 9.

The intersection of the axes, in the average value, divides the Cartesian plane into four quadrants to each of which it is possible to associate a different meaning (see Fig. 6).

The new graphic representation, proposed for the PAI model case-study, is much easier interpretable than the tables offered in the original research [14] and allows identifying groups of elements to focus to for additional consideration.

Fig. 6 shows the scatter plot obtained with the answers of the questionnaire in case B with the indication of each characteristic element considered.

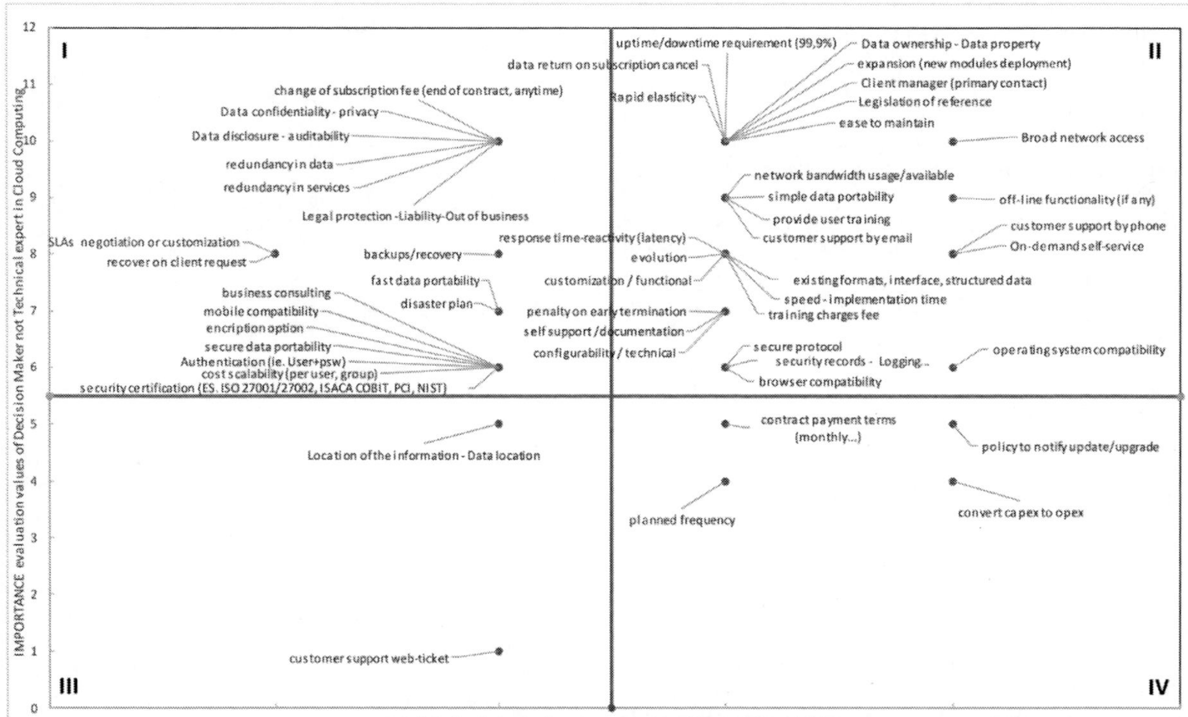

Figure 6. Graph representation of constituent elements of Case B with PAI = 2.7038 at p. 175 in [14].

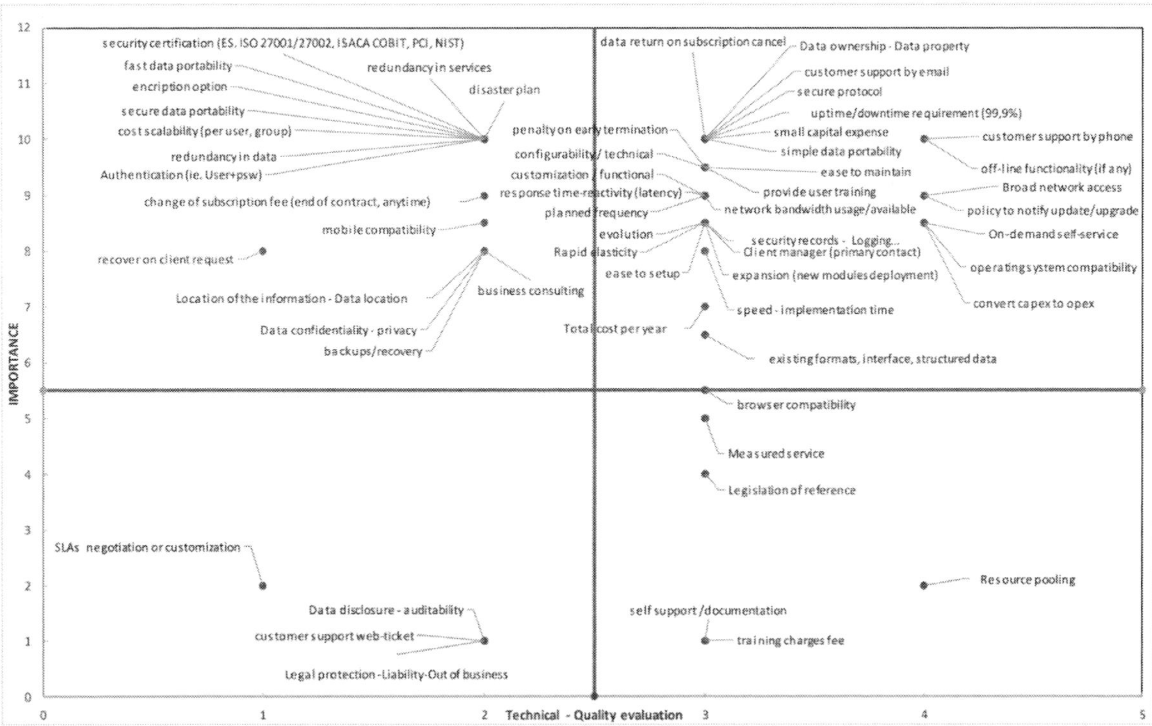

Figure 7. Graph representation of constituent elements of Case C with PAI = 2.7873 at p. 185 in [14].

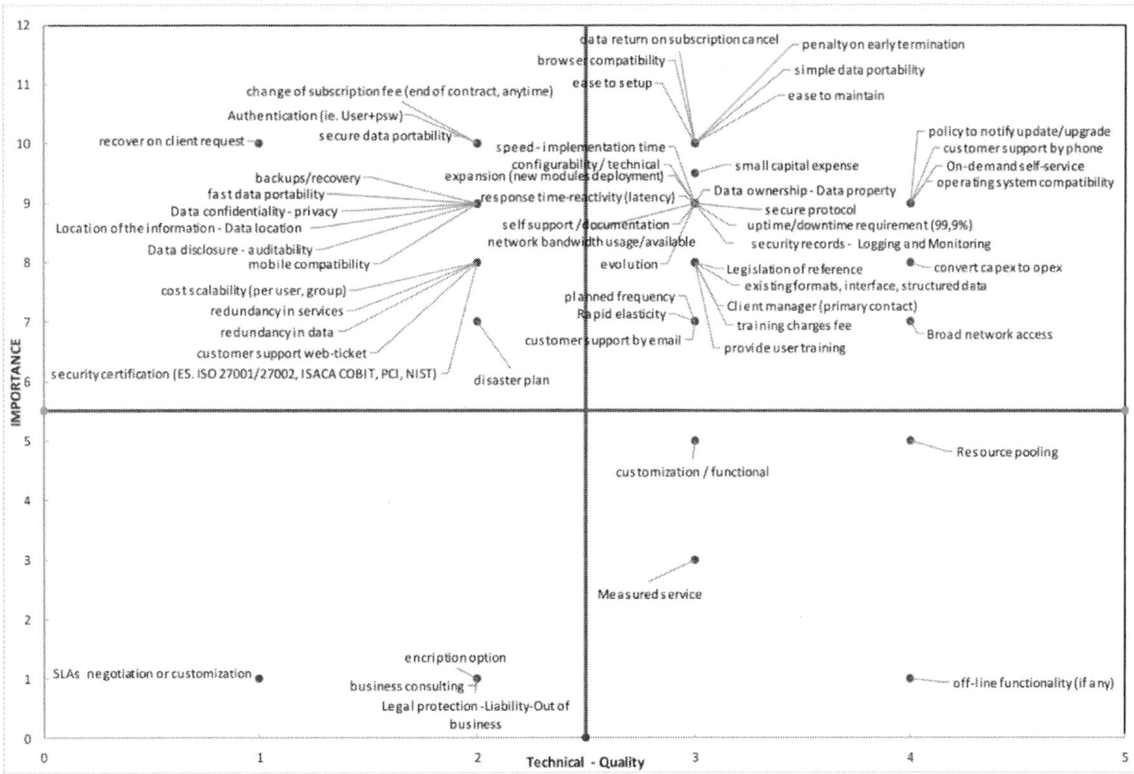

Figure 8. Graph representation of constituent elements of Case D with PAI = 2.7748 at p. 191 in [14].

With this graphic representation, the DMnTeCC of Case B can now focus his attention on the I quadrant (in Fig. 6), with the help of what was reported by the SSTE in "Technical evaluation (Rating) of the analytical elements of the quantitative model" (pp. 161-177 in [14]) for each evaluation element starting with the ones that have the high interest value (Weight) and lowest technical assessment (Rating): Change of subscription fee; Redundancy in data; Redundancy in services; Legal protection-Liability-Out of business; Data disclosure-auditability; Data confidentiality–privacy (as also highlighted in Table 28 at p. 184 in [14]).

Same considerations can be done for Fig. 7 e 8 with the appropriate case differentiation (see Table 31 at p. 190 for case C and Table 34 p. 194 for case D in [14]).

The PAI model and his graphical representation want to be an added and balanced research instrument to support the evaluation of SaaS products in a BCE.

VI. Further Works, Recommendations, and Suggested Research Agenda

The PAI data and results obtained in the three case-study in [14] refer to the same SaaS product, and if a sufficient number of cases was available they could be aggregated and analyzed further in conjunction of Fig. 9. In fact, it could be useful to address the adoption potentials of a SaaS product in a BEC using some analogies with the well-known Importance-Performance Analysis (IPA) model [25], originally developed in marketing research and progressively disseminated in social studies, with the due care.

Further subsequent studies, if sufficient data will be available, could lead in revealing solid findings for later adopters and/or could help the SaaS providers to prioritize improvements to their Software as a Service product and at the same time conform to what is defined as CC [1].

VII. Conclusion

In the Cloud Computing service models (IaaS, PaaS and SaaS), the essential characteristics are inherited among these layers through the encapsulation of the various offered technological components (that can be also automated if previously subscribed or contracted) and could be made available for the benefit of the end-users.

SaaS programs are supported on IaaS platforms and are normally developed through the use of PaaS platforms.

IaaS providers in public cloud that have accredited platforms are few and distributed in a global geographical scope (e.g., Amazon Web Services; Microsoft Azure; Google Cloud Platform and IBM Cloud, etc.).

Providers that offer SaaS applications can subcontract models of underlying services from other public cloud providers (PaaS or IaaS) by subscribing to the respective published contractual conditions in an on-demand self-service fashion.

The contractual conditions subscribed between different providers impose predetermined contractual obligations that indirectly influence (but could *"de facto"* affect) the final subscribers of the SaaS service.

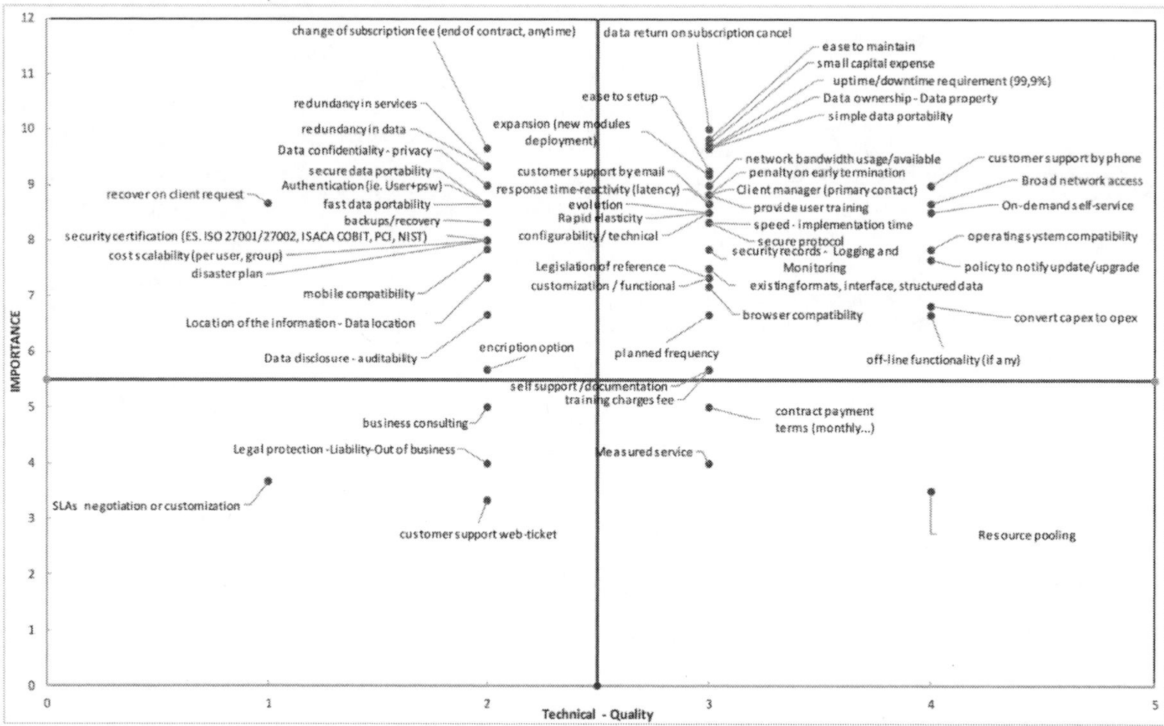

Figure 9. Graph representation of the average of constituent elements of Case B, C, and D not present as a table in [14]

When a specific SaaS service is contracted on a subcontracted platform, the subscriber of the application agrees on the use of the program, on a virtualized infrastructure, directly with the SaaS service provider (with levels of visibility and transparency most likely fragmented along the entire chain of supplied sub-contracts).

The contractual and technical responsibilities, "of and in" the services offered by the SaaS provider are shared at different levels among all the actors (all involved providers and the SaaS customers);

The complexity of evaluating the technological component, the contractual links and the offered services (incorporated or explicit), are usually underestimated or ignored until complications arise (e.g., malfunction, loss of data, unfulfilled legal responsibilities, etc.), compromising the effective use of the contracted SaaS service and/or the expected benefits.

The availability of a free trial period (free trialability) of the application is, by the authors, of deep importance to be able to appreciate the operational characteristics and verify the technical and contractual components of the SaaS services offered by the provider before committing to a paid contract.

For what reported in this paper is now possible to affirm that SaaS products for mobile devices deployed in the public cloud and available on the marketplace: (i) that comply with the CC paradigm; (ii) and have a SaaS_TFct equal to 1:1; (iii) and are actively tested (investing sufficient time and effort for their inspection); (iv) in a controlled and measured environment; (iv) during a limited cost-free trialability period offered by the provider; (v) have a lower risk and error assessment than those that cannot be tested in advance (before the contract acceptance and payment) but have, possibly, a higher initial (investment) hidden but measurable cost (SaaS_TCst).

In order to sustain the letter statement, an approach based on diverse subjects with different level of expertise /responsibility and unique measurement items has been used.

The structured approach focused on adoption evaluations of a SaaS product deployed in the public cloud, with inspection/test during the trialability period, by:

- single non-SaaS-expert user;
- decision-maker not technically expert in CC (DMnTeCC) jointly with a SaaS-Specialized-Technical-EXPERT;

using respectively:

- the Intention of Use construct (IOU) metrics;
- the Potential Adoption Index (PAI) research and additional graphic validation examples.

Trialability has been here, therefore, proposed not only as a tangible factor of Diffusion of Innovation in CC environments but also as viable reasoning and learning tool instrument in order to acquire a deeper understanding, knowledge and, data source for personal and scientific research in the evolutionary Cloud Computing paradigm.

ACKNOWLEDGMENT

With respectful humility to my *Magistri* and to all capable to stimulate exciting reasoning researches.

REFERENCES

[1] P. Mell and T. Grance, "The NIST Definition of Cloud Computing," 2011.

[2] A. Adamov and M. Erguvan, "The truth about cloud computing as new paradigm in IT," in *International Conference on Application of Information and Communication Technologies, 2009. AICT 2009*, 2009, pp. 1–3.

[3] W. Venters and E. A. Whitley, "A critical review of cloud computing: researching desires and realities," *J. Inf. Technol.*, vol. 27, no. 3, pp. 179–197, Sep. 2012.

[4] E. M. Rogers, *Diffusion of innovations*. New York; London: Free Press ; Collier Macmillan, 1983.

[5] A. Lin and N.-C. Chen, "Cloud computing as an innovation: Percepetion, attitude, and adoption," *International Journal of Information Management*, vol. 32, no. 6, pp. 533–540, December 2012.

[6] Y. Alshamaila, S. Papagiannidis, and F. Li, "Cloud computing adoption by SMEs in the north east of England: A multi-perspective framework," *Journal of Enterprise Information Management*, vol. 26, no. 3, pp. 250–275, 2013.

[7] B. Ramdani, D. Chevers, and D. A. Williams, "SMEs' adoption of enterprise applications: A technology-organisation-environment model," *Journal of Small Business and Enterprise Development*, vol. 20, no. 4, pp. 735–753, Oct. 2013.

[8] L. Morgan and K. Conboy, "Factors affecting the adoption of cloud computing: an exploratory study," 2013.

[9] L. Morgan and K. Conboy, "Key Factors Impacting Cloud Computing Adoption," *Computer*, vol. 46, no. 10, pp. 97–99, 2013.

[10] N. Alkhater, G. Wills, and R. Walters, "Factors Affecting an Organisation's Decision to Adopt Cloud Services in Saudi Arabia," in *2015 3rd International Conference on Future Internet of Things and Cloud (FiCloud)*, 2015, pp. 553–557.

[11] S. S. Nawaz and S. Gunapalan, "Evaluating the Adoption of Enterprise Applications by Small and Medium Enterprises in Sri Lanka," *European Journal of Business and Management*, vol. 7, no. 4, pp. 324–334, Mar. 2015.

[12] Fariba Safari, Narges Safari, and Alireza Hasanzadeh, "The adoption of software-as-a-service (SaaS): ranking the determinants," *Journal of Ent Info Management*, vol. 28, no. 3, pp. 400–422, Mar. 2015.

[13] S. Das and M. Dayal, "Exploring determinants of cloud-based enterprise resource planning (ERP) selection and adoption: A qualitative study in the Indian education sector," *Journal of Information Technology Case and Application Research*, vol. 18, no. 1, pp. 11–36, Mar. 2016.

[14] G. Ercolani, "Análisis del potencial del cloud computing para las PYMES: un modelo integrado para evaluar software as a service (SaaS) en la nube pública," Universidad de Murcia, Murcia, 2017.

[15] W. Sun, X. Zhang, C. J. Guo, P. Sun, and H. Su, "Software as a Service: Configuration and Customization Perspectives," in *IEEE Congress on Services Part II, 2008. SERVICES-2*, 2008, pp. 18–25.

[16] C.-P. Bezemer and A. Zaidman, "Multi-tenant SaaS applications: maintenance dream or nightmare?," in *Proceedings of the Joint ERCIM Workshop on Software Evolution (EVOL) and International Workshop on Principles of Software Evolution (IWPSE)*, New York, NY, USA, 2010, pp. 88–92.

[17] Nitu, "Configurability in SaaS (software as a service) applications," in *Proceedings of the 2nd India software engineering conference*, New York, NY, USA, 2009, pp. 19–26.

[18] B. Martens, M. Walterbusch, and F. Teuteberg, "Costing of Cloud Computing Services: A Total Cost of Ownership approach," in

Proceedings of the Annual Hawaii International Conference on System Sciences, 2012, pp. 1563–1572.

[19] F. D. Davis, "Perceived Usefulness, Perceived Ease of Use, and User Acceptance of Information Technology," *MIS Quarterly*, vol. 13, no. 3, pp. 319–340, 1989.

[20] W. J. Doll and G. Torkzadeh, "The Measurement of End-User Computing Satisfaction," *MIS Quarterly*, vol. 12, no. 2, pp. 259–274, 1988.

[21] S. Marston, Z. Li, S. Bandyopadhyay, J. Zhang, and A. Ghalsasi, "Cloud computing - The business perspective," *Decision Support Systems*, vol. 51, no. 1, pp. 176–189, 2011.

[22] G. Ercolani, "Análisis del potencial del Cloud Computing para la PYMES.," *Cuadernos de Gestión de Información.*, vol. 2, no. 1, pp. 40–55, 2012.

[23] G. Ercolani, "Cloud Computing Services Potential Analysis," presented at the CLOUD COMPUTING 2013, The Fourth International Conference on Cloud Computing, GRIDs, and Virtualization, Valencia, 2013, pp. 77–80.

[24] P. Géczy, N. Izumi, and K. Hasida, "Cloudsourcing: managing cloud adoption," *Global Journal of Business Research (GJBR)*, vol. 6, no. 2, pp. 57–70, Mar. 2012.

[25] J. A. Martilla and J. C. James, "Importance-Performance Analysis," *Journal of Marketing*, vol. 41, no. 1, pp. 77–79, 1977.

Automating the Semantic Labeling of Stream Data

Konstantinos Kotis
Dept. of Cultural Technology and Communication
University of the Aegean,
Mytilene, Greece
e-mail: kotis@aegean.gr

***Abstract*—The collection of a voluminous real-world stream data is achieved today through a large number of distributed and heterogeneous data sources. On the other hand, it is quite rare to discover and collect semantic models associated with this data, in order to be able to represent implicit meaning and specifying related uncovered concepts and relationships between them. Such semantic models, however, are the key to make the data easily available, understandable and interlinkable for its potential users and applications. Manually modeling the semantics of data requires significant effort and expertise. Most of the related work focuses on the semantic labeling/annotation of the data fields (source attributes), given that a semantic model is already provided. Constructing a semantic model that explicitly describes the relationships between the data attributes in addition to their semantic types is critical. Related works support the semantic annotation of data using existing ontologies, but there are only a few that automatically construct the ontology based on the real-world stream data that will eventually annotate (two-step process). More important, existing solutions require a manually-created training data set and its mapping to existing related ontologies/models, in order to assist in the process of learning the mapping function between the actual stream data and the related semantic model (usually via a supervised machine learning approach). This paper a) presents the problem and representative related work, and b) proposes design directions that are aligned to key requirements.**

Keywords-semantic label; ontology; stream data.

I. INTRODUCTION

In domains such as the IoT, sensor devices are used to obtain insights about the things that 'live' in the surrounding world, and to facilitate an intelligent interaction with them (sense, analyze, act). The increasing need of using the data produced by the sensor devices (stream data) inevitably leads to Big Data, which requires new scalable and efficient methods to structure and represent the underlying information and to make the data accessible, processable and interlinkable for the applications/services that use it. For instance, this is the case for accessing, integrating and reasoning with large volumes of stream data generated from moving entities (e.g., ships, airplanes), dynamic data such as weather conditions, as well as historical/static data, in order to recognize high-level critical events to support real-time decision and policy making.

Semantic technologies are used for the formal representation of the real-world sensor data, due to its advantage of conceptualizing and representing raw data in an easy but still formal and explicit way, making them machine interpretable and allowing their interlinkage to existing resources (e.g., Web, Linked Open Data cloud). For instance, representing raw numerical values of measurements of weather conditions that are measured and conceptualized by meteorological or AIS (automatic identification system) sensors, e.g., attributes, such as date, time, swell height (or height of swell), wind speed (or speed of wind), visibility, and their corresponding values such as "28/08/2017, 09.00, 1, 20, 10" and "28/08/2017, 22.00, 8, 90, 5", can be done by automatically discovering their corresponding semantics and assigning to them the appropriate semantic labels.

Typically, individual data table columns (e.g., CSV/Excel table) are mapped to ontological properties, a set of data table columns are mapped to ontological classes, and row data table rows are mapped to ontological individuals. For structured data/information such as relational databases (RDB) and Web tables, the aim is to semantically annotate/label the sources of structured data by mapping RDB and Web tables against an ontology. As recently reported [1], such a task can be decomposed into different subtasks such as table-to-class mapping, row-to-instance mapping, and column-to-property mapping.

Defining the problem of semantic labeling of a data source S with a semantic labeling function $\varphi :< \{\alpha\},\{v_i\} > \rightarrow l$ is explained in the following lines.

A data source S is a collection of ordered pairs $< \{\alpha\},\{v_\alpha\} >$, where α denotes an attribute name (e.g., 'date', 'time', 'swell height', etc.) and $\{v_\alpha\}$ denotes the set of data values corresponding to the attribute α (e.g., for α equals to the 'date' attribute the set will have values such as '28/08/2017', '30-04-2018'). Different data sources can have attributes that have different names but map to the same semantic label (e.g., 'swell height' of S_1 and 'height of swell' in S_2 are both mapped to the same property i.e., 'swell_height' of a Weather ontology). Multiple data sources are often mapped to the same ontology in many practical scenarios. The goal is to automatically learn the semantic labeling function. To assign a semantic label to an attribute in a new data source, we take an ordered pair $< \{\alpha\},\{v_\alpha\} >$ and use a semantic labeling function, which has been learned from training data, to predict its semantic label.

In the IoT domain, one of the biggest challenges is to discover and establish mappings between raw data and its intended meaning, formalized explicitly into ontological concepts, properties and/relationships between them. Such a problem is usually referred as the symbol grounding problem [2], describing the fundamental challenge of defining concepts/properties from numerical sensor data that is not grounded in meaningful real-world information. Voluminous real-world stream data are usually recorded and collected as numerical values that cannot easily be related to meaningful information without knowing the context, such as the observation time and the location of the recorded data. Such data can change over time or it can be depended on other external factors. For instance, 30 degrees Celsius in summer time can be a normal condition, however in winter time such a reading could possibly mean an error of the sensor functionality.

In contexts where real-world row data are generated in a streaming fashion by sensor devices or other data sources, the main problems related to their semantic labeling are:

- In the absence of a semantic model (ontology), how to automatically construct one by learning/uncovering the semantics 'hidden' in the data
- Given a (learned) semantic model, how to automatically, accurately and on-time compute the corresponding data-to-semantics mappings, in a continuous and iterative fashion.

While syntactic information about data sources such as attribute names (e.g., title, name, location) or attribute types (e.g., string, int, date) may provide some hints towards discovering their related meanings and form the corresponding semantic types, often this information is not sufficient for an accurate prediction. For instance, the field 'title' of a data source that records artworks is not by itself indicative of the intended meaning of its values (e.g., 'Zinnias'), i.e., it might by the case that values (titles) are meant to be related with book titles, with song titles or with artworks. This prediction can be even harder if the attribute names are used in abbreviated forms e.g., 'dob' (i.e., date of birth) instead of 'birthdate'. That is the main reason why related approaches focus on learning data semantics using the data values rather their attribute names.

The general idea behind existing related approaches is to learn a semantic labeling function from a training set of data that has been previously semantically labeled in a manual fashion. Then, when presented with a new data source of the same topic/domain, the learned semantic labeling function can automatically assign semantic types to each attribute of the new source. The training data consists of a set of semantic types and each semantic type has a set of data values and attribute names associated with it. Given a new set of data values from a new source, the goal is to predict the top-*k* candidate semantic types along with confidence scores using the training data.

In the example of Artworks, the semantic types are 'title' of 'Artwork', 'name' of 'Person', and 'label' of 'Museum'. By simply labeling the attributes with those types however, is not sufficient. Unless the relationships between the columns are explicitly specified ('museum', 'painter'), a precise model of the data cannot be obtained. For instance, a person could be the owner, the painter, or the sculptor of an artwork, but in the context of a specific example data for paints, only the semantic relation of 'painter' correctly interprets the intended relationship between an artwork and a person. Thus, to build a rich semantic model that fully represents the intended semantics of the data, another step that determines the relationships between the attributes of the data sources in terms of the properties in the ontology is necessary.

Moreover, in terms of solving the same problem presented above, but for stream (mainly numerical) data as input, one is facing with even more challenging issues. Due to the nature of stream data (data arrives so rapidly in large volumes, usually with no structure or metadata attached to it), techniques such as dimensionality reduction and time-windowing of data, as well as statistical/probability techniques for analyzing the distribution of numeric values corresponding to a semantic label as well as linking those labels to each other, are required.

This paper presents a) a number of recent related works that try to solve the abovementioned problems, and b) design directions aligned to technological requirements that must be satisfied towards the goal of automating the semantic labeling of stream data. It is structured as follows: Section 2 provides background knowledge of key technologies, Section 3 presents the related work, Section 4 presents the proposed design directions towards efficiently approaching the problem, and Section 5 concludes the paper, also stating future work plans.

II. Background Knowledge

A. *Semantic Labeling*

Semantic labeling (or annotation), in the most common cases, is the process of attaching additional information to various concepts (e.g., people, things, places, organizations etc.) in a given text or any other unstructured or structured content (e.g., video, RDB, Web tables). When a document (or another piece of content, e.g., video) is semantically labeled it becomes a source of information that is easy to be interpreted, combined and reused by computers. As described by OntoText [3], to semantically annotate concepts in the sentence "Aristotle, the author of Politics, established the Lyceum", we need to identify Aristotle as a 'person' and Politics as a 'written work of political philosophy'. Then we can index, classify and interlink the identified concepts in a semantic graph database (e.g., GraphDB), in order to be able to add (link) other information about Aristotle such as his date of birth, his teachers, and his works. Politics can also be linked to its subject, to its date of creation etc. Given the semantics about the above sentence and its links to other (external or internal) formal knowledge, algorithms will be able to automatically answer questions such as: who tutored Alexander the Great, which of Plato's pupils established the Lyceum. In other words, semantic labeling/annotation enriches content with machine-processable information by linking background information to extracted concepts.

For structured data/information, such as relational databases (RDB) and Web tables, the aim is to semantically annotate sources of structured data by mapping RDB and Web tables against an ontology. Such a task can be decomposed into different subtasks such as table-to-class mapping, row-to-instance mapping, and column-to-property mapping [1]. There are many studies on mapping data sources to ontologies and several approaches have been proposed to generate semantic Web data from databases and spreadsheets [4]. RDB schemas are easy to handle when computing 1-1 mappings (table-to-class and field-to-property correspondences). The D2RQ [5] and Ontop [6] Ontology-Based Data Access (OBDA) approaches, introduces custom mapping languages that enables users to define mapping rules between tables of relational databases and target ontologies in order to annotate and publish semantic data in RDF format. R2RML [7] is a W3C recommendation for expressing customized mappings from relational databases to RDF datasets. Writing the corresponding mapping rules by hand however, is a time-consuming task. The users need to have a good understanding of the way source tables can be most effectively mapped to the target ontology. They also need to learn the syntax of writing the mapping rules.

In recent years, some efforts were introduced towards automatically inferring the implicit semantics of tables. Polfliet and Ichise [8] use string similarity methods between column names and names of the ontological properties in order to discover the corresponding mappings. Wang et al. [9] use the header of Web tables along with the values of the rows to map the columns to the attributes of the corresponding entity that is represented in a rich and general purpose taxonomy of facts (built from a corpus of over one million Web pages and other data). This approach can only deal with the tables containing information of a single entity type. Limaye et al. [10] use YAGO ontology [11] to annotate Web tables and generate binary relationships using machine learning approaches. This approach is limited to the labels and relations defined in the YAGO ontology. Venetis et al. [12] presents a scalable approach to describe the semantics of tables on the Web, leveraging a database of class labels and relationships that are automatically extracted from the Web. Although these approaches are very useful in labeling and publishing semantic data from tables, they are limited in learning the semantics relations: they only infer individual binary relationships between pair of columns. They are not able to find the relation between two columns if there is no direct relationship between the values of those columns.

Moreover, other related work exploits the data available in the Linked Open Data (LOD) cloud to capture the semantics of the tables and publish their data as RDF. Munoz et al. [13] present an approach towards mining RDF triples from the Wikipedia tables by linking the cell values to the resources available in DBpedia [14]. This approach is limited to Wikipedia. In Mulwad et al. [15], the Wikitology [16] is used to link cells in a table to Wikipedia entities. Wikitology is an ontology which combines some existing manually-built knowledge systems such as DBpedia and Freebase [17]. They query the background LOD to generate initial lists of candidate classes for column headers and cell values and candidate properties for relations between columns. Then, they use a probabilistic graphical model to find the correlation between the column's headers, cell values, and relation assignments. The quality of the semantic data generated by this category of work is highly dependent to how well the data can be linked to the entities in LOD.

In Karma [18], a graph from learned semantic types and a domain ontology is built. Then the graph is used to map a data source to the ontology interactively. In this work, the system uses the knowledge from the pre-defined existing domain ontology to propose models to the user, who can correct them as needed. The system remembers the semantic type labels assigned by the user, however, it does not learn from the structure of previously modeled sources.

In terms of stream data, the aim is to automatically annotate real-world data flows, in real-time, with semantics that are already available before-hand (for the training dataset) [19]–[21] or not i.e., extract/uncover the real-world semantics on-the-fly, during the annotation process [22]. In a real-time stream processing and large-scale data analytics for IoT and Smart City applications' context, the semantic annotation process of heterogeneous data for automated discovery and knowledge-based processing is sometimes referred as data virtualization [23][24][25].

B. Ontology learning

Ontology learning concerns the process of constructing an ontology from data/information source(s), in an automatic or semi-automatic manner, to minimize or eliminate cost, effort and time-consuming human involvement [26]. The process extracts the concepts and relationships between them from a corpus of natural language text or other sources of data and information, and encodes them in an ontology language (e.g., OWL). As building ontologies manually is extremely labor-intensive and time-consuming, there is great motivation to fully automate the process in several application domains. A typical text-based process of ontology learning, starts by extracting terms and concepts from plain text using techniques, such as part-of-speech tagging and phrase chunking. Then, statistical or symbolic techniques are used to extract relation signatures, often based on pattern-based or definition-based hypernym/hyponym/meronym extraction techniques.

A representative work that learns and constructs ontologies from text documents is presented in Wang et al. [27], introducing an automatic learning approach to construct terminological ontologies based on different text documents. In Lin et al. [28], a learning approach that constructs an ontology automatically without the requiring training data is presented. Other related approaches include the learning of lightweight ontologies from query logs [29], aiming at the efficient retrieval of Semantic Web documents. In another related work [30], a new ontology is automatically constructed by utilizing representations of entities, their attributes and relations, learnt using unsupervised machine learning techniques on facts extracted from Wikipedia tables. Furthermore, a challenge in the automatic transformation of an RDB model into an ontology is how to label the relationships between concepts [31]–[33]. This challenge depends heavily on the correct extraction of the relationship types, since RDB models does not store the meaning of relationships between entities but it only indicates the existence of a link between them [33].

Several works have been conducted in providing sensor data with semantic annotations. In Sheth et al. [34] semantics are used to represent and structure real-world data, however, automatically transforming the raw data into the semantic representation in this work remains an open issue. Dietze et al. [35] describes the problem of symbolic grounding and the semantic sensor Web, and introduces an approach that uses conceptual spaces to bridge the gap between sensor measurements and symbolic ontologies in an automatic manner. In Stocker et al. [36] a system to identify and classify different semantic types of road vehicles passing a street is presented, using vibration sensors and machine learning algorithms. In Ganz et al. [22], a knowledge acquisition method is proposed that processes real-world stream data to automatically create and evolve domain ontologies, based on concepts-labeling rules that are automatically extracted from external sources.

C. *Ontology matching*

In recent years, ontology matching has received much attention in the Semantic Web community [37]. Ontology matching finds the correspondence between semantically related entities of different ontologies. Semantic annotation can benefit from some of the techniques developed for ontology matching. For example, instance-based ontology matching exploits similarities between instances of ontologies in the matching process. A semantic labeling algorithm can adopt the same idea to map the data of a new source to the classes and properties of a target ontology. Such an algorithm computes the similarity (e.g. cosine similarity between TF/IDF vectors) between the data of the new source and the data of the sources whose semantic models are known. Most of the work on ontology matching only finds simple correspondences such as equivalence and subsumption between ontology classes and properties. Therefore, the explicit relationships within the data elements are often missed when aligning the source data to the target ontology.

D. *Stream data mining*

Stream data, e.g., encoded in JSON, is mostly numerical and often with no rich (or any) metadata attached to it. Data arrives in a stream or streams, and if it is not processed immediately (or stored), it is lost. Moreover, the data arrives so rapidly that it is not feasible to store it all in active storage (i.e., in a conventional database), and then interact with it at the time of your choosing. The algorithms for processing streams involve summarization of the data, to make a useful sample of it and to filter it in order to eliminate most of the "undesirable" elements (e.g., stop words, noise), before it is annotated. Then the number of different elements in a stream is estimated using much less storage than would be required if all the elements were listed.

Knowledge acquisition requires several processing steps. Due to the large volume of real-world stream data, techniques are required to lower the amount (or dimensions) of the data input to make it manageable for processing algorithms such as clustering and statistical methods. In the domain of time-series analysis there has been a number of dimensionality reduction techniques such as Fast-Fourier transformation (FFT), Discrete Wavelete Transformation (DWT), Piecewise Aggregate Approximation (PAA), and Symbolic Aggregate ApproXimation (SAX). The comparative study by Ding et al. [38] reveals that SAX performs best in preserving the data features by remaining high dimension reduction (data compression).

SAX transforms time-series data into aggregated words that can be used for pattern detection and indexing. Since SAX was not developed for small constrained devices, authors in Ganz et al. [22] introduce Sensor-SAX, a modified version that has less data transmission in times of low activity in the sensor signal that is processed. In order to group similar types of patterns and events, clustering mechanisms are used. Cluster mechanisms do not require training data and can be unsupervised. However, the clustering methods rely on distance functions that map the data samples to a comparable space. The k-means clustering method provides fast computation of the groups even in large datasets. However, the biggest drawback is that the number of clusters (i.e., k) is an input parameter, and therefore should be known beforehand. In order to learn the ontological properties, a rule-mining approach can be used, similar to the one proposed in Hu et al. [39]. The authors aim at creating ontologies automatically by learning the logical rules to construct the ontology. In Ganz et al. [22] a rule learning approach is used, similar to the one of Hu et al. [39] to label the unnamed concepts in the ontology.

III. RELATED WORK

In the context of the work of Gao and Lianli [20], a Semantic Annotation and Activity Recognition (SAAR) approach is presented, integrating semantic annotation with Support Vector Machine (SVM) techniques to automatically identify animal behaviors from 3D accelerometry data streams. It enables biologists to visualize and correlate 3D accelerometer data streams with associated video streams. It also enables domain experts to accurately annotate segments of tri-axial accelerometer data streams, with standardized terms extracted from an activity ontology. These annotated data streams can then be used to dynamically train a hierarchical SVM activity classification model, which can be applied to new accelerometer data streams to automatically recognize specific activities. The approach requires a) significant human involvement, b) the creation of a training data set, and c) the use of predefined domain-specific ontologies.

Related approaches map each data value individually, typically by learning a model based on features extracted from the data using supervised machine-learning techniques. In the approach of Ramnandan et al [19], the difference is that it considers a holistic view of the data values corresponding to a semantic label, and uses techniques that treat this data in a collective manner. This way, it is possible to capture characteristic properties of the values associated with a semantic label as a whole. It supports both textual and numeric data analysis and proposes the top-k semantic labels along with associated confidence scores. For textual data, the TF-IDF-based approach is used, and for numeric data, the Kolmogorov-Smirnov (KS) statistical hypothesis test respectively. The semantics for the semantic annotation of data are automatically discovered, however the approach requires the existence of training sets, as well as of domain-specific ontologies that are used to label the training sets.

Taheriyan et al. [21] exploits external knowledge from specific domain ontologies and other semantic models learned from previously modeled sources (based on the idea that data sources in the same domain usually provide overlapping data) to automatically learn an expressive new semantic model for a new source. The new semantic model represents the semantics of the new data source in terms of the concepts and relationships defined by the exploited domain ontology/ies. The approach is based on training/sample data of the new data source against the mapped semantics of the domain ontology and the known semantic models. Although the approach can be used to learn rich semantic models from data, human involvement as well as the existence of external knowledge (domain ontology and other related semantic models) is needed. Also, the data used to evaluate the approach (museum domain) cannot be considered as the hard case of streaming data (numerical vs textual semantic labeling). Finally, supervised machine learning (training data sets) is used for the semantic labeling of the data.

Ganz et al. [22] introduces a knowledge acquisition method that processes real-world streaming data to automatically create and evolve domain ontologies, based on concept-labeling rules that are automatically extracted from external sources. They use an extended *k*-means clustering method and apply a statistic model (Markov chain model approach) to extract and link relevant concepts from the raw sensor data and represent them in the form of a domain ontology. A rule-based system is used to label the concepts and make them understandable for the human user or for the semantic analysis, reasoning tools and software. The approach is based on the abstraction of numerical values, creating higher-level concepts from the large amount of data produced by sensor devices. To do so, as in other related work [23], the symbolic aggregate approximation (SAX) dimensionality reduction mechanism [40] is used. The approach uses the extended version of the SAX algorithm, i.e., SensorSAX. The approach uses the SSN Ontology [41] as a starting point and extend it by extracting new insights from the raw sensor data to construct a topical ontology representing an extract of the observed domain.

IV. DESIGN DIRECTIONS

In this section we propose a set of design directions for future approaches, based on the specific techniques/methods of existing ones that stand-out as key choices towards achieving the highest positive impact in an automated semantic annotation framework for real-world voluminous stream (sensor) data. The aim is to design an approach that transforms raw sensor streaming data (e.g., "28/08/2017, 09.00, 1, 20, 10" or "28/08/2017, 22.00, 8, 90, 5") into meaningful semantics (e.g., "Calmness" or "Storm"), as automatically and accurately as possible, minimizing human involvement and the use of pre-defined existing domain-specific ontologies.

The focus of these design directions is towards automating (as much as possible) the transformation of raw stream data related to the continuous monitoring of moving entities (vehicles, ships, aircrafts), for instance, trajectories, weather conditions, and low-level events (e.g., start, stop, turn), to valuable annotations of higher-levels of abstraction such as: change of course (a change in the direction that vessels are moving), three-point turn (the act of turning a vessel around in a limited space by moving in a series of back and forward arcs), cold wave (a wave of unusually cold weather), calmness (an absence of strong winds or rain), atmospheric phenomenon (a physical phenomenon associated with the atmosphere). Moreover, the focus is towards investigating how these automatically generated abstractions may be used in a combined way to infer and model even more higher levels of abstractions and critical high-level events such as: trade route (a route followed by traders, usually in caravans), migration route (the geographic route along which populations of animals/humans customarily migrate), flight path (the path of a rocket or projectile or aircraft through the air), collision (an accident resulting from violent impact of a moving object), crash, wreck (a serious accident, usually involving one or more vehicles).

The hardest problem of a data-to-semantics approach that uses an unsupervised machine learning algorithm for leaning concepts from numerical data, is probably the problem of automatically labeling the learned unnamed classes and properties. In the absence of a trained data-to-semantics learning algorithm, a rule-based mechanism must be applied on clustered symbolized SAX patterns in order to automatically add names to the unlabeled concepts. Such rules can be manually defined (increasing however the undesired, in our case, human involvement), or to construct a mechanism that can automatically extract those rules. The aim is to develop such a mechanism in order to automate the process of constructing such naming rules, possible encoded in the Semantic Web Rule Language (SWRL), towards supporting the automated concept and property naming task. For instance, such a rule set in the maritime/safe-shipping application domain may look like the ones presented in Table 1.

TABLE 1. EXAMPLE RULE SET IN THE MARITIME/SAFE-SHIPPING DOMAIN

isAISdata(?ad) & isSimpleEvent (?se) & equal(?se, 'turn')	=> VesselInTurn
isAISdata(?ad) & isSimpleEvent (?se) & equal(?se, 'lost communication')	=> VesselInLostCommunication
isWeatherData(?wd) & (swell_height_m(?sh) & greaterThanOrEqual(?sh, 8)) & (wind_speed_kmph(?ws) & greaterThanOrEqual(?ws, 90)) & (visibility(?v) & lessThanOrEqual(?v, 5))	=> Storm
badWeatherConditions & vesselInTurn & ???	=> WeatherForcedChangeOfCourse (inferred knowledge)
badWeatherConditions & vesselInLostCommunication & ???	=> VesselInDanger (inferred knowledge)

Natural Language Processing (NLP) techniques and heuristic rules will be further incorporated in order to assist the process of ontology construction. For instance, the

Vessel-related concepts learned from the rule-based mechanism, VesselInTurn and VesselInDanger, can be classified under WordNet-extracted learned concept Vessel, Storm under WeatherConditions, and WeatherForcedChangeOfCourse under ChangeOfCourse. Furthermore, WordNet (open multilingual knowledge graph) semantic relations that hold between the extracted concepts can be further analyzed in order to introduce labels for the unnamed properties as well.

A two-step process is proposed and presented below in an abstract design level. The first step concerns the learning of the ontology from a specific time-window of the stream data (Figure 1) and the second concerns the semantic data annotation of the data stream (Figure 2) i.e., the use of the learned ontology for the computation and refinement of data-to-ontology mappings of the data stream. The input of the process is: a) streaming data, mainly numerical, and b) external generic semantic lexicons or knowledge graphs. The proposed abstract steps of the process are:

1. Ontology Learning (Figure 1)
   - 1.1 Pre-process stream data:
     - Transform into a specific working format (e.g., from CSV or JSON to RDF),
     - Distinguish data between textual D_{ST} (e.g., vessels' historical data) and numerical D_{SN} (e.g., AIS and weather data).
   - 1.2 Define a time window T for a subset D_S of the stream data D that will be used for the automated learning of the ontology.
   - 1.3 Analyze data for D_S using external knowledge (e.g., WordNet) and a data summarization method (e.g., SAX).
     - For textual data D_{ST}: Methods for indexing and searching of documents (TF-IDF-based cosine-similarity method). The labeling algorithm will use the cosine similarity between TF/IDF vectors of WordNet documents (focused subset of synsets) and the input document to predict candidate semantic types (WordNet senses)
     - For numerical data D_{SN}: combined analysis of a) data values (using SAX) and b) data attribute names (using lexical and semantic analysis with the aid of external semantic lexicon such as WordNet or BabelNet)
   - 1.4 Automatically construct the top-*k* candidate ontological models M_k, for D_S, using a rule-based entity naming method.
   - 1.5 Present user the candidate semantic models M_k and allow the selection and refinement of the preferred *k* model i.e., the final learned ontology.
2. Semantic data annotation (Figure 2)
   - 2.1 Repeat step 1.1 for the rest of the stream data.
   - 2.2 Repeat step 1.3 using also the learned ontology as input to the data analysis method.
   - 2.3 Automatically compute data-to-ontology mappings *m* for D_S.
   - 2.4 Based on user feedback allow the manual correction/refinement of one of more mappings of *m*.
   - 2.5 Automatically (re)compute the mappings, based on users' corrections/refinements.

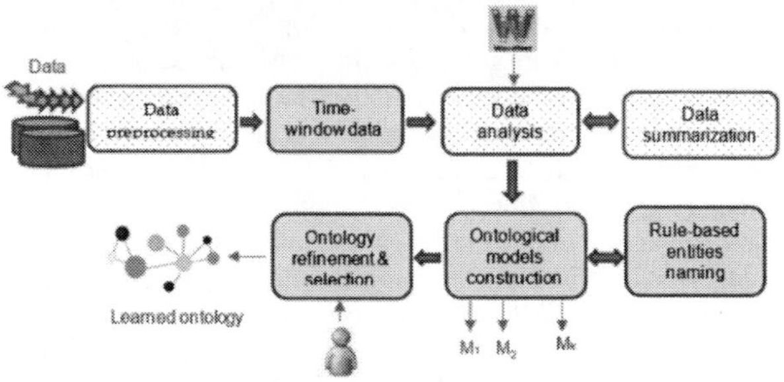

Figure 1. Ontology learning from time-window stream data

The output of the proposed process is: a) a learned-from-data domain ontology (e.g., encoded in OWL/RDF, and b) data-to-ontology mappings (e.g., encoded in R2RML).

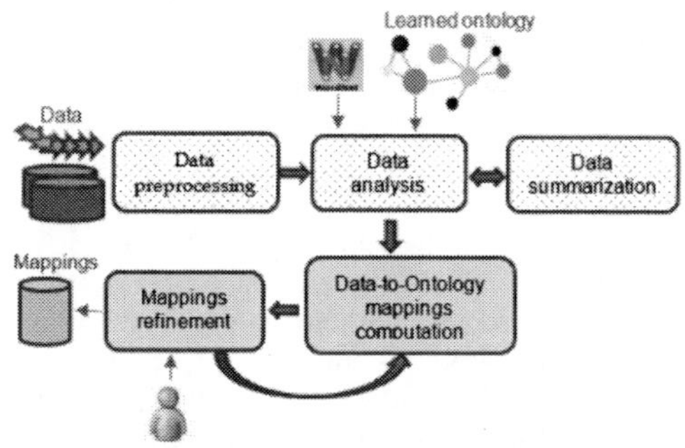

Figure 2. Semantic data annotation

The aim is to generate the learned-from-data domain ontology not just as a data-focused subset of the external lexicon source (e.g., WordNet, BabelNet), but a rich and expressive (as possible) lexicon-based ontology that reflects the intended meaning of analyzed data.

V. CONCLUSIONS AND RECCOMENDATIONS

The main problems related to the semantic annotation of stream data are: a) how to automatically construct a semantic model by learning the semantics 'hidden' in the data, b) given a semantic model, how to automatically, accurately and on-time compute the corresponding data-to-semantics mappings, in a continuous and iterative fashion.

We conjecture that there is a real need to develop approaches based on issues discussed in this paper, as well as on specific methods of existing approaches that stand-out as key choices towards achieving the highest positive impact in an automated semantic annotation framework for real-world voluminous stream (sensor) data. The need is to transform raw sensor streaming data into meaningful semantics, as automatically and accurately as possible, minimizing human involvement and use of pre-defined existing domain-specific ontologies.

The hardest problem, as identified in this paper, is related to the data-to-semantics approach that uses an unsupervised machine learning algorithm for learning concepts from numerical data: it is the problem of automatically labeling (adding names to) the learned unnamed classes and properties. In the absence of a trained data-to-semantics learning algorithm, a rule-based mechanism must be applied on clustered symbolized SAX patterns to automatically add names to the unlabeled learned concepts. Such rules can be manually defined (increasing however human involvement), or to construct a mechanism that can automatically extract them.

Based on the discussion and findings presented in this paper, the following key research actions are recommended to be integrated in related frameworks:

- Data synopses (summaries) from stream data sources, archival data, as well as detected and forecasted trajectories and events must be semantically annotated, transformed into a common form and be integrated. This task will exploit knowledge models and meta-data schemes that will be incorporated in the infrastructure, keeping them permanently up-to-date.
- Advance the related research towards automating, as much as possible, the transformation of raw stream data related to the continuous monitoring of moving entities (vehicles, ships, aircrafts), for instance, trajectories, weather conditions, and low-level events (e.g., start, stop, turn), to valuable annotations of higher-levels of abstraction.
- Develop a method for automatically learning a real-world domain-specific ontology that is needed for the semantic annotation of steam data related to moving objects' trajectories, weather conditions, and low-level events, minimizing human involvement and the usage of pre-defined external domain-specific semantics, as much as possible.
- Develop a set of novel NLP techniques and heuristic rules in order to assist the process of automated ontology construction.

REFERENCES

[1] D. Ritze and C. Bizer, "Matching web tables to DBpedia - a feature utility study," in Proceedings of the 20th International Conference on Extending Database Technology, 2017, pp 210-221.

[2] A. M. Cregan, "Symbol Grounding for the Semantic Web," in The Semantic Web: Research and Applications: 4th European Semantic Web Conference, ESWC 2007, Innsbruck, Austria, June 3-7, 2007. Proceedings, E. Franconi, M. Kifer, and W. May, Eds. Berlin, Heidelberg: Springer Berlin Heidelberg, 2007, pp. 429–442.

[3] OntoText, "Semantic Annotation example." [Online]. Available: http://ontotext.com/knowledgehub/fundamentals/semantic-annotation/. [Retrieved: Aug, 2017].

[4] S. Sahoo, et al., "A Survey of Current Approaches for Mapping of Relational Databases to RDF," W3C, 2009.

[5] C. Bizer and A. Seaborne, "D2RQ-treating non-RDF databases as virtual RDF graphs," in Proceedings of the 3rd International Semantic Web Conference (ISWC2004), 2004.

[6] D. Calvanese, et al., "Ontop: {A}nswering {SPARQL} {Q}ueries over {R}elational {D}atabases," Semant. Web J., vol. 8, no. 3, pp. 471–487, 2017.

[7] S. Das, S. Sundara, and R. Cyganiak, "R2RML: RDB to RDF Mapping Language." 2012.

[8] S. Polfliet and R. Ichise, "Automated Mapping Generation for Converting Databases into Linked Data," in Proceedings of the 2010 International Conference on Posters & Demonstrations Track - Volume 658, 2010, pp. 173–176.

[9] J. Wang, H. Wang, Z. Wang, and K. Q. Zhu, "Understanding Tables on the Web," in Conceptual Modeling: 31st International Conference ER 2012, Florence, Italy, October 15-18, 2012. Proceedings, P. Atzeni, D. Cheung, and S. Ram, Eds. Berlin, Heidelberg: Springer Berlin Heidelberg, 2012, pp. 141–155.

[10] G. Limaye, S. Sarawagi, and S. Chakrabarti, "Annotating and Searching Web Tables Using Entities, Types and Relationships," Proc. VLDB Endow., vol. 3, no. 1–2, pp. 1338–1347, 2010.

[11] Max Planck Institute for Informatics, "YAGO Ontology." [Online]. Available: http://www.mpi-inf.mpg.de/yago-naga/yago. [Retrieved: Aug, 2017].

[12] P. Venetis et al., "Recovering Semantics of Tables on the Web," Proc. VLDB Endow., vol. 4, no. 9, pp. 528–538, 2011.

[13] E. Muñoz, A. Hogan, and A. Mileo, "Triplifying wikipedia's tables," CEUR Workshop Proceedings, vol. 1057. 2013.

[14] S. Auer, C. Bizer, G. Kobilarov, J. Lehmann, R. Cyganiak, and Z. Ives, "DBpedia: A nucleus for a Web of open data," in Lecture Notes in Computer Science (including subseries Lecture Notes in Artificial Intelligence and Lecture Notes in Bioinformatics), 2007.

[15] V. Mulwad, T. W. Finin, and A. Joshi, "Semantic Message Passing for Generating Linked Data from Tables," in International Semantic Web Conference, 2013.

[16] Z. Syed and T. Finin, "Creating and Exploiting a Hybrid Knowledge Base for Linked Data," vol. 129. pp. 3–21, 2011.

[17] K. Bollacker, C. Evans, P. Paritosh, T. Sturge, and J. Taylor, "Freebase: a collaboratively created graph database for structuring human knowledge," in In SIGMOD Conference, 2008, pp. 1247–1250.

[18] C. A. Knoblock et al., "Semi-automatically Mapping Structured Sources into the Semantic Web," in The Semantic Web: Research and Applications: 9th Extended Semantic Web Conference, ESWC 2012, Heraklion, Crete, Greece, May 27-31, 2012. Proceedings, E. Simperl, P. Cimiano, A. Polleres, O. Corcho, and V. Presutti, Eds. Berlin, Heidelberg: Springer Berlin Heidelberg, 2012, pp. 375–390.

[19] S. K. Ramnandan, A. Mittal, C. A. Knoblock, and P. Szekely, "Assigning Semantic Labels to Data Sources," in The Semantic Web. Latest Advances and New Domains: 12th European Semantic Web Conference, ESWC 2015, Portoroz, Slovenia, May 31 -- June 4, 2015. Proceedings, F. Gandon, M. Sabou, H. Sack, C. d'Amato, P. Cudré-Mauroux, and A. Zimmermann, Eds. Cham: Springer International Publishing, 2015, pp. 403–417.

[20] L. Gao and Lianli, "Semantic annotation and reasoning for sensor data streams," The University of Queensland, 2015.

[21] M. Taheriyan, C. A. Knoblock, P. Szekely, and J. L. Ambite, "Learning the Semantics of Structured Data Sources," Web Semant., vol. 37, no. C, pp. 152–169, 2016.

[22] F. Ganz, P. Barnaghi, and F. Carrez, "Automated Semantic Knowledge Acquisition From Sensor Data," IEEE Syst. J., vol. 10, no. 3, pp. 1214–1225, 2016.

[23] S. Kolozali, et al., "Semantic Data Stream Annotation for Automated Framework. D3.1 Report. Real-Time IoT Stream Processing and Large-scale Data Analytics for Smart City Applications, 'City Pulse' Collaborative Project, FP7-SMARTCITIES-2013, GRANT AGREEMENT No 609035," 2013.

[24] S. Kolozali, M. Bermudez-Edo, D. Puschmann, F. Ganz, and P. Barnaghi, "A Knowledge-Based Approach for Real-Time IoT Data Stream Annotation and Processing," in Proceedings of the 2014 IEEE International Conference on Internet of Things(iThings), and IEEE Green Computing and Communications (GreenCom) and IEEE Cyber, Physical and Social Computing (CPSCom), 2014, pp. 215–222.

[25] C. Bizer, J. Volz, G. Kobilarov, and M. Gaedke, "Silk - A Link Discovery Framework for the Web of Data," in 18th International World Wide Web Conference, 2009.

[26] G. Petasis, V. Karkaletsis, G. Paliouras, A. Krithara, and E. Zavitsanos, "Ontology Population and Enrichment: State of the Art," in Knowledge-Driven Multimedia Information Extraction and Ontology Evolution: Bridging the Semantic Gap, G. Paliouras, C. D. Spyropoulos, and G. Tsatsaronis, Eds. Berlin, Heidelberg: Springer Berlin Heidelberg, 2011, pp. 134–166.

[27] W. Wang, P. Mamaani Barnaghi, and A. Bargiela, "Probabilistic Topic Models for Learning Terminological Ontologies," IEEE Trans. Knowl. Data Eng., vol. 22, no. 7, pp. 1028–1040, 2010.

[28] Z. Lin, R. Lu, Y. Xiong, and Y. Zhu, "Learning Ontology Automatically Using Topic Model," in Proceedings of the 2012 International Conference on Biomedical Engineering and Biotechnology, 2012, pp. 360–363.

[29] K. Kotis, A. Papasalouros, and M. Maragoudakis, "Mining query-logs towards learning useful kick-off ontologies: an incentive to semantic web content creation," Int. J. Knowl. Eng. Data Min., vol. 1, pp. 303–330, 2011.

[30] C. Sekhar Bhagavatula, "Learning Semantics of WikiTables," Department of Electrical Engineering and Computer Science, Northwestern University, 2013.

[31] K. Andrejs and B. Arkady, "Learning Ontology from Object-Relational Database," Inf. Technol. Manag. Sci., vol. 18, no. 1, pp. 78–83, 2015.

[32] M. Pasha and A. Sattar, "Building Domain Ontologies From Relational Database Using Mapping Rules," Int. J. Intell. Eng. Syst., vol. 5, 2012.

[33] B. El Idrissi, S. Baïna, and K. Baïna, "Ontology Learning from Relational Database: How to Label the Relationships Between Concepts?," in Beyond Databases, Architectures and Structures: 11th International Conference, BDAS 2015, Ustro{ń}, Poland, May 26-29, 2015, Proceedings, S. Kozielski, D. Mrozek, P. Kasprowski, B. Małysiak-Mrozek, and D. Kostrzewa, Eds. Cham: Springer International Publishing, 2015, pp. 235–244.

[34] A. Sheth, C. Henson, and S. S. Sahoo, "Semantic Sensor Web," IEEE Internet Comput., vol. 12, no. 4, pp. 78–83, 2008.

[35] S. Dietze and J. Domingue, "Bridging between sensor measurements and symbolic ontologies through conceptual spaces," in 1st International Workshop on the Semantic Sensor Web (SemSensWeb 2009) at The 6th Annual European Semantic Web Conference (ESWC 2009), 2009.

[36] M. Stocker, M. Rönkkö, and M. Kolehmainen, "Making sense of sensor data using ontology: A discussion for road vehicle classification." 2012.

[37] P. Shvaiko and J. Euzenat, "Ontology Matching: State of the Art and Future Challenges," IEEE Trans. Knowl. Data Eng., vol. 25, pp. 158–176, 2013.

[38] H. Ding, G. Trajcevski, P. Scheuermann, X. Wang, and E. Keogh, "Querying and Mining of Time Series Data: Experimental Comparison of Representations and Distance Measures," Proc. VLDB Endow., vol. 1, no. 2, pp. 1542–1552, 2008.

[39] W. Hu, J. Chen, H. Zhang, and Y. Qu, "Learning Complex Mappings Between Ontologies," in Proceedings of the 2011 Joint International Conference on The Semantic Web, 2012, pp. 350–357.

[40] J. Lin, E. Keogh, S. Lonardi, and B. Chiu, "A Symbolic Representation of Time Series, with Implications for Streaming Algorithms," in Proceedings of the 8th ACM SIGMOD Workshop on Research Issues in Data Mining and Knowledge Discovery, 2003, pp. 2–11.

[41] M. Compton et al., "The SSN ontology of the W3C semantic sensor network incubator group," Web Semant. Sci. Serv. Agents World Wide Web, vol. 17, pp. 25–32, 2012.

Interoperability in IoT: A Vital Key Factor to Create the "Social Network" of Things.

Antonios Pliatsios, Christos Goumopoulos
Information and Communication Systems Engineering
Dept., University of the Aegean
Samos, Greece
e-mail: icsdd18007@icsd.aegean.gr, goumop@aegean.gr

Konstantinos Kotis
Dept. of Cultural Technology and Communication
University of the Aegean
Mytilene, Greece
e-mail: kotis@aegean.gr

Abstract— **The Internet of Things (IoT) is a concept that describes the connection of various devices with built-in sensors and communication equipment to achieve the collection and transmission of data in a network. IoT devices are increasing with geometric progress, and ensuring interoperability and handling of the enormous heterogeneous data generated is of major importance for the creation of intelligent applications and services. This paper presents the state of art and current solutions on the issues of interoperability in the IoT domain, as well as the challenges and open issues. Finally, a discussion is provided on what future research should focus on and solutions are outlined to achieve interoperability in IoT systems that can lead to a "Social Network" of Things.**

Keywords- Internet of Things; Interoperability; Semantic Web Technologies; IoT platforms; ontologies; Social Network of Things; middleware; Open Linked Data, ontology alignment; reasoning mechanisms.

I. INTRODUCTION

The Internet of Things (IoT) is the next big step in the field of technology. New technologies are being developed to meet the ever-increasing demands of a new digital world where heterogeneous devices will be connected, forming a part of an IoT ecosystem [1]. IoT has the potential to bring out many possibilities of natural objects, which until recently were considered impossible. This has a significant impact on society, economic growth and in the informatics sector.

The IoT devices collect a huge amount of data using microcontrollers and sensors embedded in them connecting home users, businesses, public facilities, and business systems. These data are multimodal including video streams, images, and text data. The density of systems and technologies is becoming increasingly high and ensuring interoperability and handling of such large scale heterogeneous data will be a key factor in the development of smart applications in several areas, such as Smart Cities, Smart Homes, Smart Health, Smart Agriculture, etc. [2].

According to Noura et al. [3], the interoperability on the Internet of Things relates to the layers below: 1) Device, 2) Syntactic, 3) Networks, 4) Semantic and 5) Platform architecture. The difficulty in the communication between the various devices is not only related to the diversity of devices but also is about the way data is labelled, how devices are represented and modelled, as well as, it is about the architecture type of the different systems.

There are several definitions in the literature for interoperability. From all these definitions, we will focus on the one that is most important about our context. The IEEE defines interoperability as "the ability of two or more systems or components to exchange information and use the information exchanged" [4]. Moreover, we can define interoperability as a measure of the degree to which diverse systems, organizations, and/or individuals are able to work together to achieve a common goal [5].

The "Internet of Things" concept implies that all Things are harmoniously connected so they can communicate and they are also easily accessible from the Internet to deliver services to end-users [6]. But, to create a new "Social Network" of Things, a truly connected world, that harmoniously connects applications to Smart Homes, Smart Cities, Smart Agriculture, Smart Health, etc., it will require a real horizontal integration of devices, applications, systems and platforms.

Firstly, in this work, we attempt to define the problem of interoperability in IoT systems and then we report the current developments on this issue (Section II). Following the challenges and open issues (Section III) and existing solutions (Section IV) are discussed. As a contribuiton, solutions are proposed to enhance interoperability in the IoT field and ideas are presented on what future research should focus on (Section V) before our conclusion (Section VI).

II. INTEROPERABILITY LEVELS IN IOT

IoT interoperability is a multifaceted issue and the solutions to be addressed must be in line with many factors that are also referred to the literature as interoperability levels. A taxonomy of interoperability for IoT is based on four levels: technical, syntactical, semantic and organizational interoperability [3][7]. Below we will analyze each level individually.

A. Technical Interoperability

Technical Interoperability includes the first three levels of classification, as proposed by Noura et al. and it includes the interoperability of devices, the interoperability of networks and the interoperability of platforms.

a) Device Interoperability

Devices that are integrated into the world of IoT are becoming more and more ubiquitous. These Smart Devices / Things are either devices with a lot of computing power like smartphones and Raspberry Pi, or devices with built-in microswitches and low-power actuators, such as Arduino, Wispmote, Libelium, and others [7]. The problem of interoperability at this level is due to the inability of all these devices with different architectures and power levels to interact properly.

b) Network Interoperability

Moreover, due to the variety and heterogeneity of IoT devices, many communication protocols have been developed to cover all requirements in the IoT market. Home appliances, such as smart air conditioners, refrigerators, televisions, etc., use Wifi and 2G / 3G / 4G cellular communications. Other mobile devices use more low-power and short-range wireless technologies, such as Bluetooth, ZigBee, Beacons, RFID belonging to the WBAN IEEE 802.15.6 family. While a new category created for sensor applications is that of long-range and Low-Power Wide-Area Networks (LPWAN). Some of them are the wireless technologies LoRaWan, SigFox, NB-IoT [8]. This level of interoperability refers to the difficulty of communication of the IoT devices using different communication protocols.

c) Platform Interoperability

The IoT platform is a comprehensive suite of services that facilitates services, such as development, maintenance, analysis, visualization and intelligent decision-making capabilities in an IoT application. Interoperability issues of IoT platforms are because many of these systems are tailored for specific IoT applications. Some of the most popular platforms are Google Cloud Platform, IBM Watson IoT, ThingWorx, oneM2M, Microsoft Azure Cloud, ThingSpeak [9]. Each of the above follows its data sharing policy, it has its operating system, and this has the effect of creating heterogeneous IoT systems and increasing the problem of interoperability.

B. Syntactic Interoperability

Syntactic interoperability refers to the interoperability of data formats and encodings used in any exchange of information or services between heterogeneous systems and IoT entities. Such forms of standardization are, for example, XML, JSON and RDF. The encoding and decoding of messages are done using editorial rules, defined by a grammar. The problem of syntactic interoperability arises due to the great variety of grammars that each architecture employs and consequently, the IoT devices could not communicate properly.

C. Semantic Interoperability

Semantic interoperability is characterized as the ability to transmit information, data and knowledge among agents, services and applications in a meaningful way, inside and outside the Semantic Web [10][11]. It is the description of smart devices according to their data, services, and capabilities in mechanically comprehensible form using a common vocabulary. Semantic interoperability is achieved when the exchange of data is made harmoniously independent of the structure of the original data giving a common meaning [12]. This can be done either by existing standards or agreements on the form and importance of data or can be done using a common vocabulary either in a schema and/or in an ontological approach [13].

The use of an ontology is the most common way of adding semantics to the IoT data. It is a way of modelling information that extends the concept of the Semantic Web into the Internet of Things. The most important Semantic Web technologies have been standardized by the World Wide Web Consortium and are Resource Description Format (RDF), a lightweight data metadata model for describing ontology properties, SPARQL, and the RDF Query Language [14].

Existing solutions [11][14] suggest the use of unified ontologies to address semantic interoperability issues and automation related to the heterogeneity of data. However, the multiple possible consolidations developed by field experts [2] pose many challenges as each consolidated ontology proposes its autonomous classification. It is therefore imperative to improve ontology matching and ontology alignment [15][16] to discover the most appropriate strategies that can overcome the heterogeneity problem in the Internet of Things and bridge the semantic gap between IoT entities at the level of Information / Applications.

D. Organizational Interoperability

Organizational interoperability refers to the successful organization of a system to communicate effectively and to transmit the information in a harmonious manner [10]. To do this, the other three levels of interoperability: technical, syntactic and semantic interoperability, must be ensured. High organizational interoperability means that information has been properly transmitted irrespective of the heterogeneity of devices, networks, types of compilation and modelling of information [17].

III. CHALLENGES

With the rapid expansion of various heterogeneous devices and systems, addressing the interoperability challenges is a major issue. The IoT devices must be compatible with their devices communicate with this and this is only possible if they follow common protocols and communication standards. Below we present the most important interoperability challenges in IoT.

A. Heterogeneous Connected Devices/Things

One of the most important challenges in IoT systems is the interoperability of connected devices. Some of the most important issues are:

- Heterogeneous equipment from different manufacturers: Devices not manufactured by the same manufacturer cannot communicate correctly [18].
- Incompatibility between different platforms. Some of them are Evrythng (www.evrythng.com), ThingWorx

(www.thingworx.com), Xively (www.xively.com), Google Cloud IoT, Yaler (yaler.net), Microsoft Azure IoT [9].
- Incompatibility of different versions: Newer devices do not take backward compatibility issues.
- Different communication protocols / formats (IEEE 802.11, IEEE 802.15, LoRaWan, SigFox).

B. *Multimodal, High Heteogeinety Data*

IoT Systems collect data from different distributed sensors. These data are multimodal, including heterogeneous data, such as video streams, images, audio, and simple text [2]. How to integrate these distributed data from multisource is a key challenge for IoT development and for implementation of new innovative smart applications.

Moreover, communication between heterogeneous devices generates a large volume of real-time, high-speed, and uninterrupted data streams. These data streams include structured, semi-structured and unstructured data. When heterogeneous and various sensor data are acquired, multisource data should be merged to create a comprehensive and meaningful view for further utility [19].

C. *Syntactic interoperability between Things*

As discussed previously, syntactic interoperability involves packet and data networking mechanisms. Thus, when the above challenges are overcome, there is still a need to ensure that the data flow is interoperable between different networks and between a combination of devices. Translation functions to networks or on some devices, gateways or in the form of intermediate software sitting on the edge of one network are most likely to be necessary [20].

Moreover, IoT frameworks prefer to use popular and tried-and-tested solutions to increase syntactic interoperability. These solutions include the messaging protocols CoAP, XMPP, AMQP, MQTT, DDS and Hy-LP, as well as the DPWS, UPnP, and OSGi [21]. However, these solutions only offer cross-domain compatibility and usually operate as closed silos with a close application focus, enforcing specific data formats and interfaces.

D. *Semantically Incompatible Information Models*

As mentioned in the previous section, ensuring semantic interoperability is very important to address the inability to exchange and reuse data. Unfortunately, even today, IoT systems consist of semantically incompatible information models, such as incompatible general ontologies that offer different descriptions or even understandings of resources and processes, and thus are a barrier to the development and adoption of the IoT.

Most of the existing semantic tools and techniques, such as Linked Data, ontology alignment and ontology matching [14][15] have been created primarily for Internet resources. Existing models provide the basic description frameworks, but alignment between different models and frameworks are required. In addition, the capacity of the natural environment and the resource constraints on IoT systems have not been taken into account [16]. Future work in this area should provide capability, security and scalability and provide solutions that are easily adapted to limited and distributed resource environments.

IV. EXISTING SOLUTIONS

A significant research effort has been devoted to providing solutions in the direction of increasing interoperability at all four levels presented in Section III. In this section, we examine solutions provided by six related projects (AGILE, BiG-IoT, VICINITY, Open-IoT, INTER-IoT, and Machine-to-Machine Measurement (M3) Framework). These six projects are developing interoperability solutions at different interoperability levels and for this purpose were chosen to be analyzed in this particular work.

A. *BIG-IoT*

BiG-IoT [22][23] focus on addressing the semantic and organizational levels of IoT interoperability issues by creating the BiG-IoT API. It is about a generic web platform that unifies multiple platforms and different middlewares.
The Web API and semantic information representation models are defined in cooperation with the Web of Things Interest Group at W3C, expanding the standards of this community. The project has chosen schema.org as a basic vocabulary of concepts.

Through the API, which has a defined architecture, it is easier to create applications and services for heterogeneous platforms. To increase the level of interoperability at semantic, but especially at the organizational level the IoT API is framed by the following functions [19][24]:
- Identity management for registering resources.
- Discover resources according to user-defined search criteria.
- Access metadata, and data (download data as well as publish / record feeds).
- Work with forwarding commands in Things.
- Vocabulary management for semantic descriptions of concepts.
- Security, including identity management, authorization and key management.
- Billing that allows you to make money through payment and billing mechanisms.

B. *INTER-IoT*

The INTER-IoT project aims to comprehensively address the lack of interoperability in the IoT realm by proposing a full-fledged approach facilitating "voluntary interoperability" at any level of IoT platforms and across any IoT application domain, thus guaranteeing a seamless integration of heterogeneous IoT technology [23][25].

INTER-IoT is based on the above main functionalities to address technical and syntactic interoperability:

- Techniques and tools for providing interoperability among and across each layer of IoT platforms.
- A global framework called INTER-FW for programming and managing interoperable IoT platforms, including INTER-API and several interoperability tools for every layer.
- Engineering Methodology based on the CASE tool for IoT platforms integration/interconnection.

Regarding the main types of interoperability (technical, syntactic, semantic), INTER-IoT enables all of them [18]. Universal syntactic and semantic interoperability among any platform with different data formats and ontologies is possible through the INTER-IoT DS2DS solution. Moreover, other INTER-IoT layers (D2D and N2N) can provide organizational interoperability among smart elements, enabling connectivity to the network.

C. *VICINITY*

The VICINITY project aims at interfacing cloud-based platforms from various application domains by providing "interoperability as a service" for the Internet of Things [26]. The proposed interoperable platform is presented as a virtual neighborhood, a "social network" where users can share access to their smart objects without losing control. The project team has thoroughly reviewed all existing standards and platforms, selecting those needed to build a service or increase interoperability.

The project is not so concerned with technical interoperability. For communication between devices, wireless networks like Wi-Fi and ZigBee are mainly used. VICINITY's main goal is to increase semantic interoperability. Using the standard W3C Web Language Ontology, specific ontologies are developed in a variety of areas, such as ontologies for energy and building, etc., extending the SAREF reference ontology [27] interoperability.

VICINITY ontology network is composed of cross-domain ontologies, addressing the modelling of general concepts like time, space, web Things. It will represent the information for exchanging IoT descriptor data between peers. Domain-oriented ontologies aim to cover vertical Domains, such as Health, Transport, Buildings, etc.

D. *AGILE*

The AGILE project builds a modular open-source interoperable Gateway solution (hardware and software gateway) for the IoT focusing on the physical layer, network communication layer, processing, storage, and application layers [22]. The AGILE software modules are addressing functions, such as device management, communication networks like area and sensor networks and solution for distributed storage. Moreover, AGILE approaches include security features that allow users to share data in a trusted way.

The AGILE project focuses on technical interoperability both at hardware and software level [23][25]. Within the project, various popular and low-cost technologies, such as Raspberry Pi are being developed and expanded. This creates the "Gateway Maker", a proposal to create interoperable gateways that will be used for multi-purpose and heterogeneous purposes. At the same time, the project provides open-source code and a web-based environment (Node-Red) for developers to develop new, innovative applications. The project does not address any approach to the semantic and organizational level of interoperability.

E. *Open-IoT*

Open-IoT focuses on increasing semantic interoperability [28]. In the framework of the project, a middleware platform was created that allows semantic integration of applications on the cloud. For information modelling, the ontology of W3C (SSN) sensor networks are used as a common standard for the semantic integration of various IoT systems. Appropriate infrastructures collect and semantically comment on the data of the different sensors. Also, another semantic technique called Linked Data is used to enrich the data and interface it.

Open-IoT innovates with other programs as it implements a platform with modules for collecting data and applications in cloud computing infrastructures, modules for creating semantically interoperable applications, and applications for mobile sensors. The implementation of semantic techniques in the cloud is something that adds value to the project and makes it stand out from other similar solution. These functionalities provide a basis for the development of novel applications in the areas of smart cities and mobile crowdsensing, while also enabling large scale IoT experimentation and increase the level of organizational interoperability. The project does not address any approach to the technical and syntactic level of interoperability.

F. *Machine-to-Machine Measurement (M3) Framework*

The M3 Framework project focuses on addressing the lack of semantic interoperability in IoT. The framework of the project assists the developers in semantically annotating M2M data and in building innovate applications by reasoning on M2M data originating from heterogeneous IoT systems and domains. To increase the level of interoperability at syntactic, but especially at the semantic level the M3 Framework is framed by the following layers [30]:

- Perception layer, which consists of physical IoT devices, such as sensors, actuators and RFID tags.
- Data acquisition layer, which focus on collecting raw data from IoT devices/sensors and converting them in a unified way, such as RDF/XML compliant with the M3 ontology. These formats are compliant with the M3 ontology, an extension of the W3C SSN Observation Value concept to provide a basis for reasoning.
- Persistence layer, which takes over to store M3 in a database to store semantic sensor data which called triple store.

- Knowledge management layer, which is responsible for finding, indexing, designing, reusing and combining domain-specific knowledge, such as ontologies and datasets to update M3 domain ontologies, datasets and rules.
- Reasoning layer, which infers new knowledge using reasoning engines and M3 rules extracted from Sensor-based Linked Open Rules (S-LOR) [31].
- Knowledge query layer executes SPARQL (a SQLlike language) queries on inferred sensor data.
- Application layer, which employs an application (running on smart devices) to parse and display the results to end-users.

V. DISCUSSION

To conclude the degree of interoperability maturity, we summarize in Table I the tools of state-of-art platforms that were analyzed in section IV, which attempt to solve interoperability issues at the layers discussed in Section II.

At technical and syntactic level AGILE, VICINITY and INTER-IoT attempt to provide solutions by creating Generic Gateways and device to device modules that integrate several wireless and wired technologies. All of these need to be incorporated into supported technologies like families of Low Power and Wide Area wireless networks (LoRaWan, SigFox, etc.), as well as other short-range wireless indoor technologies, such as Beacons.

A recurring aspect is that most efforts are focused on addressing the semantic interoperability challenge. VICINITY platform uses the standard W3C Web Language Ontology and implements cross-domain ontologies, whereas Open-IoT extends SSN ontology, and uses semantic tools such as Linked Data. BiG-IoT expands the standards of WoT and uses vocabulary management for handling semantics tools. Moreover, INTER-IoT increases semantic interoperability compared to the rest of the platforms by introducing different data formats and ontologies through the INTER-IoT DS2DS solution. In addition, M3 Framework Project addressing the semantic interoperability by innovative semantic tools, such as M3 ontology tools, reasoning engines and M3 rules extracted from S-LOR.

The solutions developed in this direction are promising, but they are still at an early stage. The proposed frameworks do not take into account the limitations of IoT systems, i.e., low device resources, energy consumption, mobility, etc. Moreover, the ontologies that are created are complicated and not interoperable with each other and focus mainly on the interoperability of specific fields rather than on a general solution. Besides that, the tools for ontology alignment and ontology merging, solutions that can radically improve interoperability levels, have not been particularly emphasized. Certain future research should focus on this direction so that future ontology engineers are given powerful "light" tools, such as ontology alignment tools for low-power devices or tools to implement "light" ontologies for cross-domains.

In addition, as already mentioned, organizational interoperability will be realized provided that all other interoperability levels are properly addressed. In this context, BiG-IoT creates a common and generic Application Programming Interface (API) between the different IoT middleware platforms. Open-IoT implements a cloud-based middleware platform with innovative tools and functionalities. Also, VICINITY project creates a framework that follows the philosophy interoperability as a service for "Internet of Things Neighborhood" with many modules and tools. Moreover, the INTER-IoT platform increases the levels of organization interoperability with INTER-API, which includes several interoperability tools for every layer. Finally, M3 Framework project with innovative semantic engines and solutions at the Application layer, which parses and displays the results to end-users, increases the organizational interoperability level.

TABLE I. INTEROERABILITY LEVELS COVERAGE BY THE EXAMINED RESEARCH PLATFORMS.

Interopera-bility level / Project	Technical level	Syntactic level	Semantic level	Organiza-tional level
AGILE	Yes (Maker's Gateway)	Yes (Maker's Gateway)	No	No
Open-IoT	No	No	Yes (extend SSN ontology, Linked Data)	Yes (extend SSN ontology, Linked Data)
VICINITY	Yes (Generic Gateway supports common networks (Wifi, ZigBee,))	Yes (OWL Lang.)	Yes (VICINI-TY Onto-logies)	Yes (interopera-bility as a service)
BiG-IoT	No	No	Yes (expand the standards of WoT, vocabulary manage-ment for handling semantics)	Yes (BiG-IoT API)
INTER-IoT	Yes (DS2DS)	Yes (DS2DS)	Yes (DS2DS)	Yes (INTER-API)
Machine to Machine (M3) Frame-work	No	Yes (Data acquisi-tion layer)	Yes (Knowle-dge mana-gement layer, Reasoning layer)	Yes (Application layer)

To address the problem of interoperability, equal emphasis should be placed on all levels of interoperability as they have been presented in this work. It is necessary to create tools and software modules that will seamlessly solve the problem of interoperability at all levels in parallel, and also provide solutions that are available for devices with minimal resources. In this way, an indispensable, interoperable, global IoT ecosystem will be created in the form of a new "Social Network" of Things.

Taking under consideration, the open issues and shortcomings of the state-of-art frameworks, as presented in this survey, we aim to design/implement a framework/architecture called "Social Network" of Things framework that consists of modules, tools and functionalities that will increase interoperability at all levels.

Firstly, at the level of technical interoperability, it is proposed to extend the AGILE and VICINITY solutions as well as other solutions from similar platforms and to create an architecture that includes even more interoperable devices. Expansion of tools, such as Maker's Gateway by supporting technologies and new widespread technologies, such as Arduino, Wispmote, Beacons, Libelium products, etc., are promising to make device compatibility much easier. New data collection and raw data filtering tools should be added to the entire system, so data going to the cloud can be edited with edge computing techniques. Additionally, these new technologies should be also compatible with the new wireless technologies of the LPWAN family (LoRaWan, SigFox, NB-IoT).

Also, at the level of syntactic and semantic interoperability, the new architecture should include new tools creating interoperable ontologies that will extend the existing solutions that have been analyzed in this paper. Initially, it is necessary to create an interoperable middleware framework with new innovative semantic modules, through which heterogeneous devices will be interconnected. Moreover, with the successful implementation and development of the proposed framework and the creation of a "Social Network" of Things where all devices and systems can communicate seamlessly, many innovative applications could be spawned in various fields leveraging on the raw data collected. Consequently, the level of organizational interoperability will increase rapidly.

The new architecture, as shown in Figure 1, consists of Perception, Transmission, Middleware and Application layers. The Perception layer contains all the IoT heterogeneous physical devices, such as Beacon sensors, ZigBee sensors, LoraWan sensors, actuators, etc. from which all heterogeneous data are derived. The Transmission layer, comprises the following modules:

- *Data collection module*, to get data from different types of sensor devices
- *Data integration module* which converts the heterogeneous data in a unified way, such as RDF, XML and JSON.

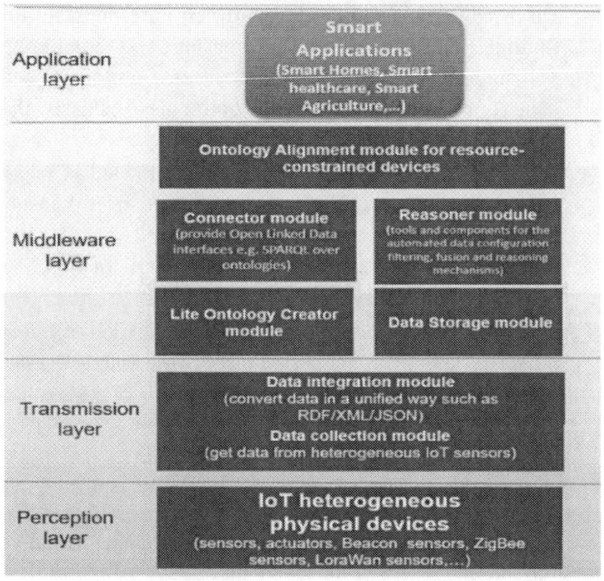

Figure 1. Overview of "Social Network" of Things Architecture.

The Middleware layer contains components and functionalities that can be divided into several functional modules as follows:

- *Data Storage module,* which contains tools to store semantic IoT Data to a cloud database.
- *"Lite" Ontology Creator module*, which includes tools for creating interoperable "light" ontologies and semantic structures, and methods to enrich with metadata and create reusable data, to enable semantic interaction and interoperability between the various heterogeneous "Things", offering a significant advantage compared to existing syntactic interactions.
- *Connector module*, to provide Open Linked Data interfaces e.g. SPARQL (SPARQL Protocol and RDF Query Language) over ontologies for internet-connected objects within the physical world abstracted by the middleware to interact with the "Social Network" of Things.
- *Reasoner module*, which includes tools and components for the automated data configuration filtering, fusion and reasoning mechanisms, according to the problems/tasks at hand.
- *Ontology alignment module for resource-constrained devices*, which includes tools for ontology merging, matching, and alignment related to the dynamics and complexity of the IoT systems.

The top layer is the Application layer. It implements and presents the results of the other three layers to accomplish disparate applications of IoT devices. The Application layer is a user-centric layer which executes various tasks for the users. It contains the innovative smart application of various fields, such as Smart homes, Smart cities, Smart healthcare, Smart agriculture, Smart buildings, etc.

VI. CONCLUSION

Addressing interoperability in IoT systems is a crucial key factor for IoT development. There is an urgent need to address the problem at all levels of IoT interoperability and to take into account the limitations of IoT systems.

In this context, we report the current developments on this issue, comparing the solutions of six major research platforms, and we discuss the main open issues and challenges. Finally, we propose to design and implement a framework/architecture that utilizes tools and methods that increase interoperability at all levels simultaneously and address the issue with low-cost devices and minimal computing resources, such as common IoT devices.

REFERENCES

[1] F. Shi, Q. Li, T. Zhu, and H. Ning, "A survey of data semantization in internet of things," Sensors, vol. 18, no 1, pp. 313, 2018.

[2] K. N. Kumar, V. R. Kumar and K. Raghuveer, "A Survey on Semantic Web Technologies for the Internet of Things," 2017 International Conference on Current Trends in Computer, Electrical, Electronics and Communication (CTCEEC), Mysore, pp. 316-322, 2017.

[3] M. Noura, M. Atiquzzaman, and M. Gaedke, "Interoperability in internet of things: Taxonomies and open challenges," Mobile Networks and Applications, vol. 24, no. 3, pp. 796-809, 2019.

[4] J. Radatz, A. Geraci, and F. Katki, "IEEE standard glossary of software engineering terminology," IEEE Std, vol. 610121990, no. 121990, pp. 3, 1990.

[5] A. Tolk, and J. A. Muguira, "The levels of conceptual interoperability model," In Proceedings of the 2003 fall simulation interoperability workshop, Citeseer, vol. 7, pp. 1-11, 2003.

[6] A. Gyrard and M. Serrano, "A Unified Semantic Engine for Internet of Things and Smart Cities: From Sensor Data to End-Users Applications," 2015 IEEE International Conference on Data Science and Data Intensive Systems, Sydney, NSW, pp. 718-725, 2015.

[7] A. Glória, F. Cercas and N. Souto, "Comparison of communication protocols for low cost Internet of Things devices," 2017 South Eastern European Design Automation, Computer Engineering, Computer Networks and Social Media Conference (SEEDA-CECNSM), Kastoria, pp. 1-6, 2017.

[8] R. S. Sinha, Y. Wei, and S. H Hwang, "A survey on LPWA technology: LoRa and NB-IoT" Ict Express, vol. 3, no. 1, pp. 14-21, 2017.

[9] A. Bröring et al., "Enabling IoT Ecosystems through Platform Interoperability," in IEEE Software, vol. 34, no. 1, pp. 54-61, 2017.

[10] L. Seremeti, C. Goumopoulos, and A. Kameas, "Ontology-based modeling of dynamic ubiquitous computing applications as evolving activity spheres," Pervasive and Mobile Computing, vol. 5, no. 5, pp. 574-591, 2009.

[11] M. Noura, A. Gyrard, S. Heil and M. Gaedke, "Automatic Knowledge Extraction to build Semantic Web of Things Applications," in IEEE Internet of Things Journal, 2019.

[12] P. Murdock et al., "Semantic interoperability for the Web of Things," 2016.

[13] H. Veer, and A. Wiles, "Achieving Technical Interoperability-the ETSI approach, European Telecommunications Standards Institute," Accessed: Sep, 2008, 20, 2017.

[14] P. Barnaghi, W. Wang, C. Henson, and K. Taylor, "Semantics for the Internet of Things: early progress and back to the future," International Journal on Semantic Web and Information Systems (IJSWIS), vol. 8, no. 1 pp. 1-21, 2012.

[15] K. Kotis, A. Katasonov, and J. Leino, "Aligning smart and control entities in the IoT," In Internet of Things, Smart Spaces, and Next Generation Networking, Springer, Berlin, Heidelberg, pp. 39-50, 2012.

[16] M. Ma, P. Wang and C. Chu, "Ontology-Based Semantic Modeling and Evaluation for Internet of Things Applications," 2014 IEEE International Conference on Internet of Things (iThings), and IEEE Green Computing and Communications (GreenCom) and IEEE Cyber, Physical and Social Computing (CPSCom), Taipei, pp. 24-30, 2014.

[17] I. P. Zarko et al., "Towards an IoT framework for semantic and organizational interoperability," 2017 Global Internet of Things Summit (GIoTS), Geneva, pp. 1-6, 2017.

[18] K. Rose, S. D. Eldridge, and L. Chapin, "The Internet of Things : An Overview Understanding the Issues and Challenges of a More Connected World," 2015.

[19] H. Cai, B. Xu, L. Jiang and A. V. Vasilakos, "IoT-Based Big Data Storage Systems in Cloud Computing: Perspectives and Challenges," in IEEE Internet of Things Journal, vol. 4, no. 1, pp. 75-87, 2017.

[20] M. Elkhodr, S. A. Shahrestani, and H. Cheung, "The Internet of Things: New Interoperability, Management and Security Challenges," 2016.

[21] G. Hatzivasilis, K. Fysarakis, O. Soultatos, I. Askoxylakis, I. Papaefstathiou, and G. Demetriou, "The industrial internet of things as an enabler for a circular economy Hy-LP: a Novel IIoT protocol, evaluated on a wind park's SDN/NFV-enabled 5G industrial network," Computer Communications, vol. 119, pp. 127-137, 2018.

[22] T. Jell, A. Bröring and J. Mitic, "BIG IoT – interconnecting IoT platforms from different domains," 2017 International Conference on Engineering, Technology and Innovation (ICE/ITMC), Funchal, pp. 86-88, 2017.

[23] G. Hatzivasilis et al., "The Interoperability of Things: Interoperable solutions as an enabler for IoT and Web 3.0," 2018 IEEE 23rd International Workshop on Computer Aided Modeling and Design of Communication Links and Networks (CAMAD), pp. 1-7, Barcelona, 2018.

[24] S. Žitnik, M. Janković, K. Petrovčič and M. Bajec, "Architecture of standard-based, interoperable and extensible IoT platform," 2016 24th Telecommunications Forum (TELFOR), Belgrade, pp. 1-4, 2016.

[25] G. Fortino et al., "Towards multi-layer interoperability of heterogeneous IoT platforms: The INTER-IoT approach," In: Integration, interconnection, and interoperability of IoT systems. Springer, p. 199-232, Cham, 2018.

[26] Y. Guan et al., "An open virtual neighbourhood network to connect IoT infrastructures and smart objects — Vicinity: IoT enables interoperability as a service," 2017 Global Internet of Things Summit (GIoTS), Geneva, pp. 1-6, 2017.

[27] L. Daniele, F. den Hartog, and J. Roes, "Created in close interaction with the industry: the smart appliances reference (SAREF) ontology," In International Workshop Formal Ontologies Meet Industries, Springer, Cham, 2015.

[28] J. Soldatos et al., "Openiot: Open source internet-of-things in the cloud," In Interoperability and open-source solutions for the internet of things, Springer, Cham, pp. 13-25, 2015.

[29] OpenIoT Consortium. [Online]. Available from: http://www.openiot.eu/ 2019.07.25.

[30] A. Gyrard, S. K. Datta, C. Bonnet and K. Boudaoud, "Standardizing generic cross-domain applications in Internet of Things," 2014 IEEE Globecom Workshops (GC Wkshps), Austin, TX, pp. 589-594, 2014.

[31] A. Gyrard, M. Serrano, J. B. Jares, S. K. Datta, and M. I. Ali, "Sensor-based linked open rules (S-LOR): An automated rule discovery approach for IoT applications and its use in smart cities," In Proceedings of the 26th International Conference on World Wide Web Companion, pp. 1153-1159, 2017.

Innovative Micro Authentication Server (MAS) Providing Trusted Authorization Services To Mobile Users Equipped with TLS Token

Simon Elrharbi
Ethertrust
Paris, France
Simon Elrharbi@EtherTrust.com

Pascal Urien
Telecom ParisTech
Paris, France
Pascal.Urien@Telecom-ParisTech.fr

Abstract— **This paper introduces an innovative Micro Authentication Server (MAS), providing trusted authorization services to mobile users equipped with Transport Layer Security (TLS) token. This platform was developed in the context of the PODIUM French Fonds Unique Interministeriel (FUI) research project whose goal is to define an Information Infrastructure (IT) referred as mobile cloud platform, deployed in emergency situation.**

Keywords-Security; TLS; Authentication; RACS; Portal

I. INTRODUCTION

In case of crisis, the rapid deployment of homeland security, military and civil defense means, takes place in a context of a multitude of risks and threats. In particular, the IT infrastructure based on physical and mobile networks is a main target for hackers and attackers. This infrastructure, commonly referred as "mobile cloud", provides ad hoc communication, information storage, and computing resources. It delivers services, such as multimedia instant messaging, fast computing of indoors and outdoors 3D mapping. Its security requires strong network access control, and security policy enforcing data confidentiality, resource authentication, electronic signature, and traceability.

Against this background, an ICT research project, PODIUM [1] has been launched to address these needs. It's funded by the French government through the FUI (Fonds Unique Interministeriel). It involves THALES, ETHERTRUST, ANEO, LUCEOR, NEXEDI, IGO, SDIS 13 and the UPMC-LIP6 from university of Paris 6. This consortium intends to develop a platform and a secure mobile cloud, which is also expected to be local and ad hoc, in order to respond to emergency situations.

This paper focuses on security and control access for the mobile network of the tactic, mobile and local cloud. This infrastructure needs to be autonomous, broadband and accessible only to security services, thanks to ergonomic and strong authentication mechanisms.

The users of the tactical and mobile cloud platform may belong to different sectors and trades (geographical or functional), exchanging information through different formats (SMS, chat, GPS, photos, video streams, etc.), and through different means of communication (mobile phones, fixed PCs or laptops, etc.) according to the Bring Your Own Device (BYOD) principle. Hence, according to these constraints, security and trust concepts are critical issues for mobile applications, as well as corporate applications, since they deal with secret cryptographic keys or PKI resources, which both require secure and trusted storage for user's private keys. In addition, privacy and traceability of users must never be exposed to an un-trusted party, and must be independent of any manufacturers.

The underlying security paradigm of the proposed solution is based on that the digital identity of user or machine is fully represented by X509 certificate, associated to asymmetric keys. The certificate does not contain vulnerable data that might be used by an attacker. Only the owner of the private key (that never travels through the network), identified by the X509 Common Name (CN) attribute, can use the certificate. The IP address is linked to its owner by means of authentication procedure. This mutual authentication is performed thanks to the TLS protocol. Trust is enforced by TLS processing in tamper resistant Secure Elements.

Two main features should be considered for the security and access control architecture. First is the connection of users to the mobile communication network, and second is their access to different applications and crisis data, which are used and exchanged.

The wireless mobile network is based on Access Points (APs) providing wireless local area networks (WLAN). APs are connected to an infrastructure made of WiMesh routers, wired routers, switches or hubs, which provides IP services to specific operating area. Additional features include Captive Portal (CP) and Access Control List (ACL) in order to manage users within the Wi-Fi network.

In this paper, we introduce an innovative micro authentication server (MAS), which provides authentication and trusted authorization services to mobile users, equipped with NFC TLS Token (see Figure 1).

We designed a "Captive Portal" in order to manage the authentication for IP addresses. According to Wikipedia, a "Captive Portal is a web page accessed with a web browser that is displayed to newly connected users of a Wi-Fi network before they are granted broader access to network resources".

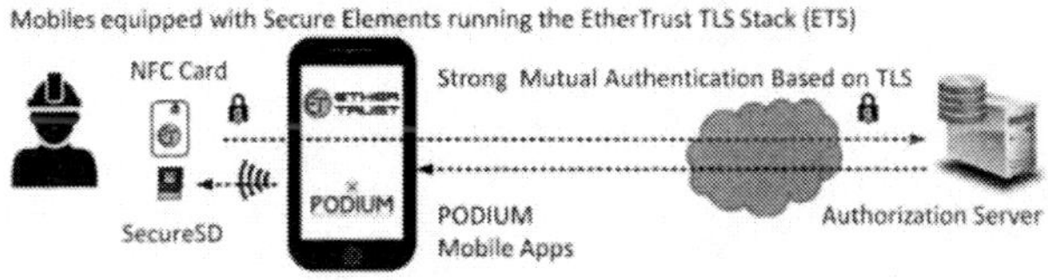

Figure 1. Authentication and Authorization services based on micro authentication server and TLS token.

In our context, the CP IP address is known and shared by mobile cloud users. The users need to sign-up to connect to the mobile network via an Access Point, and are identified by their IP and MAC addresses for getting access.

An important part of the end-user experience is the login process that he must proceed to access to the wireless access point (usually a form requesting login and password). The Access Point enables the scaling of the number of devices supported on the deployed mobile network that may add up quickly. The "login" and "password" requested for access to services will consist of a certificate and a signature, respectively. The approach adopted here is that the allocation of captive portal services must be the result of strong authentication based on the EtherTrust TLS Stack (ETS) technology combining digital certificate and TLS protocol implemented in secure elements [8].

Some mobile cloud services require specific authorizations. Because in a BOYD context the security of smartphone is unknown, the micro authentication server acts as hardware Secure Module (HSM). To reach this goal it runs a RACS server [6] managing a grid of smartcards. According to RACS, user authentication is based on TLS and certificate. A smartcard, typically hosting a private key is remotely used for signing procedures.

The structure of the paper is as follows: first, a description of the different hardware and software components incorporating the captive portal and by extension the micro authentication server using the ETS technology. Then, we focus on the implementation of the trusted authorization services designed to mobile users equipped with TLS Token.

II. HARDWARE ARCHITECTURE

The hardware architecture is described by Figure 2. The micro authentication server (MAS) is built over a Raspberry PI3 board, smartcard readers, PKCS#11 smartcards, Wi-Fi access points, Android smartphone and NFC javacard [9].

The system overall block diagram of the micro authentication server is illustrated by Figure 3. A Raspberry Pi3 board manages an Apache WEB server and a RACS server dealing with PKI smartcards. The captive portal is based on iptables resources. The TLS stack used for mobile authentication purposes is running in a NFC javacard.

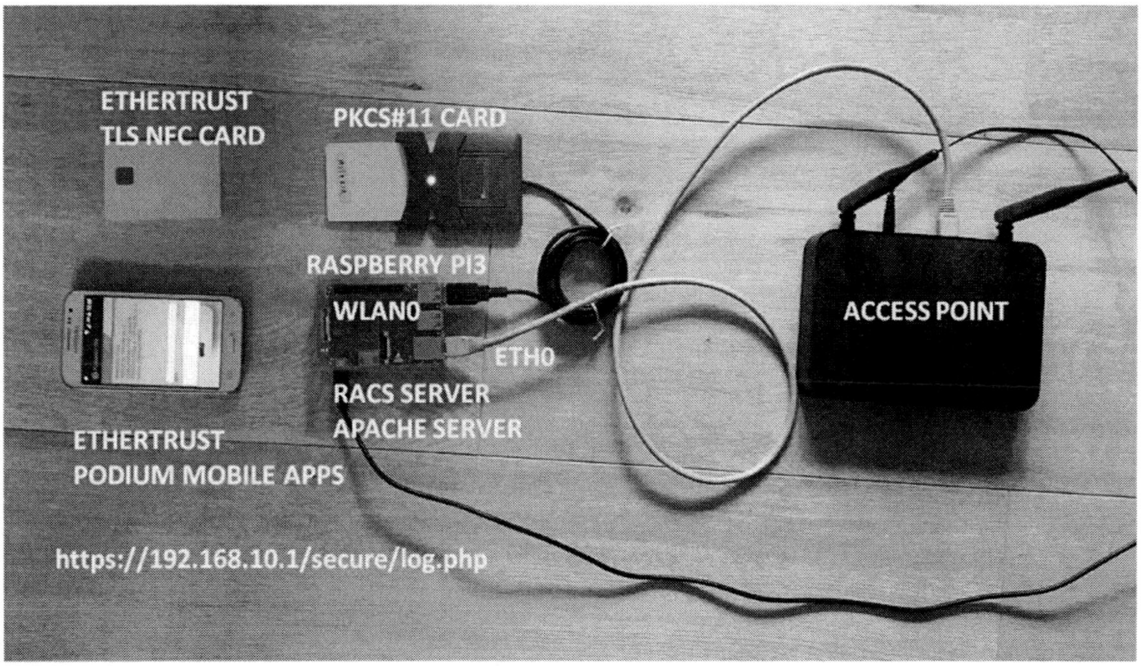

Figure 2. authentication server (MAS) providing trusted authorization services To Mobile Users Equipped with TLS Token through a captive portal

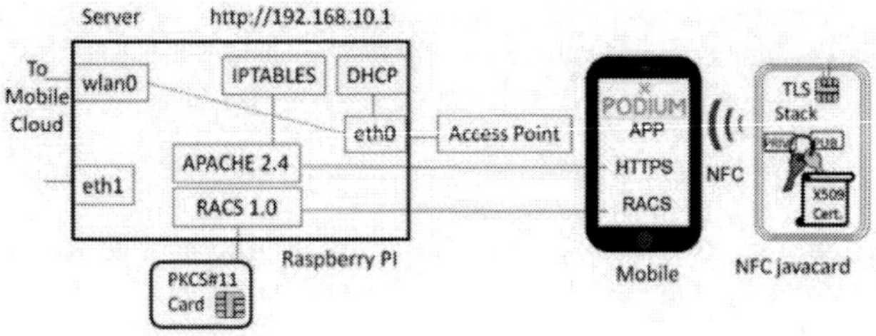

Figure 3. System overall block diagram of the Micro Authentication Server (MAS), providing trusted authorization services to mobile users equipped with TLS token through a captive portal.

A. *Raspberry Pi3*

A low-cost computing environment is supplied by the Raspberry Pi3 (Model B+), which is a multi-purpose advanced reduced-instruction set computing (ARM) processor based credit card sized computer.

The Raspberry Pi 3 Model B+ is a 64-bit quad core processor running at 1.4 GHz. The device connectivity combines dual-band 2.4 GHz and 5 GHz wireless LAN, Bluetooth 4.2/BLE, Ethernet and 4xUSB 2.0 ports. A Secure Digital (SD) memory card slot is also present for loading operating system and data storage.

Raspbian is a provided operating system (OS), but there are various other ARM-Linux OS variants that can run on it. The OS is flashed onto the micro SD. The running device can either be accessed directly using a USB keyboard, mouse and display or via a LAN port by creating a secure shell (SSH) session remotely.

B. *Smartcard Reader*

The smartcard reader is fitted with ISO7816 connectivity requiring the card is manually inserted into the reader by the user. It contains a built-in chip used for electronic processing. The built-in chip acts as a communication controller, passing data to and from the host system and the smartcard and performing functions needed for complete sessions, including: card activation and deactivation, cold/warm reset, ATR response reception, data transfers and configurable timing functions for smartcard activation time, guard time and timeout timers.

Thanks to PCSC-Lite [7] resources, smartcard readers are supported by Raspbian operating system.

C. *PKCS#11 smartcard*

The PKCS#11 standard defines APIs for cryptographic token. The set of objects stored cryptographic smartcards includes certificates and asymmetric keys, such as RSA public private keys.

Smartcard, also known as *Secure Element* (SE), is a confined and secure computing environment in which cryptographic calculations, readings, writes or deletes of sensitive data to be protected in non-volatile memories.

D. *Wi-Fi Access Point*

The Wi-Fi access point is configured as a transparent MAC bridge between IEEE 802.3 and IEEE 802.11 local area networks. It gets an IP address from the micro server (i.e., the Raspberry Pi board), and doesn't provide IP routing services.

E. *Android Smartphone*

An Android Smartphone runs the PODIUM application. It comprises two main elements involved with NFC communications. First, an NFC interface following the ISO 14443 standards. Second, a *Secured Element* (SE) in which host applications (such as PODIUM Applet) and keys are stored. The architecture of mobiles handsets may support several SE of different types: SIM card, embedded SE, or a secure memory card.

F. *NFC smartcard*

Smartcard also known as secure Element (SE) is a tamper resistant microcontroller, equipped with host interfaces such as ISO 7816, ISO 14443, SPI, or USB, whose security is enforced by multiples hardware and logical countermeasures. The security level of both electronics chips and associated operating system are ranked by certifications according to the *Common Criteria* (CC, ISO 15408) standards.

Near Field Communication (NFC) smartcard means that smartcard communicates over a 13.56 MHz air interface, in accordance with ISO/IEC-14443 and NFC Forum standards.

III. SOFTWARE ARCHITECTURE

Software components are divided in two categories: micro authentication server and mobile applications.

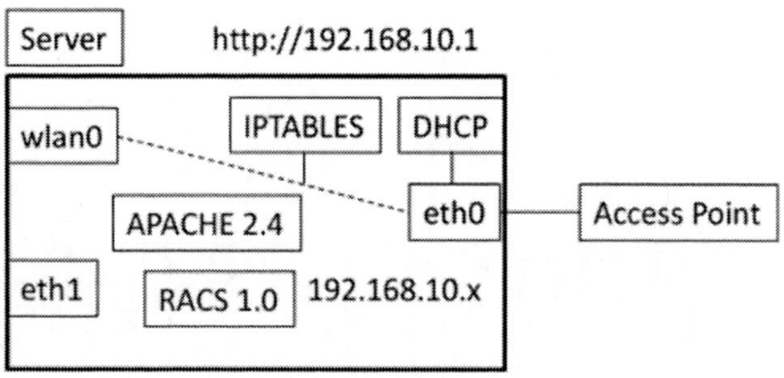

Figure 4. Software architecture of the micro authentication server.

The micro authentication server (see Figure 4) is configured with two network interfaces: Wi-Fi (wlan0) and Ethernet (eth0); an optional additive Ethernet interface (eth1) may be provided by an USB Ethernet token. The Ethernet port delivers DHCP services. The features of iptables [2] are used to enable routing services between network interfaces. An apache server is configured in order to provide user's authentication over TLS, thanks to X509 certificate. Authenticated users can download scripts that control their connectivity to the mobile cloud, i.e., send commands to iptables. They can also access to a RACS server, which requires a certificate in order to use dedicated secure elements.

A. *IP tables*

The iptables program [2] is used to set up, maintain, and inspect the tables of IP packet filter rules in the Linux kernel. It is executed with root privileges.

Three commands (see Figure 5) are needed to manage the server routing context, in order to set a route, delete a route, and dump the route list:

- the append command sets a route for a client (with an IPclient address) between interfaces eth0 and wlan0.
- the delete command deletes a route for a client (with an IPclient address) between interfaces eth0 and wlan0.
- the dump command reads the filter rules

append	sudo iptables -t nat --append POSTROUTING -s IPclient -o wlan0 -j MASQUERADE
delete	sudo iptables -t nat --delete POSTROUTING -s IPclient -o wlan0 -j MASQUERADE
dump	sudo iptables-save

Figure 5. iptables main commands.

B. *Raspberry Pi Network Configuration*

IP Forwarding	in /etc/sysctl.conf, uncomment the line : #net.ipv4.ip_forward = 1
DHCP for interface eth0	in /etc/network/interfaces, replace the line : iface eth0 inet manual, by the lines auto eth0 iface eth0 inet static address 192.168.10.1 netmask 255.255.255.0
DHCP server	sudo apt-get install isc-dhcp-server
DHCP server for interface eth0	in /etc/default/isc-dhcp-server, add the line: INTERFACES="eth0"
DHCP server configuration	in /etc/dhcp/dhcpd.conf set the parameters: subnet, netmask, range, broadcast-address, routers, domain-name domain-name-servers

Figure 6. Setting the micro authentication server network configuration.

The following operations (see Figure 6) are needed in order to configure the MAS network features:

- enable IP forwarding (i.e. packet routing between network interfaces (i.e. eth0 and wlan0) ;
- enable DHCP service on the Ethernet interface (eth0);
- install a DHCP server;
- associate the DHCP server to the Ethernet interface;
- set the DHCP server working parameters.

C. *Apache 2.4 server*

At the time of writing, the Apache2.4 version was not released for Debian systems. We manually installed it, i.e. we performed source downloading and local compilation. This version is needed in order to disable the TLS ticket option, which is not supported by the current TLS smartcard client.

The WEB server is configured with a certification authority (CA), an X509 certificate and its associated private key. Files located in a protected directory (/secure) can be downloaded only by HTTPS requests, implying client strong authentication, based on its X509 certificate.

The easiest way to design a WEB user interface is to encapsulate iptable commands in bash script (see Figure 9). This approach requests to authorize scripts with root privileges. The user's root privileges are controlled by the etc/sudoers file. The line detailed by Figure 7, enables the root privilege for a bash script (script.sh).

As illustrated by Figure 8, a remote user is authenticated by its certificate, which embeds its identity (the CN attribute).

```
daemon ALL=(ALL) NOPASSWD: /bin/bash
/usr/local/apache2/sbin/script.sh *
```

Figure 7. The sudoers file, needed for script execution with root privilege.

```
<?php
if ($_SERVER['SSL_CLIENT_VERIFY'] != "SUCCESS")
{ Header("HTTP/1.0 401 Unauthorized"); exit; }
echo " Welcome " ;
echo $_SERVER['SSL_CLIENT_S_DN_CN'] ;
echo " IP="; echo $_SERVER['REMOTE_ADDR'] ; echo " ! " ;
$cmd = 'sudo /bin/bash /usr/local/apache2/sbin/script.sh ' .
$_SERVER['REMOTE_ADDR'];
$result = exec($cmd);
?>
```

Figure 8. Exemple of php page (on.php) performing user authentication, and establishing a route with iptables.

```
#!/bin/bash
a="sudo iptables -t nat --delete POSTROUTING -s "
b=" -o wlan0 -j MASQUERADE"
c="$a$1$b"
$c
a="sudo iptables -t nat --append POSTROUTING -s "
b=" -o wlan0 -j MASQUERADE"
c="$a$1$b"
echo $c
$c
```

Figure 9. A script that establihes a route for a given IP address betwen eth0 and wlan0

D. *RACS 1.0 server for Raspberry Pi*

The RACS (Remote APDU Call Secure) protocol is described by an IETF draft [3].

RACS servers manage grid of secure elements (usually smartcards). Remote users are authenticated thanks to the TLS protocol, dealing with strong mutual authentication relying on client and server certificate and associated private keys.

An open implementation is available for Raspberry Pi systems [4].

More details on RACS are available in [6].

E. *Ethertrust TLS stack (ETS Applet)*

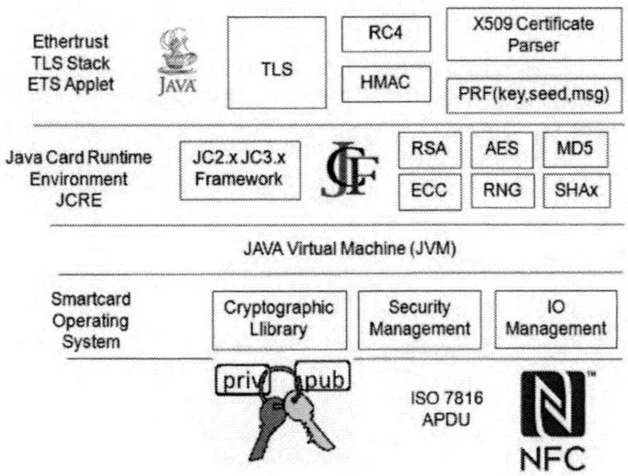

Figure 10. The ETS Applet, in a javacard software environment.

The ETS TLS (see Figure 10) stack is an applet written for javacard [9] that fully processes TLS sessions [8]. The application size is about 20KB for the client only applet. The time required to open a TLS session is about 10 to 2 seconds, depending on the device manufacturer. The four TLS flights of a full session are fully processed by the smartcard. The ETS applet always uses an X509 certificate for client authentication. Upon success the ephemeral session keys, used for record messages encryption and integrity checking, are transferred to the mobile. So, each time the NFC card is tapped against the mobile, a new TLS session is started and afterwards transferred to the mobile.

F. *PKCS#11 Java Card Applet*

The MUSCLE (Movement for the Use of Smart Card in a Linux environment) project developed an open javacard application (the MUSCLE Applet [5]), which provides PKCS#11 services.

This application generates asymmetric key pairs. It is protected by a PIN code, and computes PKCS#1 signature.

G. *Mobile Podium Application.*

The mobile application comprises a HTTPS and a RACS client. The TLS layer is provided by the TLS smartcard. The application is started by tapping the NFC card against the mobile.

As depicted by Figure 11 the server address, the RACS TCP port, and the script (on.php) needed for logging purposes are configured by the user.

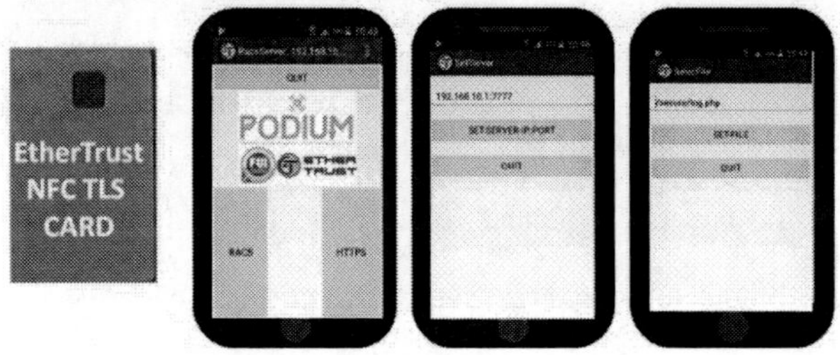

Figure 11. PODIUM Mobile Application.

IV. AUTHORIZATION SERVICES

In this section we detail the portal WEB interface, the authentication procedure, and the signature service.

A. *WEB interface*

As illustrated by Figure 12 the portal is controlled by three main scripts, on.php for connection to the mobile cloud services, off.php for disconnection, and list.php that collects iptables information.

Scripts located in the /secure directory require a valid certificate for the TLS client, whose access rights are verified

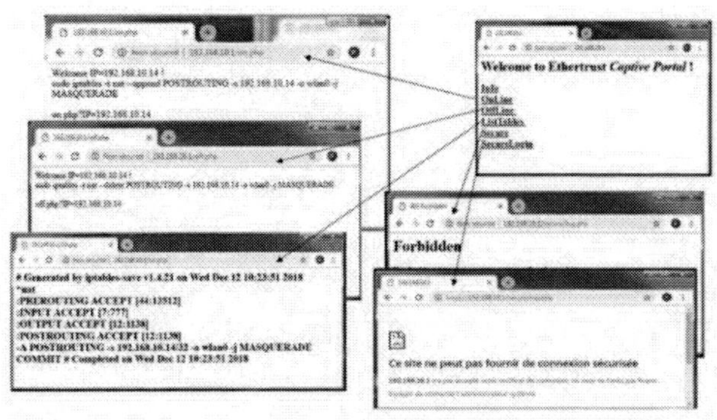

Figure 12. Illustration of the WEB interface with the portal, which comprises hree main scrips on.php, off.php, and list.phpPortal Service

B. *Portal Service*

The user taps his TLS NFC card against the mobile, and selects the HTTPS service, performing the https://server.com/on.php URL A TLS session is started between the smartcard and the server. The chip is identified by the CN attribute stored in the X509 certificate (client in Figure 13). The script on.php enables the access to the mobile cloud, thanks to iptables resources. An HTTP response is returned to the mobile, whose content is displayed by the mobile (see Figure 13).

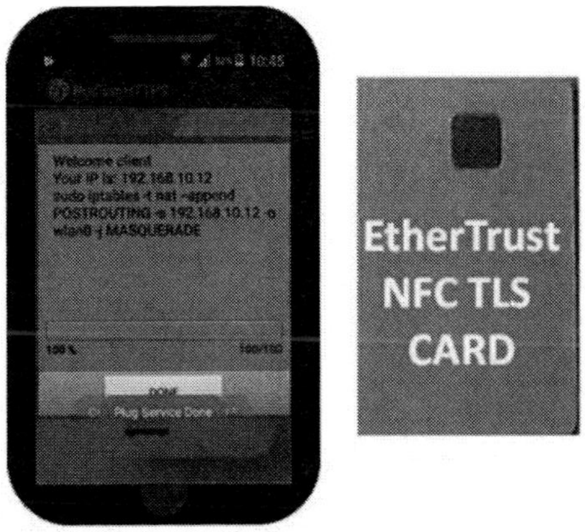

Figure 13. The user screen after a sucessfull authentication with the portal

The server returns the CN attribute found in the X509 certificate ("Client"), and the IP address. The iptables command, started from then php script, is also echoed for debugging purpose.

C. *Signature Service*

Figure 14. The Electronic Signature Service

The user taps his TLS NFC card against the mobile, and selects the RACS service (see Figure 11). A TLS session is opened between the smartcard and the RACS server. The chip is identified by the CN attribute stored in the X509 certificate. Upon success the user selects a smartcard, belonging to the grid hosted by the RACS server, to which it is authorized to access according to its rights. Thereafter, it sends a value to sign to a PKCS#11 chip. The returned signature is displayed by the mobile application (see Figure 14).

V. CONCLUSION

In this paper, we introduce an innovative micro authentication server, dealing with TLS NFC token. We believe that this technology could be applied in IT platforms in which interactions are performed from mobiles, in a BOYD context, whose security level is unknown.

The main advantages of our approach are the following:

- Mutual strong authentication based on standardized technology, i.e. TLS.

- On the client side all operations are computed in a tamper resistant environment.

- No credentials or authentication procedures are handled by the smartphone.

We are currently working on a new generation of TLS token, compatible with TLS 1.3.

REFERENCES

[1] The PODIUM FUI20 project, http://m.competitivite.gouv.fr/toutes-les-actualites/actualite-23/les-resultats-du-20eme-appel-a-projets-du-fui-regions-58-nouveaux-projets-873.html, july 2015, [retrieved: May, 2019]

[2] IPTABLES Manual, http://ipset.netfilter.org/iptables.man.html, , [retrieved: May, 2019]

[3] IETF DRAFT, Remote APDU Call Secure (RACS), https://datatracker.ietf.org/doc/draft-urien-core-racs

[4] RACS_0_1, https://github.com/purien/racs_0_1/tree/master/raspberrypi3_bin/racs_0_1, [retrieved: May, 2019]

[5] Muscle Applet, https://github.com/OpenSC/OpenSC/wiki/Muscle-applet, [retrieved: May, 2019]

[6] P. Urien, RACS: Remote APDU call secure creating trust for the internet", 2015 International Conference on Collaboration Technologies and Systems, CTS 2015, Atlanta, GA, USA, June 2015

[7] PCSC Lite, https://github.com/LudovicRousseau/PCSC, [retrieved: May, 2019]

[8] P. Urien and M. Betirac, A Triple Interfaces Secure Token -TIST- for Identity and Access Control in the Internet Of Things, the Second International Conference on Smart Systems, Devices and Technologies, SMART 2013, 2013 - Roma, Italy

[9] Z. Chen, Java Card™ Technology for Smart Cards, O'Reilly, 2000

Business Case Evaluation Methodology (BCEM) for Factories Digitalization

A quantitive approach to digital transformation assessment in industry domains

Roberto Rocca, Giacomo Tavola, Filippo Boschi, Paola Fantini, Marco Taisch
Department of Management, Economics and Industrial Engineering
Politecnico di Milano
Via R. Lambruschini 4/b, 20156, Milano, Italy
email:{roberto.rocca, giacomo.tavola, filippo.boschi, paola.fantini, marco.taisch}@polimi.it

Abstract— **In the last years, the fast evolution towards automation and digitalization of production systems is forcing companies in re-thinking their business strategies and models. To overcome manufacturers' conservatism, migration strategies and business case evaluations are required to assess, support and guide adoption of the next generation of smart production systems. This paper proposes a Business Case Evaluation Methodology (BCEM) to support companies that aim to migrate from legacy automation systems towards the Industry 4.0 paradigm. The aim of the proposed approach is to assess the profitability of the investment in advanced technologies for the decentralization of industrial automation control architectures, evaluating opportunities and mitigating the risks of migration from technical, operational, human and business perspectives. The methodology implements an iterative approach starting from the definition of the current business and operational status of the factory and the identification of business goals; progressing towards the identification and evaluation of possible migration paths; ending with the selection of the optimal one according to a cost-benefit analysis. The paper presents two exemplary applications in real industrial environments, developed in the scope of FAR-EDGE European Project.**

Keywords-Industry 4.0; digital factories; migration strategy; business case evaluation; investment assessment.

I. INTRODUCTION

Due to volatile and fast moving markets, increasing competition, as well as more complex products and production processes, industrial companies are facing increasingly intricate challenges [1]. Among these, digital transformation represents one of the biggest challenge that a company has to face nowadays [2], since it represents not only a technical issue, but also a cultural shift. In fact, the change does not only affect processes, but they require a shift from the present company values toward a continuous improvement philosophy. Within the modern industrial environment, this transformation refers to the processes that lead to the adoption of the Industry 4.0 (I4.0) paradigm. Even if the term has existed for some time, only a few organizations can claim to have reached a mature implementation. I4.0 refers to the industrial exploitation of Cyber-Physical Systems (CPS) for the intelligent decentralization in the factory. The result is the so called "smart factory" where, Information and Communication Technology (ICT), Internet of Things (IoT), Customer-to-Machine (C2M), Customer-to-Customer (C2C), Machine-to-Machine (M2M) communications [3]–[5] are integrated with distributed sensing, processing and actuating capabilities. Altogether these technologies enable a new paradigm for production management, driven by a better situation awareness, built on collection and analysis of big data. For the companies, in order to compete on the market, it is crucial to be able to promptly address market challenges with leading strategies [6]. That implies the adoption of flexible, lean, fast, agile, efficient, systems with prompt and reactive decision-making process. In spite of the benefits, the important impact of the potential technological and organizational changes has prevented many companies from adopting a full I4.0 strategy or even systematically investing in I4.0 capabilities [1]. Two relevant common barriers are: (i) high investment costs due to a lack of I4.0 suitability of the existing production infrastructure and (ii) missing transparency or quantification of benefits [1]. Moreover, this change has to be driven by clear managerial leadership. Accordingly, there is a fundamental need for assisting companies in the transition to I4.0 technologies/practices, and guiding them for improving their capabilities in a standardized, objective, and repeatable way [7]. The intent of this paper is to present a Business Case Evaluation Methodology (BCEM) that gives support to the companies that intend to migrate towards factories digitalization, considering a holistic approach from the technical, operational, human and business perspective.

The rest of this paper is organized as follows. Section II describes the BCEM for factories digitalization assessment. Section III describes two methodology application cases developed within the FAR-EDGE European Project context. Finally, Section IV draws some final conclusions.

II. BUSINESS CASE EVALUATION METHODOLOGY FOR FACTORIES DIGITALIZATION

The starting point of a migration path is commonly referred to as AS-IS situation, while the final goal is named TO-BE situation. Figure 1 shows the framework of the migration process and BCEM proposed in this paper.

The figure frames the steps 2-3-4-5 under the concept of Blueprint migration [8]. Blueprint refers to an early plan that

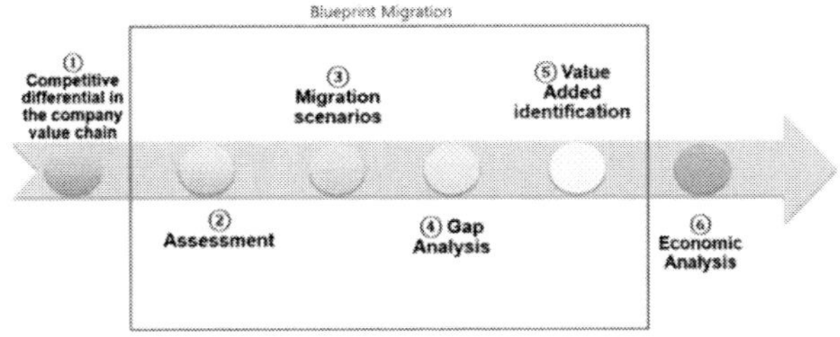

Figure 1. Business Case Evaluation Methodology framework

explains how something might be achieved. The comparison of the different strategies implies the comparison of several features, such as risks, migration design time, migration execution time, downtime, costs and effort [9].

In addition to the company managers involved in the assessment, the methodology requires a collaboration with OEMs and solution providers.

The procedure is described in the next sections, following a stepwise order.

A. *Step 1. Competitive differentials in the company value chain*

The digital transformation should not be considered as a stand alone solution, but rather considered as a powerful lever to be integrated within the strategic processes of the enterprises. For this reason, the first step of the methodology aims to open the way toward digital transformation, trying to assess the potential benefits for the enterprise value creation and business model, taking into account the competitive landscape.

By identifying the relevant Key Performance Indicators (KPIs), applying the Strengths, Weaknesses, Opportunities and Threats (SWOT) analyses and an adaptation of the Porter's value chain model, different ways of designing the digital transformation can be analyzed.

In fact, the SWOT analysis [10][11], is very suitable since it guides the identification of business changing factors through a clear and meaningful way. It can be used effectively to build organizational and competitive strategy in a migration context.

KPIs definition is a fundamental activity in order to clarify the desired impact of the project implementation, accordingly to the SWOT analysis outcome related to internal and external business changing factors

Porter's model highlights the main activities (primary and secondary) that allow the company to create value and, although its original formulation requires to be revised in order to overcome the functional segments of the classic corporate structure, it is still valid [12][13].

Overall this first section set the strategic frame for developing the Blueprint Migration and performing the economic analysis.

B. *Step 2. Technical, Operational and Human assessment*

The main goal of BCEM Step 2 is to clearly define the AS-IS situation in the technical, operational and human dimension. The three-dimensional structure has been adopted to offer a holistic perspective on the migration. To assess the various issues related to the three dimensions a maturity model has been developed and exploited within the context of FAR-EDGE EU project [8]. The maturity model rate from 1 to 5 the digital maturity or readiness of the considered aspect: the value 1 indicates a low or non-existent development, while 5 refers to a cutting edge implementation [14]–[18]. The assessment in Step 2 maps a first overview of the application context where the company is interested in reaching a higher maturity level. The final framework will be completed in Step 3 after the consulting of external experts.

C. *Step 3. Migration matrix and scenario definition*

The tool for the holistic representation is the Migration Matrix [8] and it allows to map the AS-IS and the TO-BE scenarios. It is used as a tool to conceptualize and measure the readiness or maturity of the enterprise regarding some specific target state. In this way, it is possible to identify the AS-IS situation of overall dimension analyzed, enabling the possibility to define the starting point for the digital transformation. There could be more than one way to reach the desired result and the TO-BE scenario could not be unique. In fact, a collaboration with OEMs and solution providers is required at this point in order to assess the feasibility of the scenarios and provide solutions able to improve the KPIs defined in Step 1. It can be referred to a mutually exclusive situation when more than one solution is considered to solve the same industrial problem (e.g., different technologies or resources are involved). On the other hand, the TO-BE scenarios can be referred to a mutually inclusive situation, when more than one solution is considered to solve different industrial problems. Once the scenarios are fully determined, then their description in the final Migration Matrix is portrayed. Initially, the rows are characterized, then for each one of these, the five maturity levels are specified. The final result implies one Migration Matrix for each scenario where it is depicted only one AS-IS status and one specific TO-BE status. The selected alternatives are then evaluated according to the business strategy, considering also outcome of BCEM Step 1.

D. *Step 4. Gap analysis*

Gap analysis between AS-IS and TO-BE scenarios represents an outcome of the collaboration with solution providers. Required components, possible integrations and steps for application are the three main steps to carry on. Required components represent a detailed list of the additional components, operations, and new professional skills required for each scenario migration. Possible integration to the defined architectures has to be taken into account since they enable system flexibility and easier future updates: a non-quantitative data which should be considered when deciding which migration to choose. Then, the steps required for the implementation of each scenario include costs and time evaluation for the overall migration completion which are very relevant in the economic analysis. Steps for application provides general instructions for the implementation of the technology starting from the AS-IS status.

E. Step 5. Value added identification

The value added section aims to justify the efforts spent by the company on the use case implementation. The complete definition of the scenarios allows to foresee the quantitative and qualitative improvement of the system. Value added has a double meaning:

- KPI improvement. A quantitative and measurable increase of system performance with respect to the AS-IS situation.
- Unmeasurable advantage. A benefit derived from the new system which has a positive impact on one of the three migration dimensions (e.g., flexibility of a specific process). The unmeasurable advantages of the scenario have to be coherent with the value added relative to the technological enablers selected in the scenario.

Every scenario can count on different features and peculiarities, hence the KPIs improvement and the unmeasurable advantages could differ from one another. For this reason, the metrics needed for the KPIs improvement calculation are case specific.

F. Step 6. Economic analysis

A cost-benefit analysis to justify the investment in digital transformation is the last step of the methodology. This analysis is performed comparing the TO-BE situation with respect to the AS-IS situation and it deals with quantitative results. The unmeasurable advantages and disadvantages which cannot be translated in economic value are not part of Step 6. First, the KPIs improvement is translated into money and the results are addressed as Economic KPIs or Benefits. The Economic KPIs estimation is not always straightforward. Being the benefits computation use case dependent, it is impossible to provide a complete framework. Nevertheless, we can identify a common tool to be used as reference framework: the Total Cost of Ownership (TCO), that could be adopted for cost evaluation [19]. It is recognized as an industry-standard method for the economic analysis for IT and other enterprise issues due to its holistic view of costs across enterprise boundaries over time. A subdivision is made between upfront implementation costs and recurring costs.

The investment is evaluated on a fixed time interval with a Discounted Cash Flow approach and the specific case assumptions for the economic analysis have to be declared. The Net Present Value (NPV) is an economic index which measures the value acquired by the company associated with the investment. The Cash Flow (CF) of year t is computed taking into consideration the differential analysis between the TO-BE and the AS-IS scenario. Moreover, the Profitability Index (PI) is considered. It is a relative index of profitability and it is defined as the discounted cash flow divided by the discounted investments. The Internal Rate of Return (IRR) is also considered in Step 6, since it represents the maximum risk for which the investment can be considered viable. The Discounted Payback Period (DPP) represents the number of years necessary to break even from undertaking the initial expenditure recognizing the time value of money. Of course, the best case is verified when the DPP is as short as possible. NPV, PI, IRR and DPP are indexes which defines the economic success of a project, and they are also a measure to compare more than one solution, as in the case of multiple scenario evaluations. The final decision to implement or not one or more of the defined project is the final point of the methodology. The migration process defines qualitative and quantitative reasons to guide decision-making activity.

III. BCEM APPLICATION: TWO USE CASES WITHIN THE H2020 FAR-EDGE CONTEXT

The entire methodology has been developed and tested within the Horizon2020 FAR-EDGE European Project context, with the scope to perform an economic and technical analysis of the digital transformation process toward I4.0 technologies. The main goal of the project is to create a novel Reference Architecture (RA) for industrial automation, which leverages the benefits of edge computing, while using blockchain technologies for flexible, scalable and reliable configuration and orchestration of automation workflows and distributed data analytics [20]. The two BCEM application cases are represented by (i) a world's top white appliances manufacturer company and (ii) a leader company in the automotive sector. A summary of the two use cases applications, following the stepwise order that characterizes the methodology, are reported below.

A. Use case 1. Durable goods company

1) Step 1. Competitive differentials in the company value chain.

The business objectives of this company, which interest in re-shoring will allow the consolidation of production volumes in Europe, are on (i) improving quality, (ii) time to market, (iii) costs, as well as (iv) system architecture. Better and more efficient utilization of data generated at the shopfloor level can enhance both the capability of filtering defective parts and products and increase the productivity. The achievement of these objectives starts from the manufacturing field, where the investment in improving technologies can decrease the number of factory defects at the lowest cost. The FAR-EDGE technologies in this sense impact on automation, simulation and analytics, both on the technological process and on the company's organizational processes. As a starting point it has been applied a SWOT analysis in order to comprehend the strengths, weaknesses, opportunities and threats of the FAR-EDGE Architecture implementation within the company plant. FAR-EDGE projects with its innovative decentralized structure could enhance system flexibility, adaptability and reliability. The SWOT analysis and Porter's value chain analysis underlined how the sorting system of the plant represents an issue which could be solved and improved by FAR-EDGE. The support activities involved are the firm infrastructure which should lead the change. The technology development which should implement and maintain the new architecture enables the improved data management. The human resource management which is responsible for employees training and hiring digital skilled people. The primary activities, where the smooth and lean migration is focusing on, are out-bound logistics and services, nonetheless, production data should be collected from the operations in order to optimize the products dispatching. At this point, the KPIs were identified after having got a clear idea about the potential application field of the project: (i) sorter OEE, which improvement is computed as the ratio between the fully productive time and the planned production time; and (ii) sorter reconfigurability.

2) Step 2. Technical, Operational and Human assessment.

The AS-IS matrix has been developed on multiple levels, describing the technical, operational, and human aspects where the company should increase its readiness or digital maturity to reach a satisfactory solution leveraging on the FAR-EDGE platform. The use case described is almost a green field scenario: all or most of the technological content of the AS-IS system was not present. In this case, the starting maturity levels of the migration matrix are very low and the solution is built from the beginning.

3) Step 3. Migration matrix and scenario definition.

In the TO-BE system architecture, each smart object is managed by an independent Edge Node. Edge Nodes are of fundamental importance, since the information from the field can be managed and processed in each smart object in order to modify the dispatching policy accordingly. All the nodes communicate within a Distributed Ledger smart contract called Collaborative Sorting.

4) Step 4. Gap analysis.

It was possible to identify in this use case a unique migration scenario because of the specificity of the industrial problem and two main areas can be identified among the FAR-EDGE components utilized for the accomplishment of such a result: (i) Cyber Physical System: all the smart objects are represented and configured on the Distributed Ledger; and (ii) Simulation Services: its goal is to suggest an optimized sorting policy exploiting real-time data from the field. Simulation services include local monitoring and control of the real-time situation through the Edge Nodes. Collaborative Sorting recognizes the change in the state of the system and adapts the dispatching rule accordingly.

The gap analysis has also highlighted additional tasks and competences required for managing and maintaining the systems.

5) Step 5. Value added identification.

The final consultation with the experts estimates a possible growth of the KPIs identified in Step 1. The Sorter OEE will increase by 5% and the sorter reconfigurability will improve significantly. A situation dependent analysis is part of the next section of the methodology. For what concerns unmeasurable advantages, it is possible to list: (i) a synchronization between field and simulation that could be further used for other purposes; (ii) an innovative machine autonomy which creates M2M collaboration in the operational dimension. For the human dimension, the number of stressful emergency breakdown situations is reduced and the reconfiguration of the system is not manual any more. On the other hand, the IT system becomes more complex and requires that different groups of employees are trained to acquire new technical skills.

6) Step 6. Economic analysis.

Accordingly to the last step of BCEM, the economic appraisal is then performed. First of all, the upfront costs and the recurring costs have to be computed. As a second phase, the improvement KPIs are transformed into economic benefits:

- An OEE improvement has a direct effect on the throughput of the system. It has been verified that an additional 5% of the sorter OEE implies an additional 5% of the system throughput.
- The improvement of the system reconfigurability has been considered exploiting a situation analysis: the flexibility acquired will impact on the Total Cost of Change (TCC) of the system.

Finally, the Discounted Cash Flow appraisal is calculated. In this case, the TO-BE scenario implies a favorable economic perspective. Alongside a consistent initial investment, the NPV is significantly positive after 10 years. The DPP occurs slightly after the third year. In the end, the IRR has been computed, with a value of 34,9%. Since IRR is greater than the discount rate has been utilized (10%), also this index confirms the profitability of the investment in the TO-BE scenario. The results cannot be evaluated without considering the FAR-EDGE context and all the specific hypothesis has been considered.

B. Use case 2. Automotive sector company

1) Step 1. Competitive differentials in the company value chain.

The second project use case is represented by a leader company in the automotive sector. This use case exploits ERP, MES and SCADA to collect data from the sensors on the field. The digital knowledge is widespread and is part of the group strategy, in fact, they already participated to research projects related to I4.0. The mass customization causes a high complexity of the assembly systems, it provides a strategic advantage to target niche markets and meeting diverse customer needs in a timely fashion. In such a system operations standardization, production scheduling optimization, as well as scrap reduction are of fundamental importance. It is adapting to the new environment by a changed organizational structure, larger involvement of the end customer, smaller and less complex development projects and closer partner collaboration.

The qualitative analysis underlined the possibility to implement two main target KPIs for the project:

- Tools adaptation time: automatic reconfiguration of the nutrunners could decrease the setup time.
- Rework rate: a second effect would be the facilitation of the operators' job by relieving the stress of the repetitive operation of setting the right tool's parameters. This would imply an overall reduction of the rework rate due to human errors.

2) *Step 2. Technical, Operational and Human assessment.*

Thanks to the collaboration with company experts and technical solution providers, AS-IS scenario has been mapped. In particular, the assessment highlighted that the scheduling activities are not supported by simulation services and the products are chosen from the large buffer upstream the finishing lines in a "first in first out" order. This provokes delayed deliveries due to non-optimized sequencing. The high number of degree of freedom of the assembly line has to be tackled with flexible interchangeability of the operations through the station. Currently, the tools along the lines are set up manually and for this reason, could lead to erroneous parameters imposition. In this case an automatic tool able to auto reconfigure according to the activity that has to perform could dramatically reduce setup time required by the operator to tune the parameters and at the same time guarantee a standardized replicability of the single operation excluding the human error factor.

From a human competencies point of view, it can be underlined a lack of competences in the Edge computing and distributed Ledger technologies. This gap is justified by the fact that such technologies are very advanced and in some cases never used in the manufacturing world. FAR-EDGE project will have to fill this gap and guide the use cases until the achieved result.

The AS-IS matrix identifies the usual characterization of the current situation from the technical, operational and human perspectives. The migration starting point is a brownfield scenario [8]: smart objects and sensor, as well as data management already exist in the shopfloor. Summarizing, the MES is in charge of automating and distributing the order processing throughout all the shopfloor. Work performance and production performance are monitored exploiting the Factory Control System (FCS) and ERP. A CAD system is present and it is fed manually with production data but it is not able to optimize the buffer policy. The tools reconfiguration is made manually by the operator to which is not required any digital knowledge, while the skills for I4.0 belong mainly to IT department experts.

3) *Step 3. Migration matrix and scenario definition.*

The FAR-EDGE project can provide three powerful tools for several improvements in this mass customization use cases:

- Simulation services embedded in the platform could partially solve the tardy delivery problem by suggesting improved truck sequencing.
- Data Analytics could measure the assembly time of each product and produce statistics for improved decision making based on simulation.
- Automation could enable tools with Plug'n'Produce technology able to auto reconfigure the parameters avoiding assembly time losses and products unable to pass the final quality check.

The greatest change made with respect to the AS-IS architecture is the introduction of the Cloud and the Ledger infrastructure. These new items are able to enhance automation services control, namely Plug'n'Produce technology. At Cloud level cohabits the ERP and FCS technology, in this way it is possible to exploit all their functionality in a coexistence of the legacy ISA95 and FAR-EDGE architecture. The Distributed Ledger technology is exploited to create the so-called "intelligent product": every product is registered in the distributed ledger, after every activity, the ledger is updated in the nearest peer node, and then in all the other peer nodes of the network. In this way, the product carries along the assembly line the information regarding operations performed and equipment installed.

4) *Step 4. Gap analysis.*

A FAR-EDGE Gateway is required in order for the Handheld scanner, the One Spindle Nutrunner and the Edge Display to communicate with the Distributed Ledger. A FAR-EDGE adapter has two connectors and is developed using the edge automation services. It adds Plug'n'Produce support to the nutrunner by attaching the nutrunner to one port and the work cell gateway to the other. The purpose is to encapsulate the open protocol and translate to and from the FAR-EDGE interface and thus, simplify configuration.

From a practical perspective, few physical activities will change with respect to the AS-IS situation. The operator is no more in charge of setting the parameters of the tool, he would just have to scan the product on the assembly line, plug-in the nutrunner and perform the activities in the order provided on the display. The complex IT system serves the purpose of a remarkable simplification of the production operations and quality. The human dimension requires a little step forward in the comprehension and mastery of the I4.0 tools. Maintenance and IT department have to develop an expertise to be able to sustain and provide assistance for the new architecture components. Furthermore, the operators along the assembly line have to possess basic knowledge of digital technology to fully exploit the potential of the tools automatic reconfiguration.

5) *Step 5. Value added identification.*

Once defined clearly the technology that could be implemented in the project, a final impact on the measurable and unmeasurable advantages and disadvantages has been considered. The tools adaptation time will decrease by 98%. This high percentage is justified by the transition from a manual operator activity, to an automatic configuration that would just require the time to plug in the tool and scan the product. It has been estimated that the rework rate will decrease by an uncertain quantity. The reduction is due to the decrease in human error in setting the tools parameter in any reconfiguration. Due to the high level of uncertainty related to this KPI, it has been decided to exclude it from the analysis, in order to maintain as consistent as possible hypothesis. The unmeasurable effects on the system are a dramatic increase in flexibility and replicability of the processes in the exact same way. The price of this impact is a complication of the IT architecture and a slight increase in energy consumption.

6) *Step 6. Economic analysis.*

The tool adaptation time imply a cost which will be critically reduced in case of implementation. A 98% reduction on the initial value is foreseen. This operation is performed in non-planned production time, thus it does not affect the throughput of the system. The DPP of the investment occurs in the eighth year and the IRR value was computed, with a result of 14,2%. Being the IRR greater than the discount rate has been used (10%), it can be stated that both PI and IRR indexes confirm a positive investment analysis for the project.

IV. CONCLUSIONS

The paper presents a holistic methodology for business case evaluation related to digital transformation. Even if the smart technologies implementation is becoming a main trend in the manufacturing world, the path toward I4.0 is not smooth. The final objective was to provide factories struggling for the achievement of a digital transformation with a useful guide tool to define, select, monitor and reach a successful scenario. The entire methodology has been applied to FAR-EDGE project use cases. The analysis has to consider a holistic approach from the technical, operational and human perspective. The migration has been analyzed under these three dimensions, assessing how to implement the new technologies and how does they impact on revenues, KPI and business models. Nevertheless, the revolution that the new computing paradigms are introducing involves the employees firstly and their way to adapt to this kind of changes in operations. The jobs are changing thanks to the digital transformation, the people and the operations have to be harmonized to the technical renewal so to reach a perfect and deep evolution. In general, the more flexible and open to future innovation a company is, the more it will be probable that they will lead, instead of following, in the market challenge. A very challenging task is to clearly identify the impact of the most recent technologies to a specific application, so to adapt and bend their functionalities for the purpose suggested by the firm's goal. In this light, the future work could be the utilization of the method presented to build a wide database. The more migration matrices related to value added there will be, the more the methodology would be usable and precise in foreseeing the final transformation results.

ACKNOWLEDGMENT

This work has received funding from the European Union's Horizon 2020 research and innovation programme under grant agreement No 723094. In any case, the present work cannot be considered as an official position of the supporting organization, but it reports just the point of view of the authors.

REFERENCES

[1] E. Pessl, S. R. Sorko, and B. Mayer, "Roadmap Industry 4.0 – Implementation Guideline for Enterprises," Int. J. Sci. Technol. Soc., vol. 5, no. 6, p. 193, 2018.

[2] C. Aboud et al., "The Digital Culture Challenge: Closing the Employee-Leadership Gap," Capgemini Digital Transformation Institute Survey, 2017.

[3] M. Brettel, N. Friederichsen, M. Keller, and M. Rosenberg, "How Virtualization, Decentralization and Network Building Change the Manufacturing Landscape: An Industry 4.0 Perspective," Int. J. Mech. Aerospace, Ind. Mechatron. Manuf. Eng., vol. 8, no. 1, pp. 37–44, 2014.

[4] McKinsey&Company, "IIoT platforms: The technology stack as value driver in industrial equipment and machinery," 2018.

[5] R. Burke, A. Mussomeli, S. Laaper, M. Hartigan, and B. Sniderman, "The smart factory" Deloitte Insights, 2017.

[6] G. Schuh, R. Anderl, J. Gausemeier, M. ten Hompel, and W. (Hrsg) Wahlster, "Industrie 4.0 Maturity Index," Acatech Study, p. 62, 2017.

[7] E. Gökalp, Ş. Umut, and E. P.Erhan, "Development of an Assessment Model for Industry 4.0: Industry 4.0-MM," in International Conference on Software Process Improvement and Capability Determination, 2017, pp. 128–142.

[8] A. Calà, A. Luder, F. Boschi, G. Tavola, and M. Taisch, "Migration towards digital manufacturing automation - An assessment approach," in Proceedings - 2018 IEEE Industrial Cyber-Physical Systems, ICPS 2018, 2018, pp. 714–719.

[9] A. Calà et al., "Migration from Traditional towards Cyber-Physical Production Systems," in 2017 IEEE 15th International Conference on Industrial Informatics (INDIN), 2017, pp. 1147–152.

[10] E. Gürel, "Swot analysis: A theoretical review," J. Int. Soc. Res., vol. 10, no. 51, pp. 6–11, 2017.

[11] M. Helms and J. Nixon, "Exploring swot analysis – where are we now?: A review of academic research from the last decade," J. Strateg. Manag., vol. 3, no. 3, pp. 215–251, 2010.

[12] M. Hergert and D. Morris, "Accounting data for value chain analysis," Strateg. Manag. J., vol. 10, no. 2, pp. 175–188, 1989.

[13] G. Azzone and U. Bertelè, "L'impresa - sistemi di governo, valutazione e controllo" (only italian version available), 2017.

[14] M. Macchi and L. Fumagalli, "A maintenance maturity assessment method for the manufacturing industry" J. Qual. Maint. Eng., vol. 19, no. 3, pp. 295–315, 2013.

[15] M. Fiasche, M. Pinzone, P. Fantini, A. Alexandru, and M. Taisch, "Human-centric factories 4.0: A mathematical model for job allocation," in IEEE 2nd International Forum on Research and Technologies for Society and Industry Leveraging a Better Tomorrow (RTSI), 2016, pp. 1–4.

[16] M. Peruzzini and M. Pellicciari, "A framework to design a humancentred adaptive manufacturing system for aging workers." Advanced Engineering Informatics, 2017.

[17] SEI, "CMMI for Development, Version 1.3." 2010.

[18] A. De Carolis, M. Macchi, E. Negri, and S. Terzi, "A maturity model for assessing the digital readiness of manufacturing companies," in IFIP International Conference on Advances in Production Management Systems, 2017, pp. 13–20.

[19] M. S. Grobelny, "Evaluating the Total Cost of Ownership for an On-Premise Application System," 2017.

[20] M. Isaja, J. Soldatos, and V. Gezer, "Combining Edge Computing and Blockchains for Flexibility and Performance in Industrial Automation," Int. Conf. Mob. Ubiquitous Comput. Syst. Serv. Technol., no. c, pp. 159–164, 2017.

Architectural Blueprint Solution for Migrating Towards FAR-EDGE

Ambra Calà
Siemens AG, Corporate Technology,
Günther-Scharowsky-Str. 1, 91058, Erlangen, Germany
e-mail: ambra.cala@siemens.com

Filippo Boschi, Paola Fantini, Giacomo Tavola, Marco Taisch
Politecnico di Milano
Via R. Lambruschini 4/b, 20156, Milano, Italy
email: {filippo.boschi, paola.fantini,giacomo.tavola, marco.taisch}@polimi.it

***Abstract*— Over the last years, several technologies and control systems have been developed for enabling the decentralization of automation control architectures for cyber-physical production systems. However, none of these technologies are in use yet. To overcome manufacturers' conservatism, migration strategies and decision-making approaches are required to support the adoption of the next generation of smart production systems. This paper presents a migration approach tailored to the migration of legacy automation systems towards the Industry 4.0 paradigm. Considering that the implementation of a new, or even just modified production control will have a direct impact on the existing production systems, the aim of the proposed approach is to evaluate opportunities of improvement and mitigate the risks of migration from technical, operational, human and business perspectives. The methodology follows an iterative and incremental approach starting from the definition of the current situation of the factory and identification of business goals to the evaluation of possible migration paths and the selection of the optimal one according to a cost-benefit analysis. The paper presents the methodology and one of the architectural blueprints derived during the EU-project FAR-EDGE to migrate towards a cloud- and edge-based automation control architecture.**

Keywords: Industry 4.0; Decentralized automation control; Migration strategy; cyber-physical production systems.

I. INTRODUCTION

The combination of Edge-Computing (EC) with Cyber-Physical Systems (CPS) and Internet of Things (IoT) standards will virtualize the conventional automation pyramid, enhancing flexibility and scalability in integrating modern IT technologies and, consequently, increasing the efficiency and the performance of production processes [1]. Edge-computing provides a distributed architecture option, which considers a new functional layer in the Industrial Automation pyramid that places data processing and control functions at the very edge of the network and facilitates distributed real-time control and scalable data processing.

However, today manufacturers are still reluctant to adopt decentralized manufacturing technologies. They typically aim at obtaining the return on the relevant investment sustained for their production facilities and envision only sporadic and limited changes. Nevertheless, in order to reap the opportunities offered by the new technologies, changes during the whole life cycle of the devices and services should be performed. To this end, industries need to be supported with migration strategies to implement new technologies and decentralize the automation pyramid. Within the context of complex automation systems, a complete change from the legacy production systems to the emerging I4.0 compliant ones in one step, following the Big Bang approach, will have a negative impact in terms of high upfront investments, development time, and risk of production losses. On the contrary, a smooth migration strategy, that applies future technologies in existing infrastructures with legacy systems through incremental migration steps, could lower risks and deliver immediate benefits [2]. The challenge is to identify the architectural blueprints of the migration considering not only the technology dimension but also the operational and human ones from a business process point of view.

Migration strategies are expected to play an essential role to the success of the envisioned infrastructure. Therefore, FAR-EDGE will study smooth migration path options from legacy centralized architectures to emerging FAR-EDGE based one.

The paper is structured as follows: after this brief introduction, Section II outlines the FAR-EDGE project's goals and Section III presents the methodology defined and adopted within the project, while Section IV briefly describes the migration strategy and how it supports the identification of the architectural blueprints and migration paths towards the FAR-EDGE architecture by using the migration matrix. Section V presents one migration solution blueprint and its implementation roadmap based on the FAR-EDGE industrial use cases. Section VI concludes the paper with a summary and outlook.

II. FAR-EDGE PROJECT

FAR-EDGE (Factory Automation Edge Computing Operating System Reference Implementation) intends to exploit the combination among EC, CPS and IoT Technologies for virtualizing conventional automation pyramid, and enhancing production system reconfigurability [3].

To this aim, FAR-EDGE project proposes a new Reference Architecture (RA) (Figure 1) composed by:

1. Four horizontal Layers: Field, Edge, Ledger and Cloud.
2. Three functional viewpoints: Automation, Analytics and Simulation

FAR-EDGE identifies in the Field tier, which corresponds to the Level 1 in the ISA-95 pyramid, particular device called Edge Node, equipped with on board computing capabilities,

The Edge Layer includes SCADA (Level 2) and MES (Level 3) functionalities by following the Automation Pyramid terminology. In FAR-EDGE, it consists of Edge Gateways that execute all those production processes having a local scope due to time and bandwidth constraints. Finally, the Cloud layer could also include MES functionality and provides interfaces (Cloud Services) to the ERP (Level 4) of the ISA-95 automation pyramid. Compared to the Edge Layer, it includes production and business processes that do not have strict time requirements and do not bound to the factory.

The connection to the shopfloor is performed by the Field Abstraction Component that has specific requirements from the shopfloor automations and equipment. Thus, in addition to the 3 vertical functional viewpoints (Automation, Analytics and Simulation enabled by RA), a Field dimension is required, as it is a FAR-EDGE enabler. Therefore, if in some use cases specific requirements are not met in the field, the FAR-EDGE platform is not applicable.

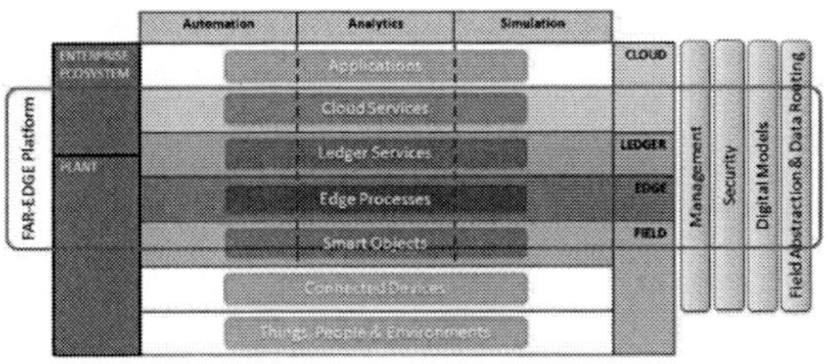

Figure 1. FAR-EDGE Platform

III. METHODOLOGY FOR MIGRATION

This section illustrates a methodological approach aiming at supporting decision makers in addressing the migration, i.e., transformation, towards FAR-EDGE. The approach encompasses the initial assessment of the current level of manufacturing digital maturity, the analysis of priorities based on the business strategy, and the development of a migration strategy. Specifically, an innovative holistic approach to develop a migration strategy towards the digital automation paradigm with the support of a set of best practices and tools is presented. The application of the approach is illustrated through the description of the blueprint solution in Section IV.

The overall approach is implemented according to the 5 steps described in Figure 2.

The identification of the factory analysis domains in Step 1 allowed a better understanding of the current situation of the production environment under technical, operational and human aspects. This task is supported by an assessment questionnaire according to the scope of the developed FAR-EDGE architecture. The second step of the FAR-EDGE Migration approach aims at the realization of the Migration Matrix and the selection of the appropriate digital maturity levels scale characterized for the three different dimensions of the factory, constituting a reference model that can be used to evaluate the AS-IS and TO-BE situations of a factory and analyse their gap. The Migration Matrix with the redefined digital maturity levels scale are described in [4].

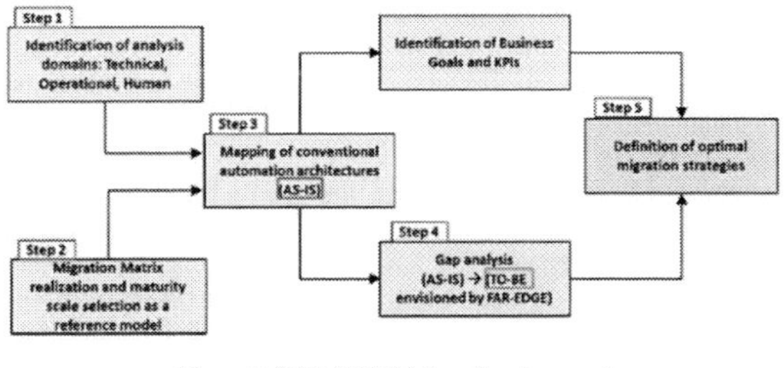

Figure 2. FAR-EDGE Migration Approach

The next step based on the mapping of the conventional automation architecture within the Migration Matrix, needed to analyse the possible different starting points of migration and to define accordingly a kind of library of reusable blueprints architectures towards FAR-EDGE.

The gap analysis between the TO-BE situation, namely the edge based distributed architecture envisioned by FAR-EDGE, and the AS-IS situation of the factory, considers the methodology described in [5] to point out the business goals and KPIs, in order to define the optimal migration strategy for the specific use cases.

Finally, the approach ends by providing a set of blueprint solution that can ensure a smooth and low risk digital transformation of traditional production systems to digital automation solutions, notably the automation, simulation and analytics solutions that are aligned to the FAR-EDGE reference architecture.

In this way, the approach provides a clear map of the current (AS-IS) and desired (TO-BE) conditions of a factory, revealing different alternatives to achieve a specific goal, by means of a digital automation system and towards the vision of digital factory.

Moreover, this approach enables the evaluation of the potential alternatives according to the business strategy, considering also strengths and weaknesses points. Based on this evaluation, the migration approach ends-up specifying adequate architectural blueprints that match the needs of the organization and the estimation of the overall benefit of the digital automation solution for the analysed production system.

IV. MIGRATION PROCESS

The first part of the migration approach previously mentioned is based on an assessment questionnaire. It has been developed in order to assess the current status of a factory at technical, operational and human dimensions. The assessment aims at evaluating the digital maturity level of a factory in comparison with the digitalization envisioned by FAR-EDGE. For this reason, the questionnaire is structured according to the main functional domains of the FAR-EDGE Reference Architecture: automation, analytics, and simulation. The "Automation" mainly concerns the capability to utilize instructions to create a repeated process that replaces an IT professional's manual work in data centres and cloud deployments. In this context, the automation accomplishes a task repeatedly without human intervention. The "Analytics" involves those activities related to multivariate analysis of a process aiming at developing a statistically based understanding, leading to process improvement and/or optimization. The "Simulation" is closely related to the digital factory concept, which offers an integrated approach to enhance the product and production engineering processes and simulation is a key technology within this concept.

In order to create a more coherent questionnaire, the interrelationship between functional domain (Automation, Analytics and Simulation) with the three dimensions applied: (Technical, Operational and Human) has been needed.

The "Automation – Technical dimension" section aims at collecting information related to the current automation system in production, i.e. the structure of the automation architecture and the legacy software and hardware. Particular relevance is also given to the type of the connectivity among these systems, and the existing security and access control mechanisms. Related topics include the monitoring support in production for errors and performance [6].

The "Automation – Operational dimension" section is related to the so-called "Orchestration" concept. This is a broader concept wherein the user coordinates automated tasks into a cohesive process or workflow for IT and the business process. In this context, automation is seen as the capability to manage and to integrate different information in an automatic way [6].

The "Analytics – Technical dimension" section is related to the possibility to utilize data and information needed to carry out the analysis to provide the value added to management approach [6].

The "Analytics – Operational dimension" section takes into account the company inclination to manage a basic manufacturing process controlling the input factors (especially chosen by decision makers) and the fixed inputs (defined by the current context) and monitoring the uncontrollable or nuisance variables aiming at evaluating and optimizing the output responses [6].

The "Simulation – Technical dimension" section sees the simulation as a technology that provides design engineers with the right tools, the right hardware—at the right time—to make better decisions. It requires Integration of CAD designs and CAE information, connecting multiple simulation models, and data synchronization of the engineering processes requiring access to all necessary product and process information [6].

The "Simulation – Operational dimension" section concerns the enabled dynamic analysis and optimization of material flow, resource utilization and logistics for all levels of plant planning from global production networks, through local plants down to specific lines. In these terms, the relevant goal of simulation is to provide all users to quickly assess the impact of their decisions on product, process, plant and resource requirements [6].

The "Human dimension" section concerns the social readiness to cope with the functional domains and the related technical and operational facets, namely it is related to the level of awareness and know how that are characterizing the company organization. It takes into account also the capability of the human resources to extract the valuable data and to carry out a disciplined engineering and scientific methods to identify and control the factors that impact the business value of the company [6].

Based on the answers of this questionnaire, different migration scenarios according to the possible technology options are investigated in order to identify the migration alternatives to go from the identified AS-IS situation to the TO-BE one [1] . To this end, a tool called Migration Matrix has been developed within the FAR-EDGE project to identify all the necessary improvements in the direction of the Industry 4.0 vision of smart factory, splitting the digital transformation in different scale-levels. Thus, the matrix represents a multiple impact dimensions, aiming at providing a snapshot of current situation of companies and suggesting which steps should be achieved in order to reach the FAR-EDGE objective in a smooth and stepwise migration process.

The migration matrix is structured in rows and columns. The rows represent the relevant application fields selected during the preparation phase with high potential of improvement by FAR-EDGE concepts implementation on the architecture. Meanwhile the columns the development steps for each application field towards a higher level of production flexibility, intelligent manufacturing and business process in the direction of a digital automation implementation [1]. The development steps are divided in five columns representing five levels of production system's digital maturity, based on the integrating principles of both the Capability Maturity Model Integration (CMMI) framework [7][8][9], and DREAMY model (Digital REadiness Assessment MaturitY) [10] .

V. MIGRATION SOLUTION BLUEPRINTS

A traditional manufacturer aims at decentralizing the current factory automation architecture and introduce cyber-physical system concepts in order to flexibly deploy new technologies and maximize the correlation across its technical abilities to support mass-customization. Target of the implementation of the FAR-EDGE platform is the reduction of time and effort required for deploying new applications by the automatic reconfiguration of physical equipment on different stations, according to the current operation, and its automatic synchronization among different information systems (PLM, ERP, and MES [11],[12]).

A factory that currently presents an automation architecture compliant to ISA-95 standards with three layers (ERP, MES, and SCADA with Field devices) could have potential issues during the integration of new applications at the MES level to obtain new functions at the shop-floor. In fact, it could be very expensive because of highly dependent on the centralized control structure of the architecture.

Moreover, it requires a long verification time and, consequently, a long delivery time to customers.

From this context, one of the project's goals was to provide a set of architectural blueprints based on the use cases that have been developed within the project. The main objective is to show the benefits of the FAR-EDGE architecture and few possible application scenarios with reference to one or more functional domains of the platform. This section presents one of these architectural blueprints, i.e. the migration towards production optimization by means of the simulation functional domain of the FAR-EDGE architecture.

A. Simulation functional domain

FAR-EDGE Simulation provides functionalities for simulating the behaviour of physical production processes for the purpose of optimization or of testing What-If scenarios at minimal cost and risk and without any impact of regular shop activities. Simulation requires digital model of plants and processes to be in-sync with the real-world objects they represent. As the real-world is subject to change, models should reflect those changes. For instance, the model of a machine assumes a given value of electric power / energy consumption, but the actual values will diverge as the real machine wears down. To detect this gap and correct the model accordingly, raw data from the Field (direct) or complex analysis algorithms (from Analytics) can be used.

To explain how a typical migration roadmap to the FAR-EDGE Simulation functionality can bring industrial benefits, the What-If scenario use case based is here described.

A traditional factory will benefit from the adoption of simulation and what-if analysis especially about the evaluation of the impacts of variations in the production conditions, including changes in the capacity, changes in the production plan, changes in the production mix, as well as the changes in physical configurations.

From a technical point of view a capacity to create a digital model to reproduce the actors and the activities carried out within the shop floor is required. Furthermore, decentralized architecture that enhances the automatic integration of data, information and results coming from the overall context of the company such as the market, the customer requirement or the internal processes, is needed. Finally, the real time and remote communication will need to be carried out for initiating and updating parameters exchange for example at the beginning of the production. This requires standard communication protocols.

Moreover, the role of employees can be affected by the new technological and operational changes. A typical design engineer should improve his/her skills and his/her know how on utilizing new technologies based on design and simulation activities and typically integrated with ICT aspects.

For example, the added implementation of communication tools in simulation process means that feedback loops are growing ever too common to the modern engineer. Feedback loops are great when it comes to affecting the design positively, but they often mean a nightmare to the untrained engineer. With the growing capability of cloud-based programs, engineer's work is now often monitored or analysed in real time. This opens up the door for collaboration and greater innovation, but it means that as engineers, we need to be able to communicate.

B. Deployment of FAR-EDGE Simulation – Roadmap Implementation

The virtual representation of the physical objects in cyber space can be used for optimization of the production processes. For example, the cyber modules have the ability to avoid getting stuck in local optimization extremes and are able to find the global maximum and minimum which results in high performance. Therefore, the integration of digital models should be considered as a first step.

In addition, the existing CAD systems will be interfaced to each other, and secondly, they will be fully integrated to enable the optimization of equipment reconfiguration through intelligent simulation tools. In the same way, the production will be optimized based on the integrated information derived from the CAD designs and then it will be automatically implemented through the intelligent tools. To this end, the production process models and their different layout versions will be first integrated with business functions, in order to align the process parameters with cost deployment and profitability measures.

From an organizational perspective, the main implications affect the roles of product designers and production engineers: they need to increase their level of cooperation to model all the relevant aspects of the manufacturing processes into the CAD. Furthermore, the production engineers have to see that the models of the CAD are connected to the models of the actual production facilities, so that the production can be simulated, planned and monitored. Therefore, the competences of the above-mentioned roles require to be enhanced with new skills concerning digitalization, modelling and simulation. Furthermore, the tasks and responsibilities of these roles have to be updated, accordingly.

The FAR-EDGE architectural blueprint for simulation and what-if analysis comprehends the following components:

- CPS Model Synchronization
  - Synchronization Services
  - Open API for Virtualization
- Edge Infrastructure
  - Data Routing & Pre-processing
  - Field Abstraction
- Ledger Infrastructure
  - Distributed Ledger

The Field Abstraction Component provides the mechanisms for configuring and controlling shop floor equipment and to receive asynchronous events and alarms from it. It is composed of informatics istance that, exploiting a bi-directional, low bandwidth communication, can exchange high frequent message. In this way, it is possible to obtain the abstraction of the low-level technical details of field components interactions.

The Data Routing & Pre-processing Component provides the mechanisms to move massive streams of data from the Field Tier to the upper Tiers of the Platform. In this case, the communication is unidirectional (upstream). Using this module, the acquisition and the pre-process of large amounts of data from heterogeneous sources can be pointed out, merging them into a common schema.

From the implementation of these two components of the edge infrastructure, it is possible to instantiate a digital model of the shop floor and to populate it with set of heterogeneous data. The digital model facilitates an intermediate step where the integration of CAD systems with other design tools can be obtained. In this way, it is possible to leave the approach in which each simulation system was fed by manually entering data from other systems (e.g. scheduling systems, production data management). In fact, through the integration of multiple software it will be possible to analyse in a single simulation environment more aspects (from those technical, operational to economic ones) facilitating the integration and orchestration ability that will be obtained through the ledger implementation.

Once the connectivity has been ensured, the next step consists in the implementation of the Ledger Infrastructure, namely Synchronization services and Distributed Ledger to enable the collection and integration of information through the Cloud and to support simulation activity and what- if analysis.

The Distributed Ledger Enabler is responsible of the decentralization of the factory automation pyramid. It maintains shared process state and shared business logic on Peer Nodes that may belong to any physical Tier of the Platform (Field, Edge, Cloud), and includes all the functionality for the enablement of Ledger Services. In this case, the Synchronization Services Component is considered as an aggregation / post-processing layer that includes all smart contacts used to support the Digital Models. These smart contracts are responsible to lead the relationship between the digital model and the changes or the event that happen in the real world, namely in the shop floor.

After Ledger implementation, the smart contract instantiation and after the connection of Field abstraction with upper tier, it is possible to obtain a fully integrated CAD systems with intelligent tools for interactive design process and consequently an automatic optimization of shop floor details based on simulation services. The last component to be implemented is the Cloud infrastructure with its Open API for Virtualization that implement the cloud service endpoints. At this point a definition of maintenance plan for cloud system and a training for its utilization and management is required.

Figure 3 represents the roadmap at technical (in blue), operational (in orange) and human (in green) dimensions towards simulation and what-if analysis by means of FAR-EDGE Simulation.

The Migration Matrix in Figure 4 represents the results, in terms of digital maturity improvement, of one of the possible migration paths towards FAR-EDGE Simulation. The technical, operational and human entities most impacted by the migration towards the scenario "Simulation and What if analysis" described above are the following:

- Simulation and visualization tools that, by the implementation of the Ledger infrastructure, are able to integrate in a digital world the results of different systems, enabling the representation of virtual aspect of overall company;
- Cyber-Physical System characteristics of the process, since the processes are integrated with digital-twin capabilities to interact each other;
- Autonomous Optimization process, since each shop floor component can be abstracted, visualized and can communicate each time has impacted by condition change;
- Production IT department, since new digital systems are introduced by external experts that will also provide continuous support;
- Simulation and design employees' skills, with the first trainings focused on the use of the new technologies implemented.

VI. CONCLUSION

The FAR-EDGE migration approach shows how migration matrices can support manufacturers by providing them with a holistic view of the required steps for migration towards the Industry 4.0 vision at different dimensions of the factory, i.e. technical, operational, and human. Based on this information

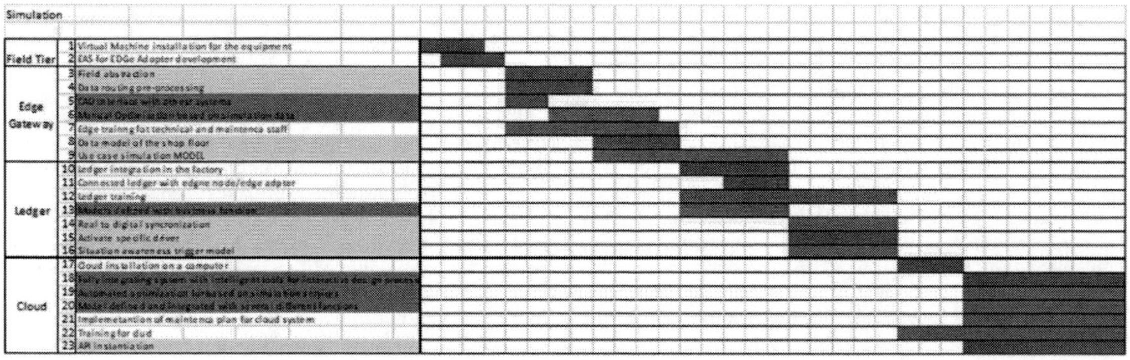

Figure 3. FAR-EDGE Simulation Roadmap for Simulation and What-If analysis scenario

MP 2 Simulation	Level 1	Level 2	Level 3	Level 4	Level 5
	3D layouts, visualization and simulation tools				
	CAD systems not related to production data	CAD systems manually feed with production data	CAD systems interfaced with other design systems	CAD systems interfaces with intelligent systems for fast development	Fully integrated CAD systems with intelligent tools for interactive design process
	Production Optimization				
	N.A.	Rare offline optimization	Offline optimization based on manual data extraction	Manual optimization based on simulation data	Automatic optimization based on simulation services
	Availability of production process models				
	N.A.	Models defined (Excel based) with limited use	Models defined with limited specific functions	Models defined and integrated with business functions	Models defined and integrated with several different functions
	Impact of digital technologies on Product Designers and Production Engineers				
	Still unclear	Identified in general terms	Analyzed	Defined	Implemented in continuous improvement

Figure 4. Migration Path (MP2) for the implementation of simulation and what-if analysis

and according to the business goals, the manufacturer can select the optimal scenario as first step of migration towards the long-term goal of complete digitalization of the factory. The solution identified within the selected scenario is then further detailed into an implementation roadmap, highlighting the necessary steps at technical, operational and human levels, in order to ensure a successful migration towards the FAR-EDGE vision.

ACKNOWLEDGMENT

This project has received funding from the European Union's Horizon 2020 research and innovation programme under grant agreement No 723094.

REFERENCES

[1] A. Calà, F. Boschi, P. Fantini, A.Lüder and M. Taisch, "'Migration Strategies towards the Digital Manufacturing Automation,'" *in The Digital Shopfloor: Industrial Automation in the Industry 4.0 Era . (Soldatos, J; Lazaro, O; Cavadini, F. Eds.)*: River Publisher, 2019."

[2] A. Calà, A. Lüder, A. Cachada, F. Pires, J. Barbosa, P. Leitao and M. Gepp "Migration from traditional towards cyber-physical production systems," in Proceedings - *2017 IEEE 15th International Conference on Industrial Informatics, INDIN 2017, 2017, pp. 1147–1152.*

[3] "FAR-EDGE – Factory Automation Edge Computing Operating System Reference Implementation." 2017.

[4] A. Calà, F. Boschi, A. Lüder, G. Tavola, and M. Taisch, "Migration towards digital manufacturing automation - An assessment approach," P*roc. - 2018 IEEE Ind. Cyber-Physical Syst. ICPS 2018*,

[5] Marco Taisch, Roberto Rocca, Filippo Boschi, Ambra Calà and Paola Fantini, "A migration methodology for factories digital transformation," in *Sixth European Lean Educator Conference (ELEC2019)*, 2019.

[6] A. Calà, F. Boschi, P. M. Fantini, A. Pagani, and F. Schildauer, "D 3.10 Blueprint Solutions and Strategies for Migrating to Decentralized Factory Automation Architectures – M20 Release," 2018.

[7] M. Macchi and L. Fumagalli, "A maintenance maturity assessment method for the manufacturing industry," *J. Qual. Maint. Eng.*, 2013.

[8] M.Macchi M., Fumagalli L., Pizzolante S., Crespo A. and Fernandez G., "Towards Maintenance_maturity assessment of maintenance services for new ICT introduction," in *APMS-International Conference Advances in Production Management Systems*, 2010.

[9] J. Zeb, T. Froese, and D. Vanier, "Infrastructure Management Process Maturity Model: Development and Testing," *J. Sustain. Dev.*, vol. 6, no. 11, 2013.

[10] A. De Carolis, M. Macchi, E. Negri, and S. Terzi, "A Maturity Model for Assessing the Digital Readiness of Manufacturing Companies," in *IFIP International Federation for Information Processing 2017*, 2017, pp. 13–20.

[11] M. Garetti, P. Rosa, and S. Terzi, "Life Cycle Simulation for the design of Product-Service Systems," *Comput. Ind.*, vol. 63, no. 4, pp. 361–369, 2012.

[12] M. Garetti and S. Terzi, "Product Lifecycle Management: Definizione , Caratteristiche e Questioni Aperte," 2003, no. January 2003, p. 16.

Digital Models for Data Analytics and Digital Twins in Industrial Automation Applications

Introduction of a Common Interoperability Registry for linking diverse functional domains

Nikos Kefalakis
IoT Group Athens Information Technology (AIT)
Kifisias Ave. 44, Marousi, 15125 Athens, Greece
e-mail: nkef@ait.gr

John Soldatos
IoT Group Athens Information Technology (AIT)
Kifisias Ave. 44, Marousi, 15125 Athens, Greece
e-mail: jsol@ait.gr

John Kaldis
IoT Group Athens Information Technology (AIT)
Kifisias Ave. 44, Marousi, 15125 Athens, Greece
e-mail: jkaldis@ait.gr

Mauro Isaja
Research & Development
Engineering Ingegneria Informatica SpA (ENG)
Via Ferrini, 47 - Loc. San Martino
53035 Monteriggioni, Italy
e-mail: mauro.isaja@eng.it

Abstract— **Digital representations of the physical world through the renowned "digital twin" concept, within industry 4.0 and Industrial Internet of Things (IIoT) environments, gave rise to several digital modelling approaches. This paper illustrates a complete digital model specifically focused on intensive Big Data operations, which is a common industry4.0 requirement. The model is established on patterns of world acclaimed standards-based digital models, as it was deployed successfully in one predictive maintenance manufacturing project and one project on edge computing with a block chain layer. Furthermore, the paper introduces the Common Interoperability Registry, a novel addition in the form of a standards-based, vendor-neutral method to map object entities belonging to different systems/databases. This facilitates discoverability and inserts a global unique identifier among entities from different functional domains.**

Keywords- Digital Twins; Digital Models for Distributed Data Analytics; Common Interoperability Registry; Industrial Internet of Things; Industry4.0; Manufacturing Plant Modelling

I. INTRODUCTION

Digital modelling of the physical world is one of the core concepts of industry digitization and the fourth industrial revolution (Industry 4.0). It foresees the development of digital representations of physical world objects and processes as a means of executing automation and control operations, based on digital operations and functionalities (i.e., at the cyber world). This concept is conveniently called "digital twin". The advent of Industry 4.0 (including models and standards, such as RAMI 4.0) has led to the identification of standards-based data schemas and data formats, which can be used for describing plants, automation operations, production systems and more. Usually, digital models are accompanied by a set of functions, which undertake the synchronization of these models with the physical world entities that they represent. Digital models serve three complementary objectives:

a) Semantic interoperability

By providing a uniform representation of the concepts and entities that comprise an IIoT deployment, they boost semantic inter-operability across diverse digital systems and physical devices. Indeed, the use of common data model provides a uniform vocabulary for describing sensors, Cyber-Physical System (CPS) devices, production systems and more.

b) Information Exchange

Digital models provide a basis for exchanging information across different similar deployments, which is closely related to the inter-operability objective.

c) Digital Operations

Digital models are a key prerequisite for performing automation and control operations at IT (Information Technology) timescales. Processes and devices can be configured through IT systems that configure and update digital models, which reflect the status of the physical world. However, this requires a synchronization, which can be challenging to implement. The functionalities of digital models should support:

- Factory and Plant Information Modelling
- Automation and Analytics Processes Modelling
- Synchronization of Cyber and Physical worlds
- Dynamic Access to Plant Information

Nevertheless, the above properties do not address issues, such as data intensive applications, similar to those faced within H2020 FAREDGE and H2020 PROPHESY. Moreover, existing digital models were found insufficient for this purpose. Section II explains why a novel model was required to be developed. Section III presents the guideline standards for our design. Section IV illustrates the new data model in detail. Section V introduces the Common Interoperability Registry (CIR), the merging problems that it solves, and its potential applications for concurrent use of different models & standards.

II. Reasoning for a New Model

The reasoning behind the introduction of a new Data Model in this paper is twofold: First, to focus on data-intensive applications like data streams, analytics, digital twins on analytics, etc., and second, to provide a CIR implementation for linking with other relevant data models. Most Industry4.0 applications are data driven and hence digital modeling of Big Data operations is a cornerstone requirement. In this respect the FAR-EDGE data model is tailored to data intensive operations, rather than lightweight automation functions. Furthermore, linking and integration of other data models is made possible through the CIR, ensuring suitability for a wider class of Industry4.0 applications. The resulting digital model has been successfully deployed in two predictive maintenance cases of H2020 PROPHESY, and two factory cases of the H2020 FAREDGE edge computing with block-chain project.

III. Standards-Based Digital Models

For over a decade, various industrial standards have been developed, and a long list of relevant digital models exists. Many standards come with a set of semantic definitions, typically used for modelling and exchanging data across systems and applications. For reviews and comparative assessments, interested readers can refer to relevant literature (e.g., [1][3][4]). The most prominent ones, which have also been driving the specifications for the relevant H2020 projects PROPHESY and FAREDGE, can be found below. Several of them are referenced and/or used by RAMI4.0.

A. *IEC 62264 B2MML*

An XML based specification and implementation of the ANSI/ISA-95 family of standards, and a very good choice for modelling interactions across entities within MES and ERP systems and their involvement in automation operations. With reference to this hierarchy, the standard covers the domain of manufacturing operations management (i.e., Level 4) and the interface content and transactions within Level 3 and between Level 3 and Level 4. Hence, the standard is primarily focused on the integration between manufacturing operations and control, rather than on pure control (i.e., Levels 1, 2, 3).

B. *IEC 61512 BatchML*

An XML based implementation of the ANSI/ISA-88 Batch Control family of standards, suitable for the modelling of ISA-88 compliant systems.

C. *IEC 62769 (FDI)*

It includes an information model that represents automation systems' topologies, including field devices and the communication networks that interconnect them, and is hence suitable for modelling information on the field layer of the factory (devices, networks), but without provisions for data analytics.

D. *ISO 15926 XMplant*

It covers the structure, the geometry and 3D models about a plant, and provides support for digital modelling of plant information, based on the ISO 15926 specification. It is a good choice for modelling the static elements and behaviors of a plant.

E. *IEC 62453 (FDT)*

The IEC 62453 Field Device Tool (FDT) by fdtgroup.org, is an open standard for industrial automation integration of networks and devices. It provides standardized software to enable intelligent field devices that can be integrated seamlessly into automation applications, from the commissioning tool to the control system. FDT supports the coupling of software modules, which have been implemented as representatives for field devices and are therefore able to provide and/or exchange information.

F. *IEC 61512 (Batch Control)*

IEC 61512 – Batch control is also referenced by RAMI 4.0. It models batch production records, including information about production of batches or elements of batch production.

G. *IEC 61424 (CAEX)*

It provides the means for modelling a plant in a hierarchical way. It supports an XML-based representation of plant information, including all components in a hierarchical structure, and adopts an object-oriented philosophy. CAEX separates vendor independent information (e.g., objects, attributes, interfaces, hierarchies, references, libraries, classes) and application dependent information, such as certain attribute names, specific classes or object catalogues. CAEX is appropriate for storing static metadata, but it not designed to hold dynamic information. CAEX can cover the modelling of the plant elements, but is inappropriate for modelling maintenance-related information such as sensor-based datasets.

H. *IEC 62714 AutomationML*

AutomationML is an XML-based open standard, which provides the means for describing the components of a complex production environment through a hierarchical structure, and it is commonly used to facilitate consistent exchange and editing of plant layout data across heterogeneous engineering tools. It relies on three other standards, namely: CAEX (IEC 62424) in order to model topological information, COLLADA (ISO/PAS 17506) of the Khronos Group in order to model and implement geometry concepts and 3D information, as well as Kinematics (i.e., the geometry of motion), and finally PLCopen XML (IEC61131) in order to model sequences of actions, internal behavior of objects and I/O connections.

I. *MTConnect*

MTConnect provides an XML-based format for exchanging data between the shop-floor and IT applications, including data about devices, topologies and component characteristics.

J. *PERFoRMML*

The H2020 PERFORM project is devoted to the development and validation of a plug-n'-produce infrastructure. Following a comprehensive review and evaluation of various data models, the PERFORM consortium has selected AutomationML as the base for building its own common data model, conveniently called PERFoRMML. It makes provisions for modelling/representing the following:

1) Machinery and Control Systems

They provide the means for modelling the topology, data types and interactions of production systems at physical machinery level. The attributes of these entities enable capturing and modelling of parameters for configurations and skills, as well as for shop-floor data to be extracted from various sources such as PLCs and databases. In particular, the following sub-entities are also modelled through proper subclasses:

- Skills (e.g., pick, place, move, weld etc.) refer to abilities, functions or tasks performed by shop-floor elements. They may possess and certain values that are relevant to be extracted (e.g., cycle time, energy consumption, and sensor data).
- Configurations provide a high-level description of a possible configuration to execute a given skill, according to a set of specified parameters.
- Products, which correspond to abstractions of given product variants, along with their core-defining characteristics to enable a process-oriented description of the product.
- Processes, which present the ordered steps required for the production of an associated product.
- Connectors, which encapsulate and abstract the information required to communicate with components in the shop-floor. The abstraction property enables to support communications regardless of the actual communication protocols (e.g., OPC-UA, MQTT) used.
- Events, modelling certain occurrences in production that require the attention of the system or its users.

2) Data Backbone entities

These model the elements necessary for interactions with the tools connecting to the PERFORM middleware. These entities can acquire data and information from the lower-level and act based on it, and they include:

- System, which is an entity representing entire production systems and therefore comprises systems information in terms of topology, products and possible simulations.
- Simulation Results, which support the representation of some simulation outcome (usually a KPI: Key Performance Indicator) in-line with the PERFORM's digital twins requirements.
- Schedules, which model the allocation of the (end-to-end) steps that need to be executed in order for the production of certain product.

For each of the two sets of entities (machinery & control, data backbone), the project specified standard based interfaces for accessing instance data of the various entities. These interfaces form the basis for an API (Application Programming Interface) as well.

IV. THE FAR-EDGE DATA MODEL

The root element of the FAR-EDGE Digital Models is the "FAR-EDGE DM" and at the next hierarchy level, a set of further XSD Schemata are designed. The FAR-EDGE Digital Models' factory data and metadata are based on the entities:

a) For factory data description:

- Data Source Definition (DSD): Defines the properties of a data source in the shopfloor, such as a data stream from a sensor or an automation device.
- Data Interface Specification (DI): It is associated with a data source and provides the information needed to connect to it and access its data (e.g., network protocol, port, network address).
- Data Kind (DK): This specifies the semantics of the data of the data source. It can be used to define virtually any type of data in an extensible way.
- Data Source Manifest (DSM): Specifies a specific instance of a data source in line with its DSD, DI and DK specifications. Multiple manifests are therefore used to represent the data sources that are available in the factory.
- Data Consumer Manifest (DCM): Models an instance of a data consumer, i.e., any application that accesses a data source.
- Data Channel Descriptor (DCD): Models the association between an instance of a consumer and an instance of a data source. Keeps track of the established connections and associations between data sources and data consumers.
- LiveDataSet: Models the actual dataset that stems from an instance of a data source that is represented through a DSM. It is t is associated with a timestamp and keeps track of the location of the data source in case it is associated with a mobile edge node. In principle, the data source comprises a set of name–value pairs, which adhere to different data types in line with the DK of the DSM.
- Edge Gateway: Models an edge gateway of an edge computing deployment. Data sources are associated with an edge gateway, which usually implies not only a logical association, but also a physical association as well.

Based on the above entities, it is possible to represent the different data sources of a digital shopfloor in a modular, dynamic and extensible way. This is based on a repository (i.e., registry) of data sources and their manifests, which keeps track of the various data sources that register to it.

b) For factory analytics description, analytics workflows and pipelines:

- Analytics Processor Definition (APD): Specifies processing functions applied on one or more data sources. Three types of processing functions are supported, including data preprocessing, data storage, and data analytics functions. These can be combined in various configurations over the data sources in order to define analytics workflows.

- Analytics Processor Manifest (APM): Represents an instance of a processor that is defined through an APD. Each instance specifies the type of processor and its actual logic through linking to an implementation function (like a Java class).
- Analytics orchestrator Manifest (AM): Represents an analytics workflow as a combination of analytics processor instances (i.e., APMs). It is likely to span over multiple edge gateways and to operate over their data sources.

V. THE CIR COMMON INTEROPERABILITY REGISTRY

A novel addition to the proposed digital model, is the Common Interoperability Registry (CIR) that enables the merging of the data models from the different functional domains. Specifically, CIR provides a standards-based, vendor-neutral method to map object entities belonging to different systems/databases that share common business context. Additionally, it:

- Enables the discoverability and relation of the registered objects and helps third party applications to combine the information provided from these systems/databases.
- Provides a global unique identifier (in a UUID format) for the registered objects.

CIR can be viewed as the infrastructure for linking objects and their information that reside in different databases, and enables the enrichment of the underlying datasets based on additional data and metadata residing in the linked databases. For instance, considering different functional domains, such as the Data Sources, the Virtualization/Simulation and the Automation, the need arises for information sharing among them. The obvious upside is that an IIoT application will be able to consult and access (through the CIR) information about the full context and observations that are related to an object, regardless of the repository they reside. Likewise, a flexible extension of the digital models' infrastructure with information (data/metadata) stemming for additional repositories and databases is possible. Nevertheless, note that this will require each new repository to be linked to objects of the project's database at the time of their deployment. The CIR provides an XML schema and a relational DB describing the specification. The OpenO&M (CIR) is open source and the latest version can be found in the MIMOSA organization GitHub. As implemented, the CIR [8] includes:

- Registry: The container object for a set of categories.
- ID: The user-defined identifier of the registry.
- Description: Description and expected use of CIR
- Category: Categories define sets of potentially related entries, such as equipment, which have alternate names on different systems.

VI. CONCLUSION AND FUTURE WORK

In the complex landscape of various standards for digital modelling in Industry 4.0, there exists no "one size fits all" solution that will prevail, until the present day. Standards are tailored to different applications, e.g., automation, simulation, digital twins, Big Data analytics, supply chain management, etc. Our needs dictated the design of a new model focused on data collection, routing and analytics i.e., typical data-intensive applications. It is based on several world-renowned, standards-based digital models. The future vision of a "Fully Digital Shopfloor" (i.e., for all production processes) will require the concurrent use of different models & standards. Hence, there is a need for more mechanisms to link those standards (like the proposed CIR), to digitally reflect the shopfloor consistently.

ACKNOWLEDGMENT

Part of this work (namely the FAREDGE DM and its further schemata) has been carried out in the scope of the H2020 FAR-EDGE project (contract number 723094), while another part (namely the CIR design and implementation) has been carried out in the scope of H2020 PROPHESY project (contract number 766994). Both projects are funded by the European Commission. The authors acknowledge valuable help and contributions from all partners of both projects, including the plants where the DM and CIR infrastructure have been validated.

REFERENCES

[1] H. Lasi, P. Fettke, H.G. Kemper, T. Feld, and M. Hoffmann, "Industry 4.0", Business & Information Systems Engineering, vol. 6, no. 4, pp. 239, 2014.

[2] A. W. Colombo, T. Bangemann, and S. Karnouskos, "IMC-AESOP Outcomes: Paving the way to Collaborative Manufacturing Systems", Proceedings of the 12th IEEE International Conference on Industrial Informatics (INDIN'14), pp. 255-260, 2014.

[3] W. Lepuschitz, A. Lobato-Jimenez, E. Axinia, and M. Merdan, "A survey on standards and ontologies for process automation" in Industrial Applications of Holonic and Multi-Agent Systems, Springer, pp. 22-32, 2015

[4] R. S. Peres et al, "Selection of a data exchange format for industry 4.0 manufacturing systems," IECON 2016 - 42nd Annual Conference of the IEEE Industrial Electronics Society, Florence, 2016, pp. 5723-5728, doi: 10.1109/IECON.2016.7793750.

[5] "IEC 62714 engineering data exchange format for use in industrial automation systems engineering - automation markup language - parts 1 and 2" in , International Electrotechnical commission, pp. 2014-2015.

[6] J.Soldatos, O.Lazaro, and F.Cavadini "The Digital Shopfloor: Industrial Automation in the Industry 4.0 Era -Performance Analysis and Applications" ISBN: 9788770220415 River Publishers

[7] S. Faltinski, O. Niggemann, N. Moriz, and A. Mankowski, "AutomationML: From data exchange to system planning and simulation," IEEE International Conference on Industrial Technology (ICIT), 2012, pp. 378–383.

[8] A. Mathew, K. Bever, and D. Brandl, "Web Service Common Interoperability Registry 1.0", OpenO&M Candidate Standard 19 June 2015, available at: http://www.openoandm.org/ws-cir/1.0/ws-cir.html [retrieved: September, 2019]

A Field Study: The Perception of Edge Computing for Production Industry

Volkan Gezer[1], Jakob Zietsch[2], Nils Weinert[2], and Martin Ruskowski[1]

[1]Innovative Factory Systems (IFS), German Research Center for Artificial Intelligence (DFKI), Kaiserslautern, Germany
Email: {volkan.gezer, martin.ruskowski}@dfki.de

[2]Siemens AG, Corporate Technology, Munich, Germany
Email: {jakob.zietsch, nils.weinert}@siemens.com

***Abstract*—The progressing digitalization of factories coincides with a growing amount of raw data being available in order to create valuable, data driven application. The Edge Computing paradigm is one of the key enablers to realize beneficial solutions, since it helps overcome obstacles such as capacity and latency restrictions or data privacy and protection requirements. However, realized industrial applications of Edge Computing Applications are rather limited as of today. Therefore, as part of the Factory Automation Edge Computing Operating System Reference Implementation (FAR-EDGE) project, a series of expert interviews covering viewpoints from both industry and academia was conducted in order to gain deeper insight on limiting factors and development challenges and expectations. The results are presented in this paper forming a brief snapshot of the current perception of Edge Computing contributing to the creation of an overall understanding of the needs of the manufacturing industry.**

Keywords–Edge Computing; Fog Computing; Survey.

I. INTRODUCTION

With the increase of raw data streams within factories, the need arises to provide processing capabilities to transform them into valuable information and act on that information in a timely matter [1]. The rising Edge Computing (EC) paradigm fulfills this need by providing both hardware and software capabilities [2]. There are currently three major reference architectures with unique features in development that focus on the challenges arising from Industry 4.0 [3]. One of them is the FAR-EDGE reference architecture, currently applied in 13 active use cases, each focusing on one or more topics in the field of automation, analytics, and simulation [4]. Common goals within the use cases are a reduction of latency, an increase of data security and privacy protection, increasing processing performance while maintaining a high level of autonomy. An ideal solution would meet or even exceed these goals while providing all services required by any production environment. The development of such an all-in-one solution, if even possible, requires a significant amount of resources and development time. For most industrial use cases, this might be an overkill contradicting with the desire of industry to solve their current challenges as soon as possible and start migrating towards architectures supporting their continues growth [5]. Therefore, focusing on fulfilling the requirements of industry stakeholders is crucial for an efficient adoption and integration of the EC paradigm. While "the research on the emerging domain is still in its infancy" [6], and only a few solutions being already deployed in industry, the question which factors are most relevant and should be prioritized in the development of reference architectures and software solutions is left unanswered. The increasing amount of surveys on EC, as well as similar paradigms [6]–[8], explicitly and implicitly cover are a large variety of essential factors and benefits for edge. However, in most cases it is neglected to present the current perception regarding the level of relevance and focus within industry and academia. In this paper, the results of a series of expert interviews conducted with both representatives of industry and academia are presented. The aim is to determine how EC is currently perceived within both domains. First, ten relevant factors for EC are rated according to their importance. Second, the necessary development distribution over the software development process is estimated. Last, the cost distribution throughout the life cycle is analyzed.

II. METHODOLOGY

This section will explain the interview questions in detail, and define how these questions contribute to the survey.

A. Overview

As described in Section I, the project builds and realizes its reference architecture in use cases defined by two industrial partners and a research partner within the consortium of the FAR-EDGE project. The project consortium also consists of several technology providers who provide software for the use cases. To interpret how these use cases and the solutions provided by technology providers match, nine expert interviews were conducted covering all aspects differentiating Edge Computing from Cloud Computing. The interviews are organized for each partner individually. The interview questions were provided beforehand. However, none of the answers of other partners were shared with anyone, whether they are involved in the particular use case or not. The interviews were recorded and the results transcribed accordingly accordingly summarizing. The following sections explain the methodology and specifically the interview questions in detail.

B. Definitions

This section will explain the questions that were asked to both kinds of partners. The interview questions are separated into five distinct sections. Although the questions were slightly different for technology providers and the use case owners, they targeted the same aspect from a different perspective. The use case owners are namely Volvo Trucks Company (VTC), Whirlpool (WHR), and SmartFactoryKL (SFK). Technology provider names are obscured for reasons of confidentiality. It is important to note that the prepared factors fostering Edge Computing applications and additional benefits aim for completeness. Even with a thorough investigation such a target is challenging to achieve. Therefore, the interviewees were encouraged to extend the list at any given moment if they see the need for it.

1) Evaluation of Relevant Factors for Edge Computing: The first part of the interview was on the evaluation of relevant factors for Edge Computing, that are preselected based on prior experience, as well as literature [2], [9], [10], to measure the use case requirements against the five imperatives of Edge Computing, namely: latency, data ownership, autonomy, quantity, and connectivity.

One of the key advantages of Edge Computing is to overcome latency constraints which are one of the reasons to prefer edge solutions over for a Cloud solution [11]. For the use case owners, the question was the measurement of the importance of the latency, whereas, for the technology providers, it was whether the solution satisfies the latency requirements of the use cases and if it helps improve the latency.

Similar to latency, data ownership, or privacy and security reasons are another cause for choosing an edge solution. Use case owners were whether they have a security issue at the moment and if the use case contains sensitive data. For the technology providers, the question was whether the data they work with is confidential, and if it leaves on-premise servers, which may cause an security issue.

Autonomy is the degree of being autonomous. In this question, it was targeted to learn if the system can govern itself without an operator, in case of a failure, etc. The use case owners were asked how autonomous they desire the solution to be. The technology providers had to answer this question by evaluating whether their solution is autonomous or not, and up to which degree.

Another benefit of Edge Computing is being able to pre-process the data at the field tier, helping reduce the network traffic and reducing the raw data that is transmitted to the Cloud. The use case owners had to answer how much data is being generated at the field tier, and whether this is a limit to increase the Quality of Service (QoS). For the technology providers, they were asked if the data being used needs to leave the Edge for decisions, and the size of the data.

The last question in relevant factors was on interactivity and connectivity. The use case owners were asked whether the actual setup needs multiple machinery to be communicated with each other for a successful production. The technology providers needed to answer if their solution always relies on the connection outside Edge, and if the solution allows even sub-components of the machinery interact with each other.

2) Importance of Additional Edge Computing Benefits: The second part of the interview was to decide on the importance of requirements of Edge Computing. These requirements were reliability, scalability, extensibility, abstraction, and interoperability, and partly taken from literature [10], [12].

An edge solution is intended to keep servicing without an internet connection. Use case owners were asked how important it is that the system works reliably, meaning how the production would be affected if a failure occurs. For the Individual Software Vendors (ISVs), it was asked whether their software can recover itself in case of a failure, and how the software affects the production in case if stops responding.

Scalability describes the capacity of the solution to adapt to its increasing users and products, whereas extensibility is more focused on the functionality. In scalability context, for the use case owners, it is asked whether they foresee an increase in the product and user base count. In the same context, the ISVs answered whether their solution supports a big number of users and products. Similarly, for extensibility, use case partners were asked whether they plan to deploy new services, devices, or functionality to their production plants. For the technology providers, we asked whether their software is extensible with minimum (re-)configuration if such deployments were made.

Modifications in the production systems may require low-level tweaks or configurations. These changes may break existing solutions. Application Programming Interfaces (APIs) introduced by abstraction can enable more straightforward configuration and better backward compatibility. Use case owners were asked if the plant structure is likely to change. Furthermore, the intention was to learn if they develop internal software which interacts with the edge solution. The technology partners answered whether their software could be used in legacy machines and if their solution introduces APIs to abstract the complexity.

Interoperability is an essential factor for complex systems since relying on a single proprietary solution may cause vendor lock-in problems in case the solution is no more updated or non-available. Working with too many solutions can also cause compatibility problems, which may require additional adapters and wrappers. The use case partners answered the degree of interaction between existing components from different providers.

3) Development Time Distribution for an Application: This part of the interview targeted the estimated time distribution (in percentage) of development for an application. Similar to Section II-B1 and Section II-B2, the definition of an application for both type of partners differ. For the use case partners, this section focused on the AS-IS and TO-BE values during the planning phase of the use case and the implementation of the solution without an edge solution. For the ISVs, this section took values for the designed or implemented TO-BE Edge application.

Time distribution values were collected in seven categories: (1) analysis, (2) design, (3) implementation and build (4) deployment, (5) testing, (6) revision, and (7) training. In the analysis, the use case partners report the time needed to analyze their non-edge solution and the current production line to create the ideas for their use cases. For the ISVs, this time includes the period for analyzing the use case to look for the solutions. Design for the use case partners includes the time to design the use case, including its requirements. For technology partners, the design time is the duration to plan the solution considering the requirements of the use cases. Training for use case owners represents the time required to train the workers or operators before introducing the edge solution. For the technology partners, it exemplifies the training time spent on instructing the edge solution.

4) Development Cost Distribution for an Application: Similar to Section II-B3, this part collected estimated cost distribution (in percentage) of development for an application. Costs are typically split among one-time costs (also called upfront costs) and recurring costs. If the solutions require no additional hardware apart from server hardware, usually, the distribution of the cost is expected to be similar to the time distribution. Upfront costs are analysis, design, implementation and build, deployment, testing, and training. Maintaining or revision costs are considered as recurring costs. As the Figure 2b shows, in this part, analysis and design costs are estimated higher than other costs.

Since determining the cost for the development the edge applications directly is challenging to upright impossible, the interview questions are designed so that the only the distribution of costs can be estimate based on the current progress of the development. At the end of the project, the estimated values will be compared with the actual numbers. If a technology provider is involved in more than one use case, the respective questions were repeated for each use case they are participating in. Additionally, contingency costs, which are unexpected costs, are going to be added after the project completion, if any exist.

5) Hardware and Software Distribution: The last part of the interview collected the distribution of the hardware and software for the TO-BE solution, to decide the tendency of the solution concerning hardware and software, in percentage. If a use case is only software-based, then the hardware questions such as reliability in Section II-B2, were unrelated.

The following section will summarize the results of the interviews explained in previous sections.

III. Results

Figure 1 summarizes the answers given to the first two parts of the interviews. The scenario column contains the use case owners, followed by the use case ID and the interviewee (actual names are obscured for reasons of confidentiality). The next two columns contain the evaluation results for the first and second part of the interview, respectively. The range from one to seven defines the importance of the attributes: one meaning not applicable, and seven being crucial. The presented attributes can be considered complete, as throughout all interviews no interview partner saw the need to adapt those in any way.

Third part of the interview is summarized in Figure 2a. The figure shows the development time distribution of six providers and three use case owners. Figure 2b depicts the development cost distribution of the edge solution. Similar to the development time distribution, the figure summarizes the answers of six technology providers and three use case owners.

IV. Discussion

Interview results showed that the technology providers and use case owners are well aligned concerning the chosen factors for Edge Computing and solutions covering additional edge criteria. The proposed list of relevant factors for Edge Computing did not have to be extended based on the interviews. Thus, the five chosen attributes - *Latency*, *Data Ownership*, *Autonomy*, *Data Quantity* and *Connectivity* - can be considered as sufficient when assessing Edge Computing implementations. As it may be noticed, one solution partner may rate the importance differently for different use cases. This is the case when the solution partner provided a different solution for that use case.

Focusing on Figure 1, the results can be interpreted in the following ways.

Unexpectedly, latency and data quantity factors were not critical due to reported low data transfer rates outside the factories. Only WHR use case requires that it has a very high importance, since the whole factory generates high traffic for actions to be taken.

For data ownership, the industrial use case owners see this criteria rather low, which might surprise at first - In the project, however, the agreement was made to not share any data meaning that even very low would already mean that their

Scenario	Use Case ID	Interviewee	Factors for EC					Additional benefits				
			Latency	Data Ownership	Autonomy	Data Quantity	Connectivity	Reliability	Scalability	Extensibility	Abstraction	Interoperability
VTC	1,2,3	Owner	4	3	7	2	6	6	7	7	6	6
		Provider #4	4	6	6	3	6	6	7	7	6	6
	4	Owner	2	3	3	2	2	6	5	5	4	6
		Provider #5	1	5	1	1	1	5	5	5	3	6
	5	Owner	3	3	7	2	6	4	6	5	6	1
		Provider #3	2	7	5	6	5	5	6	6	7	7
		Provider #2	4	7	6	7	6	5	7	7	6	7
WHR	1	Owner	6	1	7	1	5	7	1	1	5	5
		Provider #6	6	1	7	1	5	7	2	2	5	5
SFK	1	Owner	2	7	4	5	6	2	2	6	7	7
		Provider #3	2	7	5	6	5	5	6	6	7	7
	2,3,4	Owner	2	7	4	2	6	2	2	6	6	7
		Provider #6	2	7	4	2	6	2	2	6	6	7
	5	Owner	2	7	4	2	6	2	2	6	6	7
		Provider #6	6	1	7	1	5	7	1	1	5	5
		Provider #3	2	7	5	6	5	5	6	6	7	7
	6,7	Owner	2	7	4	2	6	2	2	3	6	7
		Provider #6	4	5	7	1	5	2	2	6	6	7

Legend	
1	Not applicable
2	Very Low
3	Low
4	Medium
5	High
6	Very high
7	Crucial

Figure 1. Results of the edge factors and the perceived importance of attributes

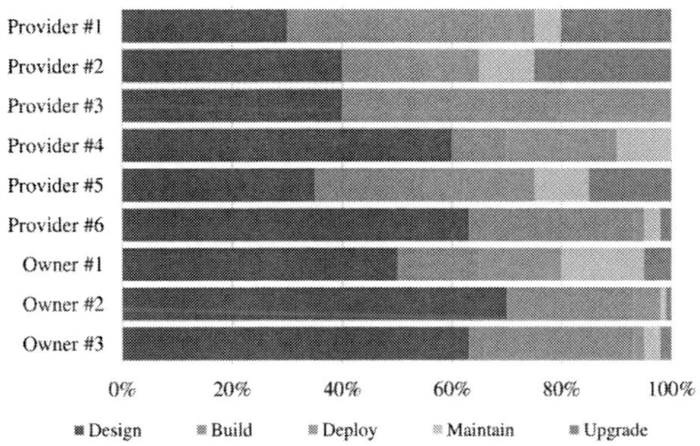

(a) Development time

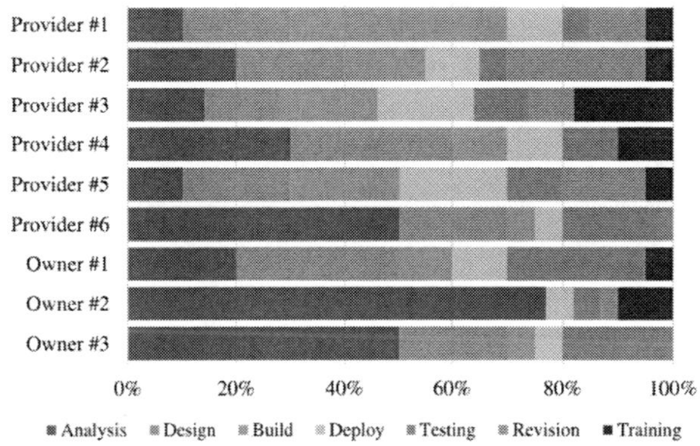

(b) Development cost

Figure 2. Distribution of development time and cost distribution for Edge Computing implementation

data will not leave the boundaries of their factory. However, the test laboratory SFK contains hardware/software that is not yet robust and is prone to cyberattacks from within the network. This increases the necessity for each device/platform to contain the data accordingly.

In automation use cases (VTC #1-#3, WHR #1, SFK #2-#7), autonomy, and in analytics use cases, scalability and extensibility factors have higher importance than others. Edge solutions are given partial responsibility of the automation tasks. This leads to Autonomy being a crucial feature in the industrial use cases, except VTC use case #4. SFK is not affected from this criteria, as the factory has already been designed to work autonomously. Similarly, importance of reliability is very high in average, for the industrial partners and the solution providers. However, as SFK is a test laboratory, the solutions are developed to test the new technology inside, before applying them in the industrial world. Therefore, reliability is not vital for the prototypical applications. SFK as a test laboratory also requires very high extensibility, since one of its goals is to provide modular factory with minimal (re-)configuration. Provider #6 in fifth SFK use case seems to provide no extensibility for this use case, however, it can be discarded as the extensibility part of the use case is satisfied by the Provider #3 in the same use case.

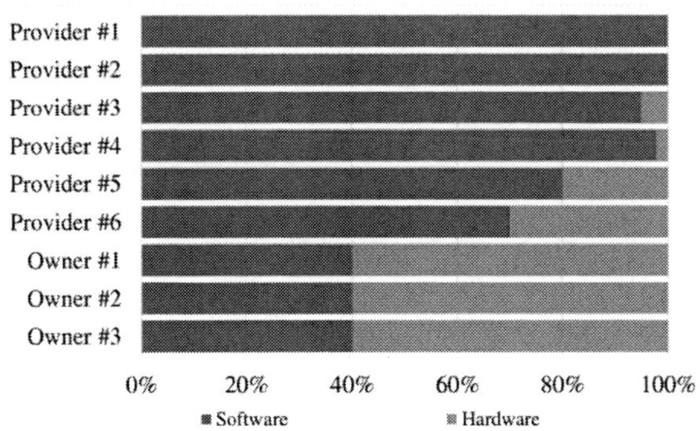

Figure 3. Hardware and Software distribution by all partners, w.r.t. their contributions to the project.

Abstraction importance is above high, as the solutions are asked to reduce the complexity of the existing systems. Vertically, except the fourth use case of VTC, which is a simulation, based on models, for all partners, it is important to increase backward compatibility for future technologies or allow legacy systems to continue functioning properly.

Interoperability is very important or even crucial for some partners. Except the fifth use case from VTC, which is an analytics use case consisting of only event identifiers, all use case owners and use case partners require and give above high attention to this factor. As the factories of the industrial partners are composed of components from different companies, interoperability will improve the efficiency once they scale, and prevent vendor lock-in problems. SFK also aims to continue the highly interoperable approach together with the solutions.

With respect to the development time distribution, the results seen in Figure 2a can be discussed as follows:

The high percentage of time spent on analysis is expected, as it means examination of the production plan for use case owners, and analysis of the given use case for the software providers. Similarly, design means sketching the use case for use case owners and designing the software for the given use case for software providers. The high training amount in analytics use cases are due to user interaction via the dashboard. However, the benefits of using analytics solutions reduce the time spent on evaluation of monitoring values, directly affecting maintenance time in the future, hence the costs. Less time requirement for deployment and testing can be explained as the deployment is mainly the software installation. Similarly, the project executes unit tests in component level during development, therefore, only final testing is conducted after deployment. Likewise, results collected for the development cost distribution shown in Figure 2b, can be interpreted as following:

The high cost requirement on design and build/implementation phase is directly related to the time values. Since most of the solutions are software-based, software development time is aligned with its costs. Use case owners and software providers agree that most resources are expected to be spent on designing and build/implementation steps. Furthermore, the costs are desired to be minimized for maintenance and upgrading after going for the edge solution.

Analytics technology provider foresees neither maintenance nor upgrade costs after deployment. This is because once the software is run, it can easily be scaled or extended to service the needs. Moreover, they do not expect to provide an upgrade to the final solution.

As mentioned in Section II-B5, the last part of the interview was to identify the percentage of hardware and software usage by the partners. As it can be seen from Figure 3, the results show that the use case partners, namely Whirlpool (WHR), Volvo Trucks Company (VTC), and SmartFactoryKL (SFKL), are the partners who contribute to the project with more hardware than software.

V. Conclusion and Future Work

Edge Computing is a recent paradigm, which moves computing power, applications and services from centralized units into the logical extremes or at the closest locations to the source and provides data processing power there. Factory Automation Edge Computing Operating System Reference Implementation (FAR-EDGE) is one of the ongoing actions on Edge Computing, which focuses on three functional domains: automation, simulation, and analytics. In this work, interviews were organized with all consortium members; firstly, to get feedback from the partners and to figure out, to which degree Edge Computing is a better alternative to the Cloud for specific use cases. Secondly, comparing the answers from use case owners and Individual Software Vendors (ISVs), to understand, how many of the important factors have been covered by the developed or in progress solutions. Thirdly, to identify the driving factors and benefits as perceived by both, solution providers and use case owners. Finally, to give a breakdown of the estimated development time and development costs to assess which step takes the most resource during development and the degree of decrease in the development time with the edge solution.

The findings in the survey are depicted in the figures in Section II-B3 and Section II-B4. Main findings from these figures can be derived as follows: (1) the industrial partners do not want to distribute their production related data, or they only plan to distribute non-identifying data, which increases the importance of data ownership, (2) except for simulation use cases or the simulation sections of the use cases, importance of abstraction is above very high, to support the legacy systems and to provide increased backward compatibility in the future, (3) automation use cases require that the autonomy is crucial for the factories due to production rates, and to reduce the amount of time for configurations or setup, (4) the solutions provided for the industrial partners need to be reliable as downtimes in factories reduce the efficiency and the productivity, however, for the test laboratory the prototypes can be deployed easier for further testing. Moreover, most of the development time and the costs are expected to be spent during the analysis and design time. Some of the use case owners target reducing the deployment time whereas some of the technology providers foresee that their solution will require neither maintenance nor upgrade.

As mentioned in Section I, this paper described the report of the initial evaluation results, which are going to be compared with the factual numbers after project is completed. This research included nine consortium members which is not yet ideal to get a clear picture. In the future, it is planned to increase the amount of participants to get a clearer view on the criteria.

Acknowledgment

This research was funded by the H2020 program of European Union, project FAR-EDGE - grant number 723094. The responsibility for this publication lies with the authors. The project details can be found under project website at: `http://www.far-edge.eu`

References

[1] D. Georgakopoulos, P. P. Jayaraman, M. Fazia, M. Villari, and R. Ranjan, "Internet of Things and Edge Cloud Computing Roadmap for Manufacturing," *IEEE Cloud Computing*, vol. 3, no. 4, pp. 66–73, Jul. 2016.

[2] W. Yu, F. Liang, X. He, W. G. Hatcher, C. Lu, J. Lin, and X. Yang, "A Survey on the Edge Computing for the Internet of Things," *IEEE Access*, vol. 6, pp. 6900–6919, 2018.

[3] I. Sittn-Candanedo, R. S. Alonso, S. Rodrguez-Gonzlez, J. A. Garca Coria, and F. De La Prieta, "Edge Computing Architectures in Industry 4.0: A General Survey and Comparison," in *14th International Conference on Soft Computing Models in Industrial and Environmental Applications (SOCO 2019)*, F. Martnez lvarez, A. Troncoso Lora, J. A. Sez Muoz, H. Quintin, and E. Corchado, Eds. Cham: Springer International Publishing, 2020, pp. 121–131.

[4] M. Isaja, J. Soldatos, and V. Gezer, "Combining edge computing and blockchains for flexibility and performance in industrial automation," *The International Journal on Advances in Intelligent Systems*, pp. 159–164, September 2017.

[5] A. Cala, A. Luder, F. Boschi, G. Tavola, and M. Taisch, "Migration towards digital manufacturing automation - An assessment approach," in *2018 IEEE Industrial Cyber-Physical Systems (ICPS)*. St. Petersburg: IEEE, May 2018, pp. 714–719.

[6] W. Khan, E. Ahmed, S. Hakak, I. Yaqoob, and A. Ahmed, "Edge computing: A survey," *Future Generation Computer Systems*, vol. 97, pp. 219–235, 2019.

[7] A. Yousefpour, C. Fung, T. Nguyen, K. Kadiyala, F. Jalali, A. Niakanlahiji, J. Kong, and J. Jue, *All One Needs to Know about Fog Computing and Related Edge Computing Paradigms: A Complete Survey*, Aug. 2018.

[8] R. Yang, F. R. Yu, P. Si, Z. Yang, and Y. Zhang, "Integrated Blockchain and Edge Computing Systems: A Survey, Some Research Issues and Challenges," *IEEE Communications Surveys & Tutorials*, vol. 21, no. 2, pp. 1508–1532, 2019.

[9] J. Zietsch, N. Weinert, C. Herrmann, and S. Thiede, "Edge computing for the production industry: A systematic approach to enable decision support and planning of edge," in *2019 IEEE 17th International Conference on Industrial Informatics (INDIN) (presented)*. Helsinki: IEEE, Jul. 2019, pp. 733–739.

[10] B. Gill and T. Bittman, "The Future Shape of Edge Computing: Five Imperatives," Gartner Website, [retrieved: Aug 2019]. [Online]. Available: https://www.gartner.com/en/documents/3880015

[11] V. Gezer, J. Um, and M. Ruskowski, "An introduction to edge computing and a real-time capable server architecture," *The International Journal on Advances in Intelligent Systems*, vol. 11(1&2), pp. 105–114, July 2018, [retrieved: August 2019].

[12] M. Ashouri, P. Davidsson, and R. Spalazzese, "Cloud, Edge, or Both? Towards Decision Support for Designing IoT Applications," in *2018 Fifth International Conference on Internet of Things: Systems, Management and Security*. IEEE, 2018, pp. 155–162.

International Academy, Research, and Industry Association (IARIA)
412 Derby Way
Wilmington, DE 19810

ISBN 978-1-7138-0042-2

CURRAN ASSOCIATES INC.
proceedings.com

First International Conference on AI-based Media Innovation (AIMEDIA 2025)

Held at DigiTech 2025

Venice, Italy
6-10 July 2025